S STREET RISING

S STREET RISING

CRACK, MURDER, AND REDEMPTION IN D.C.

RUBEN CASTANEDA

BLOOMSBURY

NEW YORK · LONDON · NEW DELHI · SYDNEY

Published by Bloomsbury USA, New York
Bloomsbury is a trademark of Bloomsbury Publishing Plc

All papers used by Bloomsbury USA are natural, recyclable products made
from wood grown in well-managed forests. The manufacturing processes
conform to the environmental regulations of the country of origin.

LIBRARY OF CONGRESS CATALOGING-IN-PUBLICATION DATA

Castaneda, Ruben.
S street rising : crack, murder, and redemption in D.C. / Ruben Castaneda.—
First U.S. edition.
pages cm
ISBN 978-1-62040-004-3 (hardback)
1. Castaneda, Ruben. 2. Journalists—Drug use—Washington (D.C.) 3. Reporters and
reporting—Washington (D.C.) 4. Crack (Drug)—Washington (D.C.) 5. Drug traffic—
Washington (D.C.) 6. Crime—Washington (D.C.) I. Title.
PN4874.C316A3 2014
070.92—dc23
[B]
2014003414

First U.S. edition 2014

1 3 5 7 9 10 8 6 4 2

Typeset by Hewer Text UK Ltd, Edinburgh

Printed and bound in the U.S.A. by Thomson-Shore Inc., Dexter, Michigan

Bloomsbury books may be purchased for business or promotional use.
For information on bulk purchases please contact Macmillan Corporate
and Premium Sales Department at specialmarkets@macmillan.com.

For Mom and Pop, who raised a survivor

CONTENTS

CHAPTER 1

THE SHOW

I should have gotten out of the car already. I should have been working the crowd, scribbling notes on the mayhem while looking for someone to interview.

But I couldn't bring myself to get out of my beat-up Ford Escort, pulled up to the curb near the intersection of 5th and O Streets Northwest.

It was the afternoon of December 20, 1990. I was a twenty-nine-year-old night police reporter for the *Washington Post*. I'd joined the paper fifteen months earlier and was anxious to make my mark, willing to do whatever the bosses asked. I routinely raced to combat zones to cover drug-crew shootings, even if the trips didn't yield many bylined stories. Single or even double gangster killings were usually relegated to the briefs column. But this assignment was different: five kids shot in a drive-by as they were walking home from school just before Christmas. Other *Post* reporters were at the scene, and chances were good that one of us was going to get our name on the front page.

Marked Metropolitan Police Department cruisers, lights flashing, were parked at odd angles in the intersection. Two TV camera jockeys recorded the aftermath of the attack. A group of spectators was clustered behind the bright yellow crime-scene tape, gawking at the bloody clothes and shell casings scattered on the street and sidewalk. Your typical crime scene, in other words—but one that looked as dangerous to me as a sniper's alley. One of those spectators could recognize me, pick me off as I stepped out of the car. For the moment, doing my job wasn't important. Staying safe was.

There were men and women of all ages in the crowd, along with some school-age boys and girls. I locked in on the faces of the teenage males and young men. I had to be sure that none of them knew me—knew *about* me, that is.

The shooting had taken place just four blocks from S Street Northwest, where once, sometimes twice, a week I drove my girl Champagne to make crack buys. Champagne was a "strawberry"— a streetwalker who traded sex for drugs.

All the S Street slingers knew Champagne. And all of them knew me and my car, at least by sight. I'd become such a regular customer that some dealers called out, "Hey, amigo!" whenever they saw me.

Most of the S Street dealers no doubt lived in the neighborhood. What if some of them were among the rubberneckers behind the yellow tape? Would they say anything if they saw me approach a cop with my notebook out? Would one of them try to shake me down in exchange for his silence? Would he tell his boss—whoever he was—the dealer who was running the street? If the S Street kingpin found out that one of his loyal customers was a *Washington Post* reporter, what would he do with that unlikely nugget? Would he use the information as a bargaining chip if the cops tried to take him down?

If the story of my tawdry double life leaked, local TV news would be all over it. It could be weirdly ironic enough for the national networks, too. *Post* executive editor Ben Bradlee would probably summon me to his glass-walled office and furiously curse at me before firing me, I imagined.

I sighed, disappointed with myself for not having come up with a good, or at least plausible, excuse to dodge the assignment, after an editor had called me at home and asked me to clock in early.

I usually thrived at crime scenes. My street instincts were good. Most reporters went straight for whatever police or fire officials happened to be on hand. I worked the edges, talking to the people others overlooked. Civilian witnesses were my priority. I'd talk to them before they vanished or were scooped up by the cops. I'd usually speak with police later, since they weren't going anywhere.

A few months earlier, I'd covered a killing at a blue-collar apartment complex near the Maryland state line. A man had been fatally stabbed inside one of the units. Outside the building, a police commander talked to a couple of detectives. Thirty feet away, a cluster of Latino men and women watched the police in silence.

I wandered over and talked to them in Spanish. A couple of the men described what had happened. Two guys had been arguing. One of them pulled out a knife. He stabbed the victim and ran. They gave me the name of the culprit. When a detective headed toward the building, I cut him off and asked if he had a suspect.

"No," he said.

"Would you like one?"

That detective turned into a good source.

But this afternoon, my instincts were useless. I sat in my car and stared hard at one of the spectators. He was wearing a black knit cap and appeared to be in his early twenties. He looked vaguely familiar. Where had I seen him?

I closed my eyes and rubbed the bridge of my nose. I couldn't stay in the car forever.

Had I smoked myself into a corner? Was I about to become an embarrassing footnote in the national crack epidemic?

At the time, no U.S. metropolis was getting hit harder by crack than D.C. In the eastern half of the city, bodies were dropping nightly in violence propelled by crack turf wars. Washington became known not simply as the nation's capital but as its murder capital. A local TV station devoted a half hour to the carnage every night with a program called *City Under Siege*. A few months earlier, Mayor Marion Barry had been convicted of crack possession following an FBI sting at the Vista Hotel, downtown, an arrest that stunned the city and made screaming headlines around the world.

The *Post* had gone into overdrive after the Barry bust. Reporters were assigned to keep an eye on the disgraced mayor or his house around the clock. My colleagues downed coffee to make it through their late-night Barry watches, but when it was my turn, I took a couple of hits of crack. The irony of riding a crack high while conducting surveillance on a mayor who'd been busted for possessing the same substance was lost on me.

The possibility of being outed by the S Street slingers while working this scene was not. Earlier in the year, I'd covered a quadruple murder on the very corner where Champagne and I made our buys. But that was on a freezing, snowy night, not an overcast afternoon, and any slingers who'd been out scattered when the gunplay began and stayed away when the cops swarmed onto the block.

The man in the black cap wandered away from the knot of gawkers, affording me a better view. It came to me: He resembled one of the guys I played pickup hoops with at the downtown YMCA. I wasn't sure if he was the basketball player, but I was relieved: I hadn't seen him on S Street.

One deep breath later, I slipped my press credentials around my neck and got out of the car.

Immediately, I spotted a police commander wearing a white shirt inside the crime scene. Uniformed officers and sergeants wore blue shirts; MPD commanders of the rank of lieutenant or higher wore white. Cops, criminals, firefighters, and reporters referred to them as "white shirts." Hands in his jacket pockets, the commander was speaking with some onlookers on the other side of the tape. That was unusual—most police officials didn't talk to civilians on the street.

I wandered over, planted myself among the spectators, and waited. From the gold bars on the shoulders of his jacket I could tell he was a captain.

A few minutes later, as he retreated from the crowd, I stepped up to the tape and called out, "Captain!" half-expecting him to ignore me. But he turned, walked over, and met me at the tape. I read the nameplate on his jacket: HENNESSY.

I introduced myself as a *Post* reporter, asked if he could help me with what had happened, and prepared for the verbal stiff-arm. Most of the white shirts I'd encountered on the street ran from indifferent to hostile.

To my surprise, the captain said, "Lou Hennessy" and extended his hand. "Not a lot I can tell you right now. Five kids were shot. They're at the hospital now. We're looking into the possibility it was a drive-by, but that's preliminary."

I asked a few questions. Hennessy answered every one. He didn't provide much detail, but I could tell he was trying to be helpful.

I thanked him and was turning away when he said, "Listen, if you hear anything, would you let me know? Sometimes you guys hear things before we do." He reached into his jacket pocket and handed me his business card.

A white shirt who makes nice with reporters? Smart, I thought as I waded into the crowd looking for someone to interview.

As I walked away, Hennessy turned his attention back to the crime scene. The victims were between the ages of six and fourteen. If any of them died, homicide would take over, but it looked as though they were all going to make it. If they did, the case was his.

A lot of captains would stay out of the fray and let their underlings go after the suspects. Not Lou Hennessy. Investigating was his favorite part of the job. Besides, he figured, he had to get the shooters off the street quickly, before the momentum for payback became unstoppable.

Most of the victims attended the same middle school. Lou called the principal. He asked whether there had been any trouble lately. The principal gave him the name of a sixteen-year-old kid who, with his friends, had been feuding with a rival crew. Lou went to his home. The kid's mom was respectful and cooperative. She agreed to let her son go downtown to police headquarters for a talk.

Lou participated in the interview. The kid gave it up right away, describing a neighborhood beef. He and his friends were gunning for a thirteen-year-old boy who was known for stabbing kids in the neck. They had cooked up a drive-by attack, the kid said.

They needed a car. A local crack fiend had lent them his Toyota in exchange for a few rocks, the teenager told Lou. Two of his friends had fired handguns from the moving vehicle. He gave up one of the names. That boy gave up another name. Investigators went to that home, and that kid gave up one more name.

Lou worked through the night. His detectives scooped up four of the five suspects within sixteen hours of the shootings. A couple of weeks later, cops in Los Angeles picked up the fifth kid, who was hiding out with relatives.

The quick work had kept the peace. There was no payback.

The rest of my own night wasn't quite as exemplary. After interviewing Lou, I talked to a handful of bystanders, then drove to the *Post* and wrote up notes for the reporter who was writing the story. I stopped worrying about landing on the national news and losing my job.

As the night wore on, my mood brightened. I'd escaped—and the 5th and O assignment was good for a few hours of overtime. My next paycheck would be fat. I typically used only on weekends, but now I could afford to be spontaneous.

Instead of going straight home after my shift, I cruised around the badlands just east of downtown, where winos milled around outside liquor stores and dealers, strawberries, and junkies roamed streets lined with apartment buildings, small churches, and turn-of-the-century row houses. I quickly found Champagne, working one of her usual corners. She smiled when she saw my car, knowing she was about to get high.

I pulled over and unlocked the passenger door.

Champagne looked both ways for cops, then got in.

In very different ways, Lou Hennessy and I were both profoundly shaped by the crack epidemic. As a veteran police officer, Lou had seen huge swaths of his hometown descend into crack-trade chaos. He would devise an approach to go after the most violent players in the city's drug trade.

As a *Post* crime reporter, I chronicled the burgeoning bloodshed in the city's combat zones, even as I contributed to the pathology with my own addiction. I would cover Lou's inroads against the city's most prolific killers—until we came up against city and newsroom politics.

Lou was thirty-four when I met him. He'd been on the police force for seventeen years, having joined as a cadet in 1973. Lou started out working as a patrol officer in tough sections of Northwest and Northeast Washington. He was smart, calm, dedicated, and determined to do what he could to stem the violence.

Investigating shootings like the one at 5th and O provided a strange kind of refuge for him. He wouldn't go home until the case was put down. That meant working twenty-four or forty-eight hours straight, which meant no sleep. That wasn't such a bad thing—no sleep meant no nightmares.

They'd started about the time crack hit the city in the mid-eighties. He dreamed of gunmen, their faces featureless, coming for him in a dark room. Some of them had handguns. Some wielded shotguns.

"Get away, motherfuckers!" Lou would scream. Lately, his wife, Loraine, told him, he'd started sleepwalking toward the dresser, where he kept his service revolver. Loraine didn't scare easily, but Lou could tell she was afraid he might grab his gun and shoot her without knowing it.

I, meanwhile, was determined to write as much as I could about the carnage. By the time of the 5th and O drive-by, I'd been a crack user for a little more than two years. I'd first tried the drug on another reporting assignment, when I was working for the *Los Angeles Herald Examiner*.

Staffers at that paper had minimal supervision, and I got away with more than most. I was a regular at Corky's, a dive bar across the street from the *Herald Examiner*'s offices on South Broadway. I hit the place three or four times a week after work, and now and then I got an early start.

In mid-September 1988, I was assigned an immigration story. After working the phones for a few hours, I headed out to find some interviewees. I drove west on Olympic Boulevard, past high-rises crowded with poor Central Americans, grimy motels frequented by streetwalkers, and concrete fast-food stands sporting sun-blasted peach and teal paint jobs and adorned with signs boasting of THE WORLD'S BEST TACOS or L.A.'S BEST BURGERS.

It was a tough area, perfect for my mission. Central American gangsters controlled the streets, the parks, the alleys. Some blocks belonged to the gang known as Mara Salvatrucha, or MS-13. Others were ruled by the 18th Street gang. In their wifebeaters and jeans, gangbangers openly peddled marijuana, heroin, and crack. At some intersections, the slingers covered every corner, keeping a sharp eye out for LAPD black-and-whites—or anyone who looked like he didn't belong.

Buttonholing strangers for interviews wouldn't work in a full-on crack zone. The street dealers might figure me for a cop. Maybe they'd leave. Maybe they'd make me leave.

I needed a relatively quiet street. A mile or so west of

downtown, I hung a right and took inventory: a cheap little motel, a couple of apartment buildings, some single-family homes. No slingers in sight. With my notebook and pen tucked into my back pocket, I hopped out of my car and wandered up the street, looking for someone to interview.

The girl quickly caught my eye. She was standing under a little awning in front of the motel. Apparently in her early twenties, she had fair skin, jet-black shoulder-length hair, and a beauty-pageant-worthy body clothed in cutoffs and a tank top. She looked like a rising starlet, someone you'd see in a cheesy sitcom or a shampoo commercial.

She busted me checking her out and threw me a quick smile. I smiled back. She waved me over.

The interviews could wait.

"Hi," she said. "Haven't seen you around here before."

"I don't live around here. I'm on a work assignment. What's your name?"

"Raven. How about you?"

"Ruben."

"So, Ruben, do you work *all* the time?"

"What do you mean?"

Raven twirled her fingers through her hair. "Do you party?"

"Why are you asking?"

Was she flirting? Was I that lucky? Raven took something out of her back pocket. She opened her hand, displaying a small plastic baggie. It contained a white, square-shaped chunk about the size of an M&M.

"Got some rock," she said. "Give you a hit, no charge."

Crack was raging through the poorest sections of the city. Though it was relatively new to L.A., the drug was already taking on a mythic quality. Doctors warned that even one hit could hook someone, hopelessly and forever.

Time stopped. I knew the little chunk in Raven's hand was dangerous.

I pictured the junkies I'd seen during reporting forays to Skid Row: homeless, desperate men who crawled on the pavement, searching for stray bits of crack. Dead-eyed women who worked the streets offering their bodies so they could score another hit.

"I'm not lying," Raven said. "First one's free. You won't find a better deal."

I pushed the images of desperate addicts out of my mind—no way I'd become one of *them*. I'd smoked pot four times and had never gotten very high. I'd smoked PCP twice. I'd hallucinated for a couple of days but quickly returned to my normal routine. If I could avoid becoming hooked on pot and PCP, what harm could there be in trying one hit of crack?

I looked over one shoulder, then the other. No foot traffic, civilian motorists, or LAPD cruisers were in sight. Forty feet away, westbound traffic was flowing on Olympic Boulevard as downtown workers headed home in the direction of upscale Mid-Wilshire, Hancock Park, the Fairfax District, and beyond, toward tony Brentwood and finally Santa Monica, with its golden sunsets and cool ocean breezes.

Shadows were creeping onto the street. Late afternoon was giving way to twilight, my favorite part of the day. It signaled the end of the workday, a time to relax, maybe hit Corky's with some *Herald Examiner* pals—though any time after noon worked for me, and I didn't need any company to knock back a few drinks. I was twenty-seven, old enough to know better, young enough to feel invincible.

A few hours earlier, I'd gone to Corky's and downed two gin and tonics with my lunch. The lingering buzz from my lunchtime drinks had made me stupid cocky.

"Sure," I said.

Raven reached back into her pocket and pulled out a glass pipe. Its filter was blackened from repeated use.

She reached into her pocket again and brought out a lighter, then removed the rock from the baggie and cut it in half with her fingernail. She loaded it onto the filter and tapped it until it was secure, then brought the pipe to her lips, flicked on the lighter, and put the flame to the pipe.

The rock hissed softly as it dissolved. Raven inhaled. Thick white smoke coursed through the pipe and into her mouth. She held her breath for about five seconds before exhaling a puff of white smoke, handing me the pipe, and nodding.

I glanced over my shoulder—the street was dead quiet. Olympic Boulevard might as well have been forty miles away. With darkness encroaching, passing motorists would have needed superhumanly sharp eyes to see what we were doing. I put the pipe to my lips. Raven flicked on the lighter and put the flame to the tip of the pipe.

No backing out now.

I inhaled. Smoke invaded my mouth and lungs. The rush hit me almost instantaneously, euphoria detonating in my brain and spreading quickly to every part of my body.

I wobbled and took a step backwards.

"You okay?" Raven said.

I looked into her big brown eyes. "Wow."

Raven grinned. "Keep the lighter and the pipe. And take this for the road." She handed me the other half of the rock. The waning sunlight finally surrendered to dusk.

I drove home high, alert, ecstatic—and a little scared. This feeling was *too* good. Was my world about to crash?

The next morning, I hit the same neighborhood to complete my reporting assignment, scored a couple of interviews with immigrants, and went to the office and filed my story, quick and clean.

Alone in my rented condo, I took a single hit each of the ensuing two weekends. Both highs were rapturous—though not quite as intense as the first one. I wanted that feeling back.

On a Saturday afternoon a week after I'd finished the last of my freebie samples, I started to think about just how close my place was to Raven's street. I could be there in ten minutes. I slammed down a couple of beers for courage and grabbed my car keys.

Raven was in the same spot in front of the motel when I pulled to the curb. She sauntered to my car and leaned into the open passenger window.

"I thought you might be back," she said.

"You thought right. That stuff's pretty good. Can I get another?"

Raven made a show of looking warily to one side of the street, then the other.

"There's been some plainclothes cops lurking around," she said. "I got a room. Safer to do this inside, if you don't mind."

The motel room was a dump. The mattress was thin and worn, the carpet dirty and ripped. A small TV was suspended from the ceiling. Raven, on the other hand, looked magnificent. She wore a formfitting black tank top and painted-on jeans.

I handed her a twenty. Raven opened the nightstand drawer, brought out a rock encased in a plastic baggie, and passed it to me.

My hand was on the doorknob when she offered a new deal: "Tell you what: If you buy two and let me have one of the rocks, I'll do you while you hit yours."

"Do me?"

"I'll suck on you while you hit the pipe," she said.

Raven had my attention. My last two blasts had not only gotten me euphorically high, they'd also made me hypersexual. My libido was healthy to begin with. On crack, it was turbocharged.

I let go of the doorknob and turned back to Raven. She pulled off her tank, revealing full white breasts straining against a black lace bra.

"Deal," I said.

I handed her another twenty. Raven reached into the nightstand and retrieved another rock, a pipe, and a lighter. We sat on the bed. Using her fingernails, Raven cut a big chunk of her rock, about two-thirds, and loaded it into the pipe.

"You ever been shotgunned?" she said.

"No. What's that?"

"You'll like it."

Raven lit up and inhaled. She held her breath for several seconds, then leaned toward me, as if moving in for a kiss, and pointed to her mouth. Our lips met. Raven exhaled a monster hit into my mouth. The room began to spin. I was woozy with ecstasy and desire.

"*That* is a shotgun," Raven said.

I undid my belt while Raven blew on the pipe, trying to cool it. I slid my jeans down, then my boxers. My joint was already stirring to life.

"So you'll do me while I take a hit?"

"That's how it works, babe."

Raven placed what was left of her rock atop the nightstand and handed me the pipe and the lighter. My rock was intact. I cut it in half.

She reached into her purse, on the nightstand, and took out a condom. She put the condom into her mouth, bent down, and had it around my penis in one smooth motion.

As she began working on me, I loaded my rock into the pipe, lit up, and inhaled.

The crack attacked my brain as Raven sucked me off. I held, held, held my hit. Raven's head bobbed up and down.

I exhaled and came at the same time, a beyond-belief, starbursting, epic climax. My entire body convulsed with pleasure. I lay back on the bed, limp and amazed.

Raven motioned for the pipe and the lighter. She blew on the pipe for a couple of minutes, then loaded her final chunk of rock and took a long hit. A few seconds later, she leaned over and shotgunned me as I lay supine.

As I headed out the door, with half a rock in my pocket, I asked, "How can I reach you?"

"I'm around here all the time, babe. Come see me whenever."

*

Hooking up with Raven for crack and oral sex became part of my routine for the next eleven months. I'd usually see her on Saturday afternoons, after playing pickup hoops in the morning. Now and then, if I was flush after scoring some holiday pay, I'd see her twice a week. But I was careful—at first—about limiting our encounters. I didn't want my life to spin out of control.

The truth is, by the time I took my first hit, my alcoholism was already taking me to scary places. I was reckless, compulsive, and I made bad choices. At least a dozen times in my mid-twenties, I drank to the point of full or partial blackout; the following day I could remember nothing of the previous night, or only small portions.

One night, about the time I met Raven, I got totally blasted at Corky's. I wasn't blackout drunk, but I was close to it. As best I can recall, I cruised Raven's street and didn't see her.

Frustrated, I headed home. On a downtown street, I spotted an older version of Raven. She was dark-haired and pretty. The woman was simply standing on the sidewalk, not near a bus stop, not talking to anyone. I still wanted to get high. Drunk logic took over.

I parked about a block away and wobbled over. The woman smiled at me. I took it as an invitation and asked if she partied. Sure, she said. I asked if we could party, if she'd do me, for forty bucks, as I recall.

She took a step back and made a hand signal. An unmarked LAPD sedan roared in from a nearby alley. The woman was a plainclothes LAPD cop, working vice. A couple of her colleagues swooped in, briefly put me in flex-cuffs, and sent me on my miserable way with a citation for solicitation.

Things couldn't get worse. Or so I thought.

On my way home, I stopped at a pay phone on Main Street to call my roommate. It was a system we'd developed: Whoever was out later would check in with the other, in case he had female companionship and wanted some privacy.

As I was putting a coin into the phone, a pair of muscular arms encircled my torso. The attacker lifted me off the ground, pinned my arms to my sides, and led me behind a small shack in a dark parking lot.

"Be cool," the man said. "I've got a gun."

I quickly sobered up.

My attacker was wearing gray sweats. He was about six-two, 235 pounds, I would later learn. As he took me behind the shack, out of sight of anyone on the street, I squirmed out of his grasp and looked at his waistband. No gun.

He reached around my waist and grabbed my wallet from my back pocket. I reared back and slugged him as hard as I could in the groin. He moaned and took a couple of steps back. I kicked him in the groin, ran to the street, and flagged down a passing squad car.

The cops found the would-be mugger staggering down the street a block or two away. I found my wallet in the parking lot. I'd lucked out. My attacker appeared to be drunk. If he'd been sober, he could have pummeled me, or worse.

A couple of months later, when my alleged attacker went to trial, I volunteered to the prosecutor how my awful night had started. He told the defense attorney, who asked me about it when I testified. I told the truth. The defendant walked.

A few weeks later, as I recall, I dealt with my citation. I admitted guilt, paid a modest fine, and filed the paperwork to have the incident expunged from my record. The episode should have been enough to scare me off crack and booze, or at least to prompt me to take a hard look at the direction my life was taking.

It wasn't.

I thought of Raven and crack as distractions—from personal woes as well as from ongoing career troubles. A few months after I met Raven, in the spring of 1989, I was dating Rosa, a smart, sarcastic, pretty teacher I'd met during a reporting assignment at her South Central middle school. One sticky summer night, she said she'd come over to my apartment in Figueroa Terrace, a hillside neighborhood a few miles north of downtown. I'd injured my left ankle playing basketball a few days earlier and could barely walk.

An hour before she arrived, I broke out my pipe and smoked a piece of a rock. I intended to stop there, but I ended up killing the entire thing. By the time Rosa got to my place, I was completely wired. She brought a bottle of wine, which we quickly downed. Now I was high and drunk, my inhibitions and judgment washed away. We stripped off our clothes and headed to the bedroom.

"Protection," she said. "You know I won't do it without a condom."

I knew. I *knew*. But in the moment, I simply didn't care. "Let me just start. I promise I'll cover up."

"You'd better."

I didn't.

Rosa's face morphed into a mask of horror the moment I came. She pushed me off her, jumped out of bed, and frantically dressed.

"Sorry," I whimpered. "I didn't mean to do that."

Rosa paused and looked at me, revulsion on her face. She didn't say a word. She finished dressing and went into the living room to put on her shoes. I limped in.

"Can we talk about this?"

She wouldn't look at me as she stormed out. I threw on a T-shirt, a pair of shorts, and some sneakers and hobbled after her.

Rosa saw me and marched around the corner toward her car. I followed. She stopped and stared at a concrete wall surrounding a nearby apartment complex.

"Can we talk about this, please?" I said.

Rosa stared at the wall. I pleaded for her to say something. Finally, while still staring at the wall, she said, "I had an abortion a few years ago. It was the most awful experience of my life. I vowed to never put myself in that situation again. I told you to put on a condom, and you disrespected me." Tears were welling in her eyes.

Shame engulfed me. Rosa was in emotional agony—and at risk of even more physical pain—because of me. I'd always considered myself a decent guy, and now I'd brought a world of anguish to a woman I cared about.

Over and over, I apologized and begged for forgiveness. Rosa stared at the wall and didn't say another word. After five minutes of this, I limped back to my apartment. For a week, I called and left messages. I taped a note on the door to Rosa's apartment asking for another chance.

I never heard from her again.

A few hours after I left my plaintive note on Rosa's door, I got roaring drunk and drove by Raven's street. I couldn't find her. I drove home frustrated and lonely.

My career wasn't going any better. After more than six years at the *Herald Examiner*, I wanted to move on but had nowhere to go. The *Los Angeles Times* gave me a couple of interviews, but that was it. My dream choice, the *Washington Post*, responded to my résumé and clips with a polite kiss-off letter.

I slogged through the rest of the summer. Gordon Dillow, a *Herald Examiner* columnist and drinking buddy, kept a fifth of Jim Beam in his desk drawer. It was an old-school journalist's move, and Gordon was old-school to the core. He generously shared his booze with me. I began spiking cups of soda with Gordon's whiskey. I'd sit at my desk or at a computer, getting blasted in the middle of the workday. My life had no direction.

In early August 1989, a *Post* job fell from the sky. A recruiter called: There was an opening for a night police reporter, she said. With the city's homicide rate spiraling upward, thanks to neighborhood crack wars, the paper needed to hire someone ASAP. Was I interested?

A good deed had led to the call. A few months earlier, in the spring, I'd gone for a reporting assignment to a small Catholic church in Boyle Heights, a hardscrabble section of East L.A., where volunteers were helping immigrants cobble together documents to qualify for amnesty under newly reformed immigration law. Inside a tiny community center, I saw another reporter, a middle-aged white man in a suit, struggling to interview a Latina woman. I volunteered to translate.

The journalist, Jay Mathews, was the West Coast bureau chief for the *Post*. Before I could ask, he offered to write a letter of recommendation for me. I'm certain I never would have gotten even an interview without Jay's thumbs-up. Years later, I learned that Phil Dixon, a *Post* assistant city editor who'd held a similar job at the *Los Angeles Times* in the 1980s and liked my work, had also championed my cause. In anticipation of a drug test, I abstained from crack for a long, miserable week. I flew to D.C. on a Monday, went through a gauntlet of interviews on Tuesday, flew back to L.A. on Wednesday, and was offered the job on Thursday. It turned out the paper didn't screen for drug use. I accepted without bothering to negotiate. I didn't feel the need—the first offer represented a 33 percent pay bump.

Word spread quickly through the *Herald Examiner* newsroom. That afternoon, I wandered over to the sports section and lingered to watch a tennis match on TV. A sports editor I barely knew turned to me and said, simply, "So you're going to the Show"—the sportswriters' term for the major leagues.

I was moving up from the minors.

A few days before I hit the road to D.C., I visited Raven for one final crack-enhanced tryst. I wasn't worried that my crack use was getting out of my control, but I didn't want to run the risk of getting popped in D.C. for drug possession. And I wasn't about to do anything to jeopardize my roster spot in the Show.

Raven let me into her room and took my cash. She was usually holding at least one rock, but on this afternoon she had to go out to make the buy. The room smelled of cigarettes. A dozen or so butts lay in an ashtray on top of the battered dresser. I sat on the edge of the bed, picked up the remote from the nightstand, and channelsurfed. There was no porn, just the big three networks.

President George H. W. Bush appeared on each channel, sitting behind his desk in the Oval Office. I was about to click Poppy off when he picked up a clear plastic bag. My eyes zeroed in on the big white chunk inside. Could it be?

"This is crack cocaine," the president said grimly. He poked at the monster rock. Federal agents had busted a dealer and seized his stash in Lafayette Park, right in front of the White House.

"It's as innocent-looking as candy, but it's turning our cities into battle zones, and it's murdering our children," Bush said. "Let there be no mistake, this stuff is poison."

The president asked who was responsible for the drug problem, and then provided the answer: "Everyone who uses drugs, everyone who sells drugs, and everyone who looks the other way."

I wasn't looking away. I was staring hard at the plastic bag of crack, wondering how many $20 rocks were in there.

Raven returned. She tossed two rocks on the bed.

I turned off the TV and reached for my pipe. Raven had her own glass stem, but I'd brought mine for a reason. She stripped off her shirt and bra. I undid my belt. We finished the two rocks before I could get off. Raven said she could make another buy.

"Why don't we try it with the res?" I suggested.

By now, Raven had shown me how to scrape out the gray-black residue that built up inside the pipe after repeated use. The residue was considerably stronger than any rock.

We waited about ten minutes for the res to harden. From her purse Raven retrieved a straight piece of wire, about six inches long, and a small mirror, which she placed on the bed. She removed the charred filter from the pipe and placed it near the mirror.

With the focus of a brain surgeon, Raven held the glass stem over the mirror and scraped its walls with the wire. Fine dark-gray powder spilled onto the mirror.

"Half for you, half for me. Me first," I said. Raven nodded.

With one of my *Herald Examiner* business cards, I pushed the powder into a neat little pile about the size of half a rock. Raven put the filter back into one end of the pipe. With my thumb and forefinger, I carefully loaded the res onto the filter. I brought the pipe to my lips, flicked on the lighter, brought the flame to the pipe, and inhaled.

I held the res smoke as long as I could, exhaled, and gestured to Raven. She went down on me as I lit up again.

I climaxed the moment I exhaled the last of my res. I lay woozily on the bed as Raven loaded her share of the res into her own pipe and lit up. She took a long pull, leaned down, and shotgunned me. A few minutes later, I dressed and handed my pipe to Raven.

"I won't be needing this anymore," I said.

On my final day as an Angeleno, Gordon and another *Herald Examiner* crony treated me to a final lunch at Corky's, where I downed three gin and tonics with my turkey sandwich before lurching out to my Escort for the long drive east.

Leaving Los Angeles felt like a getaway. For me, L.A. was the city of doomed romance, excessive drinking, and risky crack use. D.C. beckoned like a new lover. I was going to the Show, where I'd be working in the same newsroom as Bob fucking Woodward, racing to crime scenes in the most murderous city in the country.

On top of that, the previous month, a nationwide ABC News–*Washington Post* poll had shown that 44 percent of Americans considered illegal drugs the nation's most serious problem.

The president had just declared a war on drugs—and I was going to be a war correspondent.

CHAPTER 2

COMBAT ZONE

Marion Barry strutted across the makeshift plywood stage, chin up and shoulders back, a bemused look on his face. Boos and catcalls greeted him. He turned to the crowd, gathered for a street festival in Adams Morgan, a trendy part of town full of nightclubs and ethnic restaurants. The mayor of Washington, D.C., lifted his arm and gave the crowd a single-fingered salute.

Video footage of the event made it to the six o'clock news a day or two later, a little more than a week after my valedictory tryst with Raven. I sat in my new apartment in Washington and watched on a fifteen-inch TV perched atop a box of books as I chomped on a Roy Rogers burger and took slugs from a bottle of beer. It was mesmerizing.

Los Angeles was also led by a black mayor, Tom Bradley. An ex-LAPD cop, he was calm, dignified, widely respected—and pathologically cautious. My pal Tony Castro, a *Herald Examiner* columnist, joked that Bradley had undergone the world's first charisma bypass.

Barry was a different kind of cat. During the previous months, the *Washington Post* had published several articles quoting unnamed sources who accused the mayor of doing crack. I'd read the stories carefully. I couldn't imagine why people close to the mayor would make such a specific, damning allegation if it wasn't true. Where there's crack smoke, I figured, there's crack. I knew better than most.

Barry's image disappeared from the TV screen. The anchor moved on to the next story.

Okay, I thought, *I'm not in L.A. anymore.* In six days, I'd be starting my new job as a nighttime crime reporter, working in a city where the mayor himself might be a crackhead. Perfect.

Washington has always been lousy with journalists who are drawn to the nation's capital to cover national politics and government. Those topics never thrilled me. It seemed that most political and government reporters were at the mercy of the people they covered. The nature of their jobs required that they be spoon-fed by spin doctors. Covering a presidential press conference would be exciting exactly once, it seemed to me.

I'd be on the street, chasing the gunplay, no two nights alike. Plus I was getting an unexpected chance to start my life and my career anew.

It was exhilarating, living a short jog from the White House, preparing to work at the newspaper of Watergate fame. For the first time in a couple of years, I felt optimistic about my life and my career. I'd left all my troubles, including crack, behind in Los Angeles. I felt like one of those movie characters who escapes the bad guys on his heels by sliding under a descending metal door a moment before it slams shut.

Oh, I'd had a blast at the *Herald Examiner*. If the *Post* was a powerful, shiny battleship in the sea of journalism, the *Herald Examiner* was a leaky pirate boat populated by misfits, malcontents, dreamers, and a few burnout cases. But as much fun as I'd had working there, the paper had no future. For years, the *Herald Examiner* had been hemorrhaging cash—about a million dollars a month, according to newsroom chatter. It folded six weeks after I arrived in Washington.

But my six and a half years at the *Herald Examiner* had prepared me well for the *Post* gig. Working at a newspaper with a small staff in a big, news-rich city meant I got a chance to write about almost everything. I'd covered earthquakes, fires, L.A. City Council meetings, local and state political races, the murder of singer Marvin Gaye, and the takedown of infamous serial killer Richard Ramirez, who was dubbed—by a *Herald Examiner* editor—the Night Stalker.

When I was working in L.A., I didn't think of myself as a crime reporter, but I had the soul, instincts, and resourcefulness that any good crime reporter needs. Wailing sirens and tight deadlines made me tingly. Chasing the big story amid chaos was energizing.

The more chaotic the situation, the better. I wrote a few longer pieces, articles that took two or three weeks to research and complete. But being in the street was what got my pulse racing. And I was good at it.

When the big earthquake hit Mexico City in September 1985, the paper sent me. As the plane cruised in for landing, I surveyed a ruined city from my window seat—fires and rubble everywhere. Outside the airport, I quickly interviewed a handful of taxi drivers—not for a story, but for a short-term hire. My gut told me that a young driver named Carlos was the biggest risk taker, so I hired him.

He confirmed my instincts. Young soldiers with assault rifles manned roadblocks, preventing non-official vehicles from going into damaged areas. Carlos roared through the stricken city, improvising alternate routes around the checkpoints. When we were stopped at a military roadblock, Carlos explained with urgency that "we" were press, persuading the soldiers to let us through.

For several days I witnessed and wrote about one amazing story after another: Mass burials with quick blessings by exhausted priests. A series of rescues, after several days, of newborn babies from the rubble of a hospital that had collapsed below ground level. Dazed men and women roaming a makeshift morgue in the outfield of a baseball field, studying hideously bloated heads and other body parts to try to identify missing loved ones. I hardly slept, but I wasn't tired. I was running on adrenaline.

The first big quake had hit on Thursday, September 19, 1985. The 8.0 earthquake knocked out all communications—phones, faxes, and Western Union wires were all down. On Friday afternoon, I flew to Ciudad Juarez, just across the border from El Paso, just to get to a phone. As I was in the air, an aftershock, almost as big as the first temblor, had struck the city. I called in my first story and hopped on a jet chartered by a group of journalists to get to Mexico City, after an editor approved the $1,000 cost. I spent Friday night reporting and Saturday morning handwriting my voluminous notes and a second story. The paper was counting on me; failure to file would have been a journalistic catastrophe.

I gathered my notes and hailed a taxi to the airport. I found a check-in line for a flight to Guadalajara. A fellow *Herald Examiner* reporter was working the story from there, in an airport hotel that still had phone service. More than a hundred people were in line, anxiously waiting to check in for the flight. I had to stay in Mexico City to continue reporting, but I had to get my notes to my colleague in Guadalajara. I studied the people waiting to board the flight and zeroed in on a woman with two young kids—a boy and a girl. I introduced myself to the woman, explained that I was a newspaper reporter from Los Angeles, and told her that it was important my notes got to my co-worker. Would she deliver them?

The woman nodded. Yes, of course.

This was my one shot. I thought she would probably follow through, but I wanted to be sure. I pulled out $100 and tried to hand her the cash.

"This is for helping us," I said.

The woman shook her head vigorously. "No, I don't need any money," she said.

I looked at her children. "For the kids."

The woman thought about it for a second, glanced at her kids, and took the money. A couple of days later, I flew back to Los Angeles and learned that the gambit had worked: My story had made the Sunday paper.

*

Being a reporter gave me a ticket to parachute into drama most people would never experience. I was naturally introverted and shy, but when I was on the job I assumed another, more forceful, more confident persona.

Three years before the *Post* hired me, I'd even roamed Raven's neighborhood looking to commit a felony in pursuit of a story. President Ronald Reagan had signed an immigration reform bill. The law required employers to check new hires for papers, to confirm they were in the country legally. I pitched an idea to my editors. They weren't thrilled about having me break federal law for an article, but I ran my scheme by a contact at the immigration service. The feds *probably* wouldn't come after me, she said. That was close enough for my bosses.

I didn't shave for a day, dressed down in tattered jeans and an old T-shirt, and made for the corner of Olympic Boulevard and Alvarado Street, a couple of blocks from Raven's motel hangout. The intersection was a magnet for shady characters. Inside of five minutes, a guy asked me, in Spanish, what I needed.

"Papers," I said.

"Seventy bucks," he replied.

He led me into a little office in a corner strip mall. Another guy asked what name I wanted to use. I made one up, and he took my photo and disappeared into the back. A couple of minutes later, the photographer returned and handed me a laminated "green card" with my picture and the name I'd provided. The ID hustler told me to meet him at a doughnut shop around the corner in ten minutes. I settled into a booth and waited.

He arrived on time, nervously swiveling his head side to side, looking for federal agents, then settled into the booth across from me. He reached under the acrylic tabletop and left a card on the metal crossbar that supported it, telling me to take it and leave the cash. The document peddler quickly counted the money and slipped out of the shop. I studied my "Social Security" card. The name matched the one on my green card.

A trained federal agent would quickly make both cards as fakes. A civilian employer might not. I wrote a first-person sidebar to a longer piece. It took Congress years of contentious negotiations to pass immigration reform; it took me fifteen minutes and $70 to buy fake documents that could defeat the new law. The feds didn't come after me.

I couldn't imagine doing anything with my life other than journalism, and I didn't think it would go well for me if I did. With the right tools, it seemed, my father could fix anything under the hood of a car or in the house. Hammering a nail was the extent of my fix-it skills. And I don't think I would have thrived in a nine-to-five office job. I couldn't stand routine, and I was congenitally disheveled. I could put on a freshly pressed suit and a brand-new dress shirt and within five minutes look as if I had slept in them. But the street didn't care how I dressed, or that I couldn't fix a carburetor.

As the local news droned on, I finished my meal, swigged the last of my beer, and headed to the fridge for another. A big smile crossed my face as I envisioned what it would be like covering record-breaking violence in a city with an in-your-face crackhead mayor.

Working here was going to be *fun*.

The possibility that Barry was a crack user and the violence unleashed by neighborhood drug wars were the top two stories in the city. By the end of 1989 there would be 434 killings, in a city of about 610,000 residents.

D.C. hadn't always been so violent. Just four years earlier, in 1985, the District had recorded 148 homicides. By 1987 the number of killings had spiked to 372.

In the 1970s, illicit drug sales in the city were stable, dominated by veteran dealers who controlled specific areas. Heroin was the street drug peddled the most during that decade. Its sale was highly centralized, limited to a handful of locations, mostly just north of downtown. Lou Hennessy recalled seeing as many as three hundred smack dealers and their clients clustering late at night at the corner of 14th and U Streets Northwest, one of the primary copping zones for heroin.

The profit margin for heroin dealers in geographically small D.C. was greater than it was for their counterparts in Baltimore and Philadelphia. District pushers sold a good portion of their product to users from the nearby Maryland and Virginia suburbs, who were willing to pay more than junkies from the city.

In addition to the smack sellers downtown, a handful of seasoned drug dealers operated in other sections of the city: Mint Jelly sold powder cocaine on 9th Street Northwest, the Hartwell gang peddled coke and heroin in deep Southeast, and Big Pink—who cruised around town in a pink Cadillac—dealt smack at 4th and M Streets Northwest. They and the other old-school drug dealers had their enforcers, but they knew that violence was bad for business and didn't use it casually or promiscuously.

Around 1980, groups of Jamaicans set up shop in D.C. to deal marijuana. They never commandeered a large amount of turf, but their arrival marked an important step in the evolution of D.C. street crime as established dealers defended their corners against the newcomers. In the inevitable gun battles that ensued, the Jamaicans fought with the kind of weaponry that had been all but unseen in Washington to that point. They carried semiautomatic nine-millimeter handguns, MAC-10 fully automatic submachine guns, and Uzis. The display of Jamaican firepower sparked an arms race among local drug dealers.

The long-standing drug markets blew up when crack hit the city five years later. Open-air crack emporiums appeared in neighborhoods that hadn't hosted drug markets before. Stable heroin and marijuana corners became contested crack zones. Scores of neighborhood crack kingpins rose to power. They were younger than the old-school dealers, men in their twenties or even teens. They were suddenly making barrels of cash—and, unlike the veterans, they were impulsive and quick on the triggers of their powerful new weapons.

Bandits who used to hit mom-and-pop stores with Saturday-night specials and sawed-off shotguns started going after drug dealers, because that was where the cash was. And the dealers were firing back—when they weren't firing at one another. With frightening speed, a culture of intimidation and retaliation took hold. When Lou had joined the force, retaliatory violence was rare, witness killings almost unheard of. Suddenly each shooting required payback, and witnesses—most of whom were in the drug game themselves— were being gunned down with alarming frequency. One neighborhood in Northeast was so violent it was known as Little Beirut.

Lou watched a series of police chiefs respond with ham-handed tactics that did nothing to stanch the bloodshed. He knew he could do better.

From the moment he put on the uniform, Lou loved being, as he liked to say, *po-lice*. Not FBI, not ATF, not DEA, not Secret Service. *Po-lice*. There was excitement and a chance to do some good. And no two days were ever the same.

He became a sworn officer two years after signing up as a cadet and quickly earned a reputation as a smart, resourceful, and effective street cop. While other newbies were writing traffic tickets, Lou and his partners were taking down armed robbers and capturing people carrying illegal guns.

He had good instincts and a great training officer, Skip Enoch, who taught him the value of building a rapport with people in the neighborhoods they patrolled—blue-collar workers, civil servants, store owners, junkies, hookers, and, if they were willing, even drug dealers and thugs. Some officers maintained the standoffish attitude of a soldier occupying a hostile foreign country. Skip showed Lou that an effective cop is part of the community. A good cop knows whom in the neighborhood to call when something happens on his beat; a great cop has people calling *him*. Skip also advised Lou that he didn't have to worry about internal affairs if he beat up a handcuffed suspect: He would lock up his protégé himself if Lou ever abused someone.

A couple of years after he became a full-time officer, Lou showed that he knew how to handle himself when the guns came out, too.

In January 1977, Lou was on a plainclothes assignment in a working-class Northeast D.C. neighborhood known as Brookland, near Catholic University. He went into a Safeway to grab an orange juice while his partner waited in their unmarked sedan on the street.

Lou was standing in a checkout line when two men stormed into the store and pulled out sawed-offs from beneath their jackets. Without being told, many of the patrons and workers hit the ground; armed robbers took down the store fairly regularly, the employees and the shoppers knew the score. A few patrons and workers headed for the back of the store, away from the trouble. Lou quietly drifted to the back. He didn't want the gunmen to see him unbutton his coat and retrieve the police revolver on his hip. Fighting back his fear, Lou held the gun in his shooting hand and slipped it into the pocket of his coat.

Less than a minute later, a half-dozen squad cars roared onto the street in front of the store. As they were preparing to enter the store, the two bandits had aroused the suspicion of Lou's partner, Freddy Merkle; he'd radioed for backup moments before the duo stormed in and took out their weapons. Freddy had a feel for developing trouble; he'd been in three shootouts with robbers in the neighborhood.

The two bandits were shocked by how quickly the cops swarmed outside the store.

"The rollers are here!" one of the gunmen yelled.

Clutching the gun in his pocket, Lou walked to the front of the store, toward the gunmen. Outside, uniformed cops pulled out their service pistols and shotguns and took cover behind their cruisers.

The gunmen saw the small army of cops and panicked. One of them started screaming and swearing. He headed for the back of the store, apparently looking for an escape route. The other bandit trained his weapon at the store manager's head. Lou stepped to within a yard of that robber. The bandit didn't seem to notice Lou; he was preoccupied with the cops gathered outside the store. Lou leveled the revolver in his pocket at the man's torso. The bandit's partner was out of Lou's line of sight.

Lou tensed. His right index finger caressed the trigger of his revolver. Lou thought it through: If he shot the bandit, would the robber reflexively shoot the store manager? How would the bandit's partner react? Lou figured he was busy trying to flee. But he might start firing if Lou shot his partner. A bloodbath seemed inevitable.

To Lou, it felt like he, the bandit, and the store manager were the only people in the store. Lou kept his gun pointed at the bandit for what seemed like a half hour. In reality, it was three, maybe four minutes. The gunman menacing the manager suddenly turned his head toward Lou.

"What should I do?"

"If I were you, I'd call 911 and talk to the police," Lou said.

To his astonished relief, the bandit lowered his shotgun, walked behind a service counter, and picked up the phone. He was patched through to a police commander in the parking lot.

Minutes later, both gunmen dropped their weapons and walked out of the store with their hands in the air.

Later that night, in the police station, Lou walked up to the bandit he'd almost shot. The man was sitting in a holding area, handcuffed.

"Do you realize how close I came to killing you?" Lou said.

"Who the hell are you? You're too young to be a roller."

Lou brushed his coat aside and showed the badge and gun clipped to his belt.

"Goddamn, you *are* a roller!" the man exclaimed.

By the early eighties, Lou was working as a homicide detective, discovering that he liked jumping into investigations, gathering evidence, and figuring out ways to coax—or leverage—witnesses to talk. Lou took the sergeant's exam when he was thirty. He aced it. Same with the exams for lieutenant and captain. In a span of three years, he rose from officer to captain.

At thirty-three, he was young for a captain—and he figured he had maxed out. Tests determined promotions up to that rank; all promotions beyond it were political, approved by the mayor. Barry was known to favor certain high-ranking commanders, who in turn looked out for other white shirts in their clique. Lou never joined a faction and didn't put any energy into departmental politics—he was all about being the *po-lice*, enforcing the law and keeping the peace. Being part of the clique meant telling his chief whatever he wanted to hear, and Lou wasn't wired like that.

Beyond that, Lou believed, the city's political system for police appointments wasn't helping matters on the street. People in dozens of neighborhoods overrun by drug dealing and violence pressured elected officials for relief. The pols leaned on the police brass. The white shirts responded with a series of highly publicized sweeps, arresting dozens of street dealers at a time. These operations got great play on the TV news shows, local residents felt grateful, and the Metropolitan Police Department bumped up its arrest statistics. MPD made some forty thousand arrests between 1986 and 1988, in Operation Clean Sweep, which focused on street dealers and buyers.

But a day or two after police made arrests, the street dealers were either back out or replaced by other slingers. The buyers lined up again. The police department didn't even bother to interview arrestees to try to compile intelligence on the serious players. The real dealers and enforcers weren't on the street making retail sales, so the sweeps didn't touch them. MPD was going after garden snakes and ignoring the cobras and pythons.

Not only did the sweeps have no lasting impact, they were actually counterproductive, Lou thought. They made the police look like ineffectual amateurs.

In the city's most violent neighborhoods, detectives heard the same names over and over in the wake of a shooting. The fact that there were more than four hundred homicides in the city didn't mean that there were four hundred killers. There were a relative handful of shooters—two, maybe three dozen—killing a lot of people, Lou believed. They tended to operate in specific neighborhoods, where everybody knew who they were. Most killings weren't whodunits. The challenge was getting frightened witnesses to testify.

Lou had given the problem a lot of thought. He'd developed a plan for how to go after the most violent players in the city.

All he needed was a chance to put it into action.

Six days after Barry flipped the bird, I began my first Saturday in town with some pickup hoops at the downtown YMCA. Then I settled down to watch a college football game. After a couple of beers, I upgraded to gin and tonics. Three drinks later, I was happily drunk.

I was in no condition to drive. But in L.A. I'd gotten behind the wheel dozens of times while hammered and had never been pulled over. It was a warm, sunny September day. I wanted to explore my new neighborhood, my new city. What harm could come of that?

My street was dominated by Victorian row houses. There was an old four-story apartment building at the far end of the block, directly across the street from a church. I drove a block past the apartment building and the church and turned right, toward downtown.

I'd gone exactly three blocks when I saw her. She was standing on the corner of 13th and M Streets Northwest, near a liquor store. Her brown eyes followed each passing car. She was trying to make eye contact with motorists.

The woman was petite, with curly, dark brown hair and fair, freckled skin. She wore a calf-length black skirt, a short-sleeve blouse, and flats. She held a small black handbag. I guessed her to be about my age, in her late twenties.

She was working the street, trying to be subtle, and mostly pulling it off. The woman was pretty, but not TV-ingenue gorgeous, like Raven. She looked like someone I'd feel comfortable approaching at a party after one or three drinks.

If I'd been sober, I might have kept driving, but the beer and gin had drowned my better judgment. There'd be no harm in talking to her, I figured. I pulled over to the curb, leaned over, and rolled down my passenger-side window.

"Hi!" she chirped. "You want some company?"

Her invitation unleashed a little jolt of adrenaline, the kind I'd felt whenever I'd pulled up to the curb on Raven's street. The rush of getting high began with making the buy, and making the buy usually started with finding the girl to cop the rock.

I glanced at the street in front of me and checked the rearview mirror. Traffic was light. There were no cops in sight. The thought just popped into my head: *Why not?*

"Sure," I replied as I reached over and opened the passenger door.

The woman swiveled her head, taking a quick look down both ends of the street, then settled into my car.

"What's your name?" I said.

"Champagne."

Maybe it was her obvious street name. It could have been junkie intuition. Real estate certainly had something to do with it. Though we were only two blocks from the shiny office buildings and upscale hotels of downtown, we were in a neighborhood full of liquor stores and run-down apartment buildings, its streets populated by junkies, winos, and strawberries. I'd chosen my apartment because it was just five blocks from the main offices of the *Post*, but I think part of me was drawn to the inherent drama of the whole area.

Whatever the reason, as soon as Champagne was in my car, I just *knew*. It had been eleven long days since my last hit, and in that moment, some internal switch was flipped.

"So," I said. "Do you party?"

Champagne knew exactly what I meant. She opened her handbag and held it over the gearshift so I could see inside. The bag contained a nail file, a handful of condoms, a small mirror, a lighter, a six-inch strand of hanger wire, and a crack pipe.

Aces. I checked the rearview again. All clear.

"If I buy a rock for you, and one for me, would you do me while I'm hitting the pipe?"

"Sure."

"Are you holding?"

"No, but I know where to go. It's close by. I can get us two for thirty-five."

One more party wouldn't hurt. "You navigate."

Champagne directed me two blocks north, to Logan Circle. She had me bear right, onto Rhode Island Avenue, toward the east. We passed people engaged in ordinary Saturday-afternoon activities: a group of kids playing basketball on the outdoor court of a middle school, a handful of old people passing the time in chairs outside their building, a woman carrying a bag of groceries. They hardly looked like the residents of a city under siege from crack violence.

At 7th Street Northwest, Champagne had me turn left. Two blocks later, we hit the corner of 7th and S.

"Turn right here and park," she said.

I pulled up directly in front of a squat concrete building with a small sign that read JOHN'S PLACE. A nightclub. I killed the engine and gaped.

In front of us, a half-dozen or so sullen young men and teenagers in wifebeaters or tees and sagging shorts or blue jeans loitered in the shade of a tree in front of a row house. Across the street, an equal number of slingers leaned against a rusty railing in front of an abandoned bakery.

The two-story brick building was huge. The front spanned about thirty yards, and it looked to be more than fifty yards deep. Two sets of front doors were padlocked, and the windows were covered with plywood. Near the top of the facade, plastic letters spelled WONDER BREAD and HOSTES CAKE, a space where the second S in HOSTESS had once been. I wondered whether some young gunslinger had knocked it off during target practice.

The building seemed like some kind of giant, urban ghost ship.

My eyes flickered to the right, to our side of the street. A brick row house stood next to John's Place, then an alley, followed by four modest two-story houses.

In the middle of the block stood a large brick Victorian with circular bay windows and a large turret on top. It looked like a small castle. The lush front yard was filled with boxwoods, a rosebush, and daisies, all shaded by a large sycamore. The yard was set off from the sidewalk by a short, black iron fence. A small sign near the front door read NEW COMMUNITY CHURCH. A church? Here? In the middle of a crack zone?

To my right, just past John's Place, a thin man flipped burgers on a grill in the small front yard of his home, seemingly unconcerned about the brazen drug dealers working the block. The aroma of barbecue wafted into the car.

Within five seconds, the slingers on both sides of the street spotted Champagne and sprang to life. Their eyes lit up as they raced toward my car. Yeah, she was known on the block. I watched them close in with a combination of anticipation and horror. I imagined a team of plainclothes cops swooping in, guns drawn, as Champagne exchanged crack for cash from the passenger seat.

"The money?" Champagne asked, calm as Sunday morning.

"Not in the car," I said, my voice tense. I knew that some cities could confiscate the vehicles of motorists busted for drug buys made from a car. I wasn't sure if D.C. was one of them. "Do you mind getting out?"

Champagne shrugged. "Fine."

I handed her the cash. The street dealers surged toward her. I checked the rearview once more.

As soon as her feet hit the sidewalk, Champagne was surrounded by a dozen slingers. I figured she'd lead them into the nearby alley, on the side of John's Place, out of plain sight. I figured wrong. Champagne stayed put as the dealers formed a tight circle around her. They reached into their pockets, then held out their palms, displaying their products. Calmly, as casually as if she were inspecting fruit at a farmers' market, Champagne considered her options. I watched in anxious awe.

In Los Angeles, the Latino-gangster slingers in MacArthur Park and in Raven's neighborhood at least looked over their shoulders for cops during drug deals. Here we were, barely two miles from the White House, and neither Champagne nor the dealers were breaking a sweat.

In fact, Champagne looked bored. After what felt like a small eternity, she nodded toward one slinger and made the buy. The crack dealers retreated to their territory like football players jogging to the sideline after being removed from the game. Champagne strolled back to my car. I checked the far end of the street. Still no cops.

"How'd you do?" I said.

"See for yourself."

She opened her palm, displaying two healthy-sized chunks of rock in separate plastic baggies. Goose bumps erupted on my arms and neck.

"Nice job," I said.

I turned on the ignition, shifted into drive, and cruised past the guy barbecuing on his front lawn, the slingers, the bakery, and the church that looked like a castle.

We reached the end of the block. As I hung a right to head back to my apartment, I joked, "I guess these guys haven't heard about the war on drugs."

A quizzical expression crossed Champagne's face. "Huh?"

At my place, we sat on the edge of my bed and got right to it. Without a word, she cut her rock in half, loaded it into her pipe, lit up, and inhaled.

"Shotgun?" I asked. Champagne nodded. We leaned toward each other and she exhaled a blast of crack smoke into my mouth. The hit made me light-headed. I motioned for the pipe and lighter. She handed them to me.

"You'll do me while I do my rock, right?" Champagne reached into her handbag, brought out a condom, and broke open the wrapper.

"Ready when you are," she said. The rock was good. Champagne was good. Together, the rock and Champagne were great.

Before she left, Champagne grabbed a piece of scrap paper and a pen from my nightstand and scribbled her name and a series of digits.

"That's my pager number," she said. "Call me whenever."

Remorse kicked in as soon as she walked out the door. I padded to the bathroom and stared at my guilty-looking face in the mirror. In less than forty-eight hours, I'd be starting my job as a crime reporter at the *Washington Post*. What the hell was I thinking?

In disgust, I grabbed the paper with Champagne's number, rolled it into a ball, and fired it into a wastebasket. I downed a frozen dinner with a beer, vowed to stay away from Champagne and S Street, and went to bed.

*

The next morning, I stirred awake as slivers of sunlight angled through the blinds of my bedroom. My apartment was ten feet above street level. A rickety wooden porch ascended from the sidewalk to my door. I opened the door, stepped outside, and, for the first time, picked up the Sunday edition of the *Post*. The street was dead quiet. On the other side of the block, a middle-aged couple in their Sunday best walked toward the church at the far end of the street. Birds chirped.

I dumped milk, a banana, and some peanut butter into a blender, then reconsidered the previous night.

Champagne had been fun. She didn't dress like a hooker, so she wouldn't draw undue attention from my neighbors. She was willing to assume all the risk of copping. She held the money. She made the buy. She carried the rocks until we got to my place.

If I happened to be on S Street when the cops swooped in—if they ever did—well, there was no law against giving someone a ride. The police would know why I was there, but they'd never be able to prove it. The cops might detain me for questioning, and I might suffer some embarrassment. But so long as I wasn't charged with a crime, my bosses at the *Post* were unlikely to find out about my tawdry activities. There would be no harm, no foul. And thirty-five bucks for a rock and a blow job was a pretty sweet deal.

I stepped into the bedroom and retrieved the balled-up sheet of paper with Champagne's pager number. I carefully opened it, smoothed it out, and slipped it into my sock drawer.

If the slingers were working that brazenly in the middle of the day, S Street must be an around-the-clock operation. It was a five-minute drive from my apartment. Champagne was clearly connected. I was about to get a nice pay bump courtesy of the *Post*.

I couldn't see a downside.

CHAPTER 3

"THIS MUST BE WHERE GOD NEEDS US"

On a gray, frigid day, pastor Jim Dickerson and demolition man Claude Artis inspected a small wood-frame house on S Street Northwest. The structure stood a few feet from a four-story Victorian that Jim and his humble congregation, a dozen strong, hoped would become their spiritual home, the place they would gather for Sunday services.

It was January 1984. Cops had shooed away the heroin junkies, squatters, hookers, and hustlers who'd made the big brick house at 614 S their own for years. The building would need to be thoroughly cleaned and renovated before it would be of any use as a church. But first, Jim and Claude had to deal with the smaller house, which was also part of the property—and looked as if it might fall over in the first decent breeze.

Jim and Claude crunched their boots over the remnants of a recent snowfall as they circled the sad little building. The front door and windows were long gone. The framing was rotting. The roof looked like two big slabs of Swiss cheese. The whole sorry thing was leaning hard to one side.

Fifteen or so drug dealers were working the other side of the street, near the not-yet-derelict Hostess bakery. Delivery trucks lurched out of the huge building every twenty minutes or so. The inviting smell of freshly baked bread, muffins, and cakes filled the winter air. A couple of the slingers wandered over to a fire burning inside a rusty metal trash can on an empty lot directly across the street from the old wooden house.

The drug dealers eyeballed Jim, Claude, and the demolition man's crew. Claude hired laborers off the street. Some of them were friends with some of the slingers. Some bought drugs from them.

Claude studied the house. He was compact and muscular, with a thick neck and arms and shoulders that could have belonged to a middleweight boxer. Claude looked like someone who could handle himself in a brawl.

"This bad boy's done," he said. "It can't be saved. I best blow it up."

Jim nodded in agreement. "I'm afraid you're right. This structure's not worth saving. We're better off knocking it down."

A tall and lean forty-year-old, Jim wore wire-rim glasses and a beard. He was bald on top, with a fringe of brown hair that ran from ear to ear. He looked like he'd be at home in a college lecture hall.

The slingers who'd gathered near the fire leaned toward one another and exchanged whispers. They threw hard looks at Jim and Claude.

Silently, independently, Jim and Claude came to the same unnerving conclusion: The dope boys were using this little house to hide their stashes of heroin, methamphetamine, and Dilaudid. Now here they were, fixing to blow it up.

Jim rubbed the back of his neck. This was grief he didn't need. The minister looked at Claude. The two men were good friends. Jim asked Claude what they should do. The demo man pivoted toward the dope boys and said, "Come with me, reverend."

They were halfway across the street when Claude, in his deep, booming voice, called out, "Listen up, fellas, the reverend wants to talk with you!"

Claude had caught Jim by surprise. Jim could usually yap about anything until the seasons changed, and he'd planned on reaching out to the street dealers soon. But not this soon. Jim felt his pulse quicken as they approached the slingers.

Jim and Claude stopped on one side of the trash can. The dealers gathered on the other side, about five feet away, and stared hard at Jim, murder in their eyes.

The pastor shifted toward Claude until they were standing shoulder to shoulder. Jim blew out a white breath. He was scared, shaking, which he hoped the dope boys would mistake for shivering from the cold. *Help me, God*, Jim prayed to himself as he scanned his audience.

In the next moment, the words came to him.

"Listen, fellas. We're gonna have to blow up that little house across the street," Jim said calmly. "So those of you who have your stash there, now's the time to get it out."

The dealers looked at the house, then back at Jim.

Jim felt his neck muscles tense. He wondered: What would he do—what could he do—if the drug dealers bucked? What could he do if they declared war on him and his church?

A slinger named Chief stepped up to Jim. Chief was an American Indian, with a bronzed complexion and a ponytail that hung to his waist. He never smiled.

Could really use your help again here, God, Jim prayed to himself.

Chief extended his hand.

"Well, thank you, Reverend. Thank you so much," Chief said.

The drug dealer and the minister shook hands. Jim exhaled as a sense of relief and gratitude washed over him.

Chief and the other slingers made a beeline for the doomed house.

Jim grew up a thousand miles from S Street, in a small cracker-box house in the working-class, racially segregated town of Conway, Arkansas. He was born in Fort Smith, hard by the

Oklahoma state line, about two hundred miles from Conway. Jim was a toddler when his biological father was put in a state mental hospital. Jim's mother divorced his father and supported herself and her boy by waitressing. She met and married a doctor, and the family moved to Conway when Jim was in the third grade. Jim's mom and stepfather had two children, a boy and a girl.

Jim's stepfather was a good doctor, but he was also a binge drinker. He was kind and fun when he was sober, but when he was drunk, he would scream at the kids and sometimes beat Jim's mom. He would disappear for as long as two months at a time. Once when he was drunk, he waved around a gun and threatened to kill the entire family. Jim's mother was also an alcoholic and prescription drug addict. Young Jim never doubted that his mother and stepfather loved him and his siblings. But thanks to their alcoholism, domestic tranquillity never lasted long.

Conway was a speck of a place where everybody knew everybody else's business. What Jim's family was going through wasn't a secret. Many of the town's residents considered themselves devout Christians, and their failure to help his family angered Jim.

"I hated the hypocrisy of many of the church people. They rejected us and stayed away from our family because we were such a mess," he said. "On one level I didn't blame them—but that wasn't real Christianity." As the oldest child, Jim assumed responsibility for the family, such as giving his mom money he earned from delivering newspapers and doing odd jobs so she'd have enough money for food.

When Jim was about ten, his stepfather and mother started attending Alcoholics Anonymous meetings. Back then, in the fifties, many AA meetings were held in people's homes. Participants of different ages, races, and social classes were welcome—and all were treated the same. In an AA meeting, a wealthy banker was on the same level as a low-wage janitor. *This* is what Christianity is really about, Jim would realize later on: acceptance, compassion, egalitarianism, people with seemingly little in common coming together to help one another with a common problem. His step-father and his mother quit drinking for a year, but neither could stay sober.

Jim's home life didn't prevent him from having a good time in high school, where he was popular. An average student, Jim was a talented dancer, and he played on the football team. He graduated in 1961 and landed a job with Southwestern Bell, repairing telephone lines on poles seventy-five feet in the air. He was already spending time in bars and at the Veterans of Foreign Wars hall with some of his hell-raising childhood friends and telephone-company co-workers. A small organized-crime group operated out of the hall. In an ostensibly dry county, the hall sold booze and ran an illegal gambling enterprise.

It wasn't long before Jim became part of the group, working for tough men who had nicknames like Two Ton and Jimmy Fiddler. He did small jobs for them, transporting liquor or starting craps games, and spent a couple of nights in jail for petty crimes and bar brawls. Jim's mom warned him he was on the fast track to ruin, telling him, "Jimmy, you won't live to vote." By the time he was in his early twenties, he was miserable. To self-medicate, he popped pills and drank heavily. He would sometimes run into his mom in beer joints, nightclubs, and liquor stores.

"One day I looked in the mirror and I saw a stranger," Jim recalled. "*Who are you? Where are you going?* I was a wreck. My life had no purpose, no meaning, no value to anyone."

After one particularly hard night of drinking at an after-hours club in Little Rock, Jim and a friend were driving home when suddenly his buddy asked, "What do you think the good Lord thinks of all this, Jim?"

His pal was from a conservative, churchgoing family, and he was reflecting on his own drinking and carousing, Jim believed. But the question resonated with Jim. He'd been thinking about his own boozing, women-chasing, small-time-hoodlum-associating ways.

Jim gazed out of the car into the post-midnight darkness.

"I don't know," he replied. "But I'm going to find out."

Jim wasn't sure if he could change his life, but he was determined to try. Without any particular plan, he moved to North Little Rock, renting a room in a three-room apartment. He didn't know anybody in town. He wandered the streets, asking God to show him a sign. He started to wonder if he was going crazy, like his biological father.

One night, he got on his knees in his room and cried out: "God, if you're there, please take me. I don't know what to do." As he finished his emotional prayer in tears, Jim felt an immediate release. His pain, despair, and anger dissipated. In their place, he felt healing, peace, and a sense of joy he'd never before experienced.

Jim quit drinking and started attending support-group meetings. He also decided it was time to get past his loathing of churches. When he was a child, Jim and his family had watched an Episcopal pastor, the Reverend Rufus J. Womble, on TV every morning at 7:55. Womble emphasized compassion and the healing power of God, not fire and brimstone. Jim went to Womble's church one Sunday and met the pastor at the door after a service.

"My name's Jim Dickerson. I've decided to turn my life over to God—or Jesus—or somebody," he said, tears streaming down his face. Womble welcomed him. Jim's faith began to take root.

Jim started volunteering at a local Boys Club, working with low-income children, all of them white. The club director, Jim Wetherington, had been slowly integrating the club, bringing in a black kid here, a black kid there. After Jim had been volunteering a few weeks, Wetherington hired him to be his assistant and the program director for the club. Jim helped recruit more black children, and the pace of integration picked up.

As more blacks joined the club, most of the whites left. But slowly, over the span of more than a year, many of them returned.

The club was well run, and there weren't a lot of options for structured recreation for kids in town.

For about three years, Jim attended Womble's church. He even occasionally delivered his own sermon. Jim was a natural speaker, and Womble urged him to become an Episcopal minister. But Jim was worried about the church's lack of social activism and outreach. Jim lived in a black neighborhood and had joined civil rights marches, but he couldn't invite his black friends to church because he knew they'd be treated badly. His fellow parishioners were exclusively white, financially well-off, and socially conservative. Three days after the Reverend Martin Luther King Jr. was assassinated 130 miles away in Memphis, Tennessee, Womble's sermon didn't even mention the slaying of the civil rights leader.

"They were segregationists, and I didn't even realize it until then," Jim said. Womble and his congregation had been good to him—but he knew he couldn't stay.

In 1965, about a year after Jim began volunteering at the Boys Club, he enrolled at the University of Arkansas at Little Rock, where he double-majored in political science and sociology. One of his courses was taught by Carol Smelley, a charismatic social worker who'd been instrumental in the state in establishing group homes for juvenile girls as an alternative to incarceration.

Smelley and her husband, Wes, often had Jim and other students to their house for meals and long talks. Jim told her about his boyhood hatred of Christian hypocrisy, his days as a hell-raiser, his frustrations with the churches he'd attended—not only Womble's but also a Presbyterian church that was more concerned with social action and placed little emphasis on connecting with God as an individual. Smelley loaned Jim two books: *Call to Commitment* and *Journey Inward, Journey Outward*, both written by Elizabeth O'Connor. They told the story of the founding of the Church of the Saviour, an unconventional church in Washington, D.C.

The books had an immediate and dramatic impact on Jim. The Church of the Saviour, O'Connor wrote, aimed to "recover ... something of the vitality and life, vigor and power of the early Christian community." It was organized around small congregations and even smaller "mission groups" that explore how the Gospels are relevant to members' lives. One doesn't need to be an ordained minister to start such a congregation—in the Church of the Saviour, every member is considered a minister.

"It was the kind of church I had in me," Jim said. "It was a commitment of your life to God, a commitment that helps you live your faith according to your gifts and your calling in challenging ways. It was about more than just going to church on Sunday morning."

Smelley told Jim he should consider launching his own congregation in Little Rock and encouraged him to investigate the Church of the Saviour in person. He went to Washington in 1968 and again in 1969. The church's structure was familiar and comforting to him. "The Church of the Saviour had that AA flavor," he said. "These were small groups, with the emphasis on personal transformation and reaching out. It was very egalitarian."

On his first visit, Jim heard church co-founder Gordon Cosby preach. "Gordon said, 'The church is a laboratory for change,'" Jim recalled. "That was the opposite of what I'd seen in other churches, which were static and resistant to change."

After his second visit, Jim returned to Little Rock and continued his education. In January 1971, on a cold gray day, Jim stuffed his belongings into an old Ford and headed for D.C. "I looked like someone from *The Grapes of Wrath*, heading east," Jim recalled. He moved to Washington to join the Church of the Saviour and learn as much as he could about it, hoping eventually to found a congregation in Arkansas.

In D.C., Jim launched a nonprofit called Rehabilitation of Men and Houses. He recruited men who were fresh out of prison, jail, or detox to renovate homes. The program helped them learn or sharpen their skills and develop a work history. As word of the group spread, a couple of guys who lived at a local Mennonite service home and had carpentry experience volunteered to help out.

One night, after a day of renovating houses, Jim drove the men back to their group house, which was located at the corner of 14th and W Streets NW, in the middle of the zone that had been devastated by the 1968 riots. There he met Grace Martin, a beautiful young Mennonite woman who was also a resident of the home. Jim was immediately smitten. Grace was not.

Jim persisted. He got himself an invitation to dinner at the group house and chatted her up. Later, he took her for a walk in Rock Creek Park, where they strolled by a cemetery. Grace wanted to explore, so they climbed over the cemetery's iron fence. He was gazing at a tombstone when he heard Grace cry out in pain: She'd been climbing a memorial topped with a three-foot-tall concrete cross and lost her balance. The cross had tumbled onto her ankle, breaking it.

Jim put her on his shoulders and, somehow, scaled the seven-foot fence without dropping her. He carried Grace to his car, and an off-duty police officer who happened to be on the street led them to the emergency room at George Washington University Hospital. Because she had no insurance, Grace could stay in the facility just one night; the next day, she was taken to D.C. General Hospital, the city's public hospital in Southeast.

Grace's injury was gruesome: She had open wounds on both sides of her ankle. Fearing that an infection would invade her bones, doctors decided not to set the ankle until the wounds healed. Nurses cleaned up the wounds. But the ankle wouldn't heal. Doctors refused to release her, saying that she needed surgery and that if they allowed her to leave, they couldn't guarantee there would be a bed for her later.

For several weeks, Grace was on a surgery list, but she never made it to the operating room. She begged to be released, saying she'd come back for surgery after her ankle healed, but her doctors wouldn't budge. They insisted there wouldn't be a bed for her if she left.

Grace reached her limit during Thanksgiving week. "I had had it, so I told them I was leaving, and if they weren't going to give me crutches I would get someone to bring me some," she recalled. Hospital administrators had Grace sign a document releasing the hospital from liability if she suffered any medical complications after she left.

"I told them I didn't care where they put me when I returned for my surgery," Grace said. "They could put me on the floor or in the hall if they didn't have a bed for me." The hospital gave her crutches and released her.

Grace went home for Thanksgiving, and her ankle quickly improved. She returned to D.C. General for her surgery in December. Her ankle hadn't healed correctly, however, so doctors decided to rebreak it and insert pins. Grace had to stay in the hospital, often in horrible pain, until early February.

In all, she spent two and a half months in the hospital, restricted to her bed.

It was a perfect opportunity for a persistent suitor. Jim visited Grace every day. Little by little, he won her over. Near the end of her stay, he asked Grace to marry him.

She said yes.

Jim remained in close contact with the Smelleys and his other friends in Arkansas. He entered the Virginia Theological Seminary, where he earned a master's in theological studies. In 1975, he and Grace moved to Little Rock. But Jim's attempts to establish a church in his home state went nowhere. After a year, he and Grace returned to D.C., where he tried to launch a church out of a home in Northwest Washington, the way the Church of the Saviour had started. A handful of congregants met a few times—then didn't. Another effort was more successful and became the Community House Church. But Jim eventually left. He wanted to lead a church located in a low-income neighborhood, somewhere where people needed help.

By now, Jim and Grace had three young children: Ben, Rachel, and Andre. For a year, the family attended Jubilee Church, an offshoot of the Church of the Saviour whose members met in a coffee shop and bookstore in Adams Morgan. In 1981, Jim attempted once more to start his own church. With twelve core members, he founded New Community Church. The flock consisted of whites and blacks. All were District residents. They met for Sunday services in the office of a nonprofit group on 14th Street Northwest.

In late 1983, Jim heard about the abandoned row house on S Street and drove over to check it out. He pulled to the curb and gawked: The big house had no windows. Junkies sat on the windowsills and injected heroin. Hookers led johns into the house for quickies. Squatters ducked in and out of the place as they pleased. The rest of the block was no better, with slingers brazenly serving a steady stream of customers. The drivers of the Hostess bakery's delivery trucks sometimes had to wait for the completion of a drug deal before turning onto the block.

He walked into the house as a couple of squatters walked out. The first two floors were littered with clothes, food cartons, and syringes. The stench of human urine and feces was overpowering. Jim climbed to the second floor, then the third. He stopped in his tracks. Not long before he heard about the house, he'd had a dream: "I was in a room in a poor neighborhood. A single unadorned lightbulb was hanging from the ceiling. There was another person in the room. I couldn't tell who, but I wasn't afraid. The room was painted green."

Now, in the house on S Street, Jim stared at the walls: The paint on the third floor was green. Jim realized the person in the room in his dream was Jesus.

Jim considered the dream—and the hard reality of the junkies, hookers, squatters, and slingers who populated the street. *This must be where God needs us*, he concluded. After all, Jesus had walked easily among the sinners and the outcasts, the neglected and the rejected.

The place was perfect.

*

Crack hadn't made it to D.C. when Jim first ventured onto S Street. But the area, in the Shaw neighborhood, a few blocks east of downtown, had been a 24-7 drug emporium since the early 1970s. Among some cops, the street was known as the "Fast Lane."

Until the end of the 1960s, Shaw had been a stable, affordable, predominantly black residential neighborhood. Its turn-of-the-century row houses and World War II–era apartment buildings were occupied by laborers, nurses, civil servants, and hotel and restaurant workers. Thriving businesses lined the retail corridor of 7th Street Northwest.

Shaw was also a vibrant cultural center. The Howard Theatre, built in 1910, was located one block north of S Street. Through the decades, the venue hosted dozens of prominent black entertainers, including Ella Fitzgerald, Duke Ellington, Nat King Cole, Otis Redding, and James Brown. White artists such as Buddy Holly and Danny Kaye also performed there.

Everything began to change on the evening of April 4, 1968, with the assassination of the Reverend Martin Luther King Jr., which sparked more than three days and nights of rioting across large swaths of the city. More than eleven thousand Army troops and another three thousand National Guardsmen were deployed in response to the looting and widespread burning of businesses. When it was over, twelve people had been killed, thousands had been injured, and more than nine hundred businesses had been damaged or destroyed. More than six hundred dwellings—apartments and single-family homes—had been ruined, many by fire.

Some of the worst destruction occurred in Shaw, on or near 7th Street. Hundreds of properties were damaged or destroyed. In the span of a few angry days and nights, Shaw was transformed from a flourishing neighborhood into an urban wasteland. In the wake of the rioting, thousands of white business owners and residents, as well as many middle-class blacks, fled Washington, taking their energy and ideas—and a big chunk of the city's tax base—with them. The Howard Theatre closed in 1970.

In the eighties, while downtown Washington bloomed with new office buildings, restaurants, and hotels, the area around 7th and S languished. Nearly a decade and a half after the riots, it still resembled a bombed-out war zone. The streets remained full of abandoned brick shells and empty lots. The Howard Theatre reopened sporadically throughout the decade, then shut down again. The Hostess bakery, which employed dozens of bakers, wrappers, and truck drivers, would be shuttered a couple of years after the church took root at 614 S.

Over the years, Mayor Barry and the series of local council members who represented the neighborhood didn't do nearly enough to encourage revitalization. This failure created a leadership vacuum on S Street—one that would be filled by a charismatic and dangerous man.

It wouldn't be long before Jim crossed paths with him.

Jim moved quickly on the house. The owner owed $70,000 in tax liens. He was willing to sign over the building if Jim would assume the tax bite. Jim made some calls to a few people he knew at city hall and described his plan to establish a church on S Street. Eventually, the tax liens disappeared.

Jim drove Grace to S Street, eager to show her the future home of the church. He pulled over to the curb and pointed out the building. Grace was supportive, but Jim could tell she was nervous about the location. "She didn't even get out of the car that first day," he recalled.

Accompanied by church volunteers, Jim spent the first few months of 1984 cleaning out the house. They wore paper surgical masks to try to ward off the stench and donned work gloves to keep themselves from being pricked by one of the hundreds of used needles littering the floor. One trash bag at a time, they hauled away the detritus of junkie living.

One day, Jim wandered out to the street to chat with the drug dealers. Again, they gathered around the burning trash can.

"Listen up, fellas," Jim said. "I'm not going to turn any of you in for drug dealing. We all have to get along. And more importantly, I'm here to help you find God and change your lives, if you so choose."

The slingers didn't say anything, but a couple of them silently nodded their heads in assent.

"One more thing," Jim added. "When the church opens, all of you are welcome. You don't need to dress up. Just come as you are."

A few weeks later, a couple of plainclothes D.C. narcotics cops came to see Jim at the church. "You've got an awful drug problem on this street," one of them said. "The top floor of this house would make a great observation post."

"Let us help you out," the second officer said. "We can clean out all these street dealers."

Jim didn't need to think about it. "No, thank you," he said, politely but firmly.

Jim saw the shades of gray. He knew that most of the slingers were probably the main sources of income for their families. New Community would be untenable if people saw the church as being in league with the police. The street dealers didn't come to church, but some of their kids did.

Besides, Jim didn't trust cops. The organized-crime outfit he'd worked for in Arkansas had paid off the local police, the county sheriff, and the state police. Though he'd been on S Street only a short time, he already suspected that some D.C. cops were on the take, too. He'd seen squad cars roll into the alley on the side of the church. Drug dealers would follow the cars. The slingers would place something in the hands of the officers. The drug dealing on S Street was too brazen, Jim thought. Some cops had to be getting payoffs to look the other way.

The narcotics officers persisted: "Don't you want to be a good citizen?" one of them said.

Jim stood firm. "I'm sorry, but I can't do that. You have your job to do; I have mine. The church is here for everyone."

The two cops shook their heads and walked out.

As soon as they left, Jim marched out to the burning trash can. He summoned the drug dealers, who gathered around him.

"I want you all to know that the cops just asked me to use the church as an observation post, and I told them no," he said. "I don't condone what you all are doing out here, you're killing yourselves, each other, and your community, but I will not turn any of you in for selling drugs. However, if I ever witness any of you committing violence, I will tell the police, and if asked, I will testify against you truthfully. If you get in trouble with the law, don't bother asking me to write a letter to the judge saying what a great churchgoing guy you are.

"And remember," he added, "once it's open, you're all welcome at the church."

New Community Church celebrated its first service on S Street on April 22, 1984—Easter Sunday.

It was a bright, unseasonably cold day. The renovation was far from complete. There were no windows. There was a huge hole in the floor of the main sanctuary, in the front of the house. The congregation adapted. Worshippers sat on metal folding chairs, wearing coats and gloves and scarves, exhaling white breath. Jim threw a piece of plywood over the big hole. Grace was among the worshippers. So were Ben, Rachel, and Andre.

Jim and his volunteers kept working on the church through the spring and into the summer. Almost every day, Jim would exchange hellos with a stout man who sat on a folding chair in the front yard of his row house, next door to the church. Everyone in the neighborhood called him Baldie.

Baldie turned forty that spring. He was six feet tall, with muscular arms, big shoulders, and, of course, a bald head. He had a wife and a couple of young daughters, but he didn't seem to have a job. At times, Baldie drank beer as he sat in his yard. Sometimes he drank too much and yelled at his wife and kids.

Once, after Jim and Baldie exchanged their usual pleasantries, the church's enigmatic neighbor said, "Anything you need, just let me know. Anything at all."

Jim didn't give the offer much thought. He figured Baldie was just showboating for the new guy on the block, pretending he could get things done. Now and then, Jim heard rumors about Baldie—that he'd done time, that he owned a cache of weapons, that he had a high-priced attorney on retainer. But he dismissed them as overheated street legends.

An architect friend of Jim's visited the church in progress. He came up with an idea to close up one of the windows in the sanctuary and use the space to create an artistic crucifix using bricks. It would provide a dramatic backdrop to the altar.

Word of the plan filtered onto the street. One day, as Jim walked to the church, Baldie called out to him from his yard. "I heard about the crucifix. I know you need bricks. I'll have my guys come over to help you."

Jim humored Baldie. "Sure. Send them over. We'd be happy to have the help." Jim didn't think Baldie had any guys or could afford more than a couple of bricks.

The next day, ten of Baldie's guys showed up at the church with a wheelbarrow full of bricks. They drank beer as they worked, using the bricks to construct the crucifix to the architect's specifications.

Jim recognized some of the workers. He saw them every day— he'd even talked to a few of them. They sold drugs on the block. The picture snapped into focus: Baldie wasn't some wannabe tough guy. The slingers worked for him. Baldie was the neighborhood drug kingpin.

The next day, Jim thanked Baldie for sending his guys over with the bricks.

"You're welcome," Baldie said. "Holler if you need anything."

The offer was tempting. The fledgling church needed money. But Jim didn't want to be indebted to the drug dealer who ran the block.

He invited Baldie to church, but he never asked him about his business. He already knew enough. If he knew more, it could put him in a bad spot if the police ever started asking him questions.

A week or two after Baldie's guys brought over the bricks, Jim noticed something: The slingers usually worked seven days a week, virtually around the clock, but on Sunday mornings they melted away. During the initial phase of the renovations, the slingers hadn't bothered any church members, black or white. Now that the church was holding services, the drug dealers seemed to be ceding the block to the outsiders on Sunday mornings.

One weekday, a middle-aged suburban couple came to S Street to help out with the ongoing renovations. The two weren't part of the congregation and hadn't been in the neighborhood before. They quickly got lost. But they didn't wander S Street for long. One of the slingers led them to the church. Jim welcomed his guests and thanked the drug dealer, who went back to his crack-selling post across the street.

"I think Baldie's protecting us," Jim told Grace one morning at the breakfast table. "I think he's told his guys to watch out for us."

Grace nodded. "I think you're right," she said. By then, most of the misgivings she'd had about S Street the first day Jim took her there had faded. Like Jim, she felt God's presence on the block.

And she felt better knowing that Baldie had the church's back.

Crack began to appear on S Street and in other D.C. drug zones the year the church was launched. In 1985, it slammed the city. The transition on S Street was seamless: Baldie's guys simply started selling crack in addition to heroin and "bam," or meth. Before long, they were dealing only crack. The drug traffic increased. S Street became one of the busiest open-air drug markets in the city.

Each summer, Baldie hosted a block party. Everything was on him. He'd break out a big grill and cook burgers and chicken and fill a cooler with ice, bottled water, and cans of soft drinks. The slingers got the afternoon off. They and neighborhood residents, as well as Jim and some of his church members, would eat Baldie's food, down his drinks, and mingle. Little kids would open a fire hydrant and frolic in the gushing water.

Baldie did other things for his neighbors, too: If a struggling single mother was unable to pay the rent, Baldie would slip her some cash. If a young woman felt harassed by a too-persistent suitor, Baldie would have a word with the man. Now and then, he handed out candy to the neighborhood children, many of whom affectionately called him Uncle Baldie. And he continued to have the church's back—even if Jim never stopped telling him and his slingers that drug dealing was a "new form of slavery."

The street slingers were trapped, risking their lives and their freedom for crumbs, on behalf of a system that exploited them, as Jim saw it. Neighborhood dealers like Baldie made good money. Midlevel drug distributors, the people who provided crack, heroin, and other product to neighborhood dealers, were pulling in big cash. South American and Mexican drug cartel kingpins, who produced the drugs and transported them to the United States, raked in cartoonish amounts of money, hundreds of millions of dollars a year.

On the flip side, a burgeoning prison-industrial complex was raking in hundreds of millions of dollars by incarcerating hundreds of thousands of low-level drug dealers and addicts. Jim didn't see the street dealers as villains. They were pawns—teenagers and young men who were considered disposable by their drug-dealer bosses and society.

The establishment of a church in the middle of the block did nothing to slow down the drug dealing. And the drug dealing didn't discourage Jim and Grace from going forward with the church's mission—even if it meant leading young kids into a combat zone.

*

In the fall of 1988, the church launched an after-school program for kids from the neighborhood. It was Grace's idea. The church would offer classes in art, music, poetry—the kinds of subjects that weren't available, or weren't taught well, in the wretched public schools. It would be a good way for the church to become more involved in the daily lives of the people of the neighborhood, Grace and Jim thought.

Jim hired Cynthia Barron, a former schoolteacher with Peace Corps experience, to run the program. They started with six first graders. On a warm September afternoon, Cynthia, a pretty, willowy brunette, inaugurated the program by marching the boys and girls straight down S Street.

Dealers manned both sides of the street, as usual, but Cynthia and the kids walked to the church in peace. The dealers were protective of the kids. Baldie sat in his front yard and exchanged hellos with Cynthia as she led the children into the church.

The next spring, near the end of the school year, Cynthia was leading the kids into the building when one of Baldie's young daughters, Nicole, walked over and joined the group. She was about seven. A couple of weeks later, Nicole's sister, Angie, age four, joined, too. Neither Baldie nor his wife ever talked to Jim or Cynthia about enrolling their kids in the after-school program. The children simply showed up. Sending the girls to the program was Baldie's way of trying to be a good father, Jim figured.

Jim never asked Baldie to fill out any paperwork for the girls. Baldie wasn't much for documentation, and Jim didn't want to do anything to discourage him from continuing to send his girls to the church.

New Community had been on S Street for five years. Jim no longer simply assumed that the church had Baldie's protection.

He counted on it.

CHAPTER 4

ROOM SERVICE CHAMPAGNE

As was the case every Halloween, on October 31, 1989, a couple of *Post* reporters were sent to cover the festivities in Georgetown, where thousands of mostly white and affluent revelers partied through the night. I was dispatched to Potomac Gardens, a rundown public housing project a mile east of the Capitol, where Marion Barry was scheduled to make nice with the residents. My job was to take notes and contribute a few paragraphs to an innocuous story about how Washingtonians celebrated the holiday.

I'd already been to Potomac Gardens a handful of times during my first month on the night crime beat, to cover shootings. The complex was a collection of boxy concrete buildings between three and six stories high, surrounded by a tall wrought-iron fence that reminded me of a penitentiary. At one crime scene near the project, I'd overheard a street cop joke that the fence was there not to protect the residents but to keep the rest of the city safe from Gardens inhabitants. A violent drug crew operated in and near the housing complex. At night, it was a forbidding, dangerous place.

I arrived early and staked out a spot at the edge of a concrete courtyard inside the complex. A few minutes later, a black Lincoln pulled up. A security man in a dark suit hopped out of the shotgun seat and opened the rear passenger door for the mayor. Barry stepped out and smoothed the lapels of his charcoal-gray suit coat.

Some people in the courtyard saw him and cried, "Mr. Mayor, Mr. Mayor!" and "We love you, Marion!" Barry smiled. He waved. He sauntered toward the courtyard.

He was in friendly territory. While much of white and upper-class-black Washington viewed Barry with hostility or disdain, he was beloved in places like Potomac Gardens. In the eastern half of the city, many people believed that Barry was being unfairly persecuted by the white establishment, that reports of his cocaine use had been trumped up by his political enemies to discredit him.

Some blacks even thought there was a grand conspiracy among whites to retake the reins of city government, which would require knocking Barry out of office. The alleged scheme was known simply as "the Plan." It seemed that everyone who'd been in D.C. more than five minutes had heard about the Plan, and a surprisingly high percentage of people, mostly blacks, gave it credence.

If there was such a scheme, it wasn't troubling Barry at the moment. Smiling ear to ear, the mayor waded into the crowd. I slipped my notebook and pen from the inside pocket of my jacket and went to work.

The mayor posed for pictures with children and kissed babies. Someone turned on a boom box. Some teenagers busted moves to the music, and Barry joined them for a minute.

A handful of kids took shots at a portable basketball hoop set up on the edge of the courtyard. Barry slipped off his coat and awkwardly clanged a couple of set shots, then strutted to the front of the courtyard and faced the crowd to deliver an impromptu speech.

"This time last year, you couldn't come here," he said triumphantly. "A year ago, there were shootings every night." I stifled a laugh. The city was hurtling toward a record homicide total. I was logging double-digit miles in the company sedan every night, racing to the latest crime scene.

The crowd cheered. Some people clapped. Some pumped their fists. Some cried out, "You tell 'em, Mr. Mayor!"

Barry advised kids to stay away from drugs, then led them in a little rap: "My mind is a pearl / I can do anything in the whole wide world!" The children responded out of sync, the words all jumbled up. Barry beamed.

The routine was too much. I laughed out loud. *Barry's got a big brass pair*, I thought as I put away my notebook.

Using crack on the sly while running a city was one thing. Openly taunting the establishment, the *Post*, the feds—daring them to prove he was a junkie—was another.

Around the *Post* newsroom, reporters swapped rumors about purported Barry investigations. The FBI was hot on his trail; he could go down any day, one said. No, the investigation is on the back burner, another argued. No, the feds are ready to indict him; they're just taking their time, a third suggested.

Police were gossiping about the mayor, too. After just a few weeks on the job, I'd already encountered one particular police inspector four or five times at late-night crime scenes. In the Metropolitan Police Department hierarchy, inspectors ranked above captains but below assistant and deputy chiefs. At the time, this one was the "nighthawk," the de facto chief during late-night hours. Unlike most white shirts, he was friendly to me, providing basic information about whatever shooting I was covering and happy to chat about sports or whatever was in the news.

One night that fall, as detectives hunched over the body of a young man who'd been shot in the street, the inspector and I landed on the topic of Barry. The mayor was so paranoid about the FBI that he summoned the chief to his office every few weeks to look for listening devices, the inspector told me.

The chief, Isaac Fulwood Jr., would dutifully check the mayor's phone and lamps. He would even check under Barry's desk, the inspector said.

"He didn't know what he was doing. He wouldn't know an FBI bug unless it was labeled," the inspector chuckled. "But he went through the motions."

The story seemed goofy, and in interviews Fulwood had always insisted that he'd never done anything to interfere with an FBI investigation. But I didn't dismiss it. After all, Barry had appointed the chief, and the mayor had already shown he was willing to deal ruthlessly with MPD officials he viewed as threats. In the spring of 1982, police inspector Fred Raines reported alleged drug use by Barry to the U.S. Attorney's Office. Raines passed along accusations that Barry had snorted cocaine at a 14th Street Northwest strip club called This Is It? around Christmas 1981. When the mayor learned what Raines had done, he ordered the commander busted down to night supervisor.

Barry couldn't manipulate the FBI or the U.S. attorney, though. In 1984, a federal grand jury indicted Karen Johnson, a city employee and reportedly a onetime Barry girlfriend, on charges of selling cocaine. An informant had worn a wire and recorded her talking about dealing to Barry. Federal prosecutors pressured Johnson to testify against the mayor, but she refused. Johnson was charged with contempt of court and incarcerated for eight months.

Barry wasn't charged in connection with the Johnson case. But federal attention returned to him in December 1988. Just before Christmas, Charles Lewis, a Barry acquaintance, reportedly displayed a bag of white powder to a Ramada Inn maid and propositioned her. She reported Lewis to a hotel security officer. A hotel official called the police. Two D.C. detectives were on their way to the hotel when Barry arrived and headed to Lewis's room. The hotel manager waved off the detectives, who aborted their assignment. Six days later, U.S. Attorney for the District of Columbia Jay Stephens announced he was launching an investigation into the incident.

Then, in March 1989, the FBI arrested Lewis for selling twenty-five rocks of crack to an undercover agent in the Virgin Islands. A federal grand jury issued a sixteen-count indictment against him, charging him with conspiracy, cocaine distribution, perjury, and other offenses.

Would Barry be the next to fall?

The mayor remained unflappable. "I want to repeat that I never saw any drugs or drug paraphernalia during my visits with Mr. Lewis," he said in a statement.

What Barry didn't know was that by late summer, Lewis would agree to a plea bargain and begin talking in detail about his cocaine escapades with the mayor to a team of FBI agents and MPD internal affairs detectives. Lewis told the investigators about the times and places he'd used powder cocaine or crack with the mayor. Lewis said he'd used drugs several times with Barry in the Virgin Islands from 1986 through 1988.

And he told them about a onetime Barry girlfriend named Hazel "Rasheeda" Moore.

I was unable to resist the combination of crack and an attractive woman. The FBI bet that Barry couldn't either.

By mid-January 1990, newsroom rumors of an imminent Barry indictment had grown more persistent than ever. Meanwhile, people were getting shot in the city's combat zones virtually every night. I was riding a seemingly nonstop wave of adrenaline, racing to crime scenes when I was working, driving Champagne to S Street to buy crack for our next tryst on my off days.

The night of January 18 began routinely: I parked near Logan Circle, then walked to the *Post* for my night shift. Parking closer without getting a ticket was always tough. But just before 8:00 P.M., I decided to try again and walked back to my car. It was going to be a frigid night, and I didn't want to hike those four long city blocks after the temperature had really plummeted.

I was on M Street Northwest, driving toward the office, when two white shirts bolted into the street ten feet in front me. They sprinted toward the entrance of the Vista Hotel, to my left. A tall man in a suit and a guy lugging a TV camera were hot on their trail.

It was unlikely that a shooting had occurred in an upscale downtown hotel. Right away, I thought, *Barry?* I pulled over and ran across the street and into the hotel. The white shirts were in the lobby, talking to a serious-looking man in a dark suit.

I spotted Tom Sherwood, a reporter for a local TV news station. Tom had covered D.C. government for the *Post*; he'd left the paper about the time I'd arrived. I sidled up. Tom was gazing at the white shirts and the guy in the suit, mesmerized.

"Hey, Tom," I said. "Do you know what's going on?"

"I think the FBI just arrested the mayor for drugs."

Byline glory.

I'd left my equipment bag, with my *Post* cell phone inside it, in my car. I didn't want to leave the hotel, not for a moment. I raced to a bank of pay phones a few feet away and called Curt Hazlett, the night city editor.

"Curt, I'm at the Vista Hotel. I think Barry's just been busted by the FBI."

"Ha-ha, very funny."

"No, I'm serious. A couple of white shirts ran into the lobby, along with Tom Sherwood and a cameraman. The white shirts are talking to a guy in a suit. He may be FBI. *Something* is happening."

The mirth disappeared from Curt's voice. "Stay right there. I'll get back to you."

A couple more police commanders ran into the lobby. I stayed near the pay phone. Curt paged me about five minutes later. The reporter who'd been tracking the Barry investigation had confirmed that the FBI had busted the mayor, he said. They'd nabbed him inside a hotel room.

The news was traveling at warp speed. A radio reporter showed up, followed by a wire service guy. A white shirt went over to them and made a vertical chopping gesture—he was telling them they had to stay put.

"Do you have a credit card?" Curt asked.

"Yeah."

"Get a room—on the *Post*. The paper will reimburse you. Spend the night there, see if you can interview any staff, guests, anyone who saw or heard anything. We're working on finding out where in the hotel they busted him. As soon as I know more, I'll page you."

After retrieving my equipment bag from my car, I checked into a room on the fourth floor and for the next ninety minutes roamed all over the Vista, buttonholing guests and hotel staffers. No one knew anything about the Barry arrest. I retreated to my room and called Curt.

"Hang tight," he said. "Doesn't seem like there's much else you can do. I'll call you if anything comes up."

I sat on the edge of the bed, clicked on the TV, and channel surfed. Every station had abandoned its usual lineup of sitcoms and cop dramas to report on the Barry takedown. After an hour or so, I hadn't heard from Curt. I figured I was done for the night. I rang up room service and ordered a lobster dinner with a rum and Coke. The mixture of adrenaline and booze produced a nice buzz. I ordered another rum and Coke.

By 10:00 P.M. the news was reporting that Barry had been taken from the Vista to FBI headquarters. A dark SUV was shown rolling into an underground garage at the J. Edgar Hoover Building. A statement was issued by the U.S. attorney and the FBI: Barry had been arrested on narcotics charges in an undercover operation that was part of an "ongoing public corruption probe." It wasn't long before sources told my colleagues who were working the story that the mayor had been videotaped smoking crack.

The frenzy surrounding Barry was just starting. But the Vista portion of this party was over, which meant I was done for the night.

In one gulp, I knocked back half my drink. A crazy idea came to me. I punched in the numbers to Champagne's pager.

By now I knew it by heart. Champagne called me back almost immediately.

"Someone page me from this number?"

"Yeah, it's me. This is, uh, a work phone. Are you near Thomas Circle?"

"You know it."

"Are you holding? Do you have two?"

"You're in luck. I do."

I hesitated. Two hours earlier, the hotel lobby had been full of FBI agents and white shirts. But Barry was gone, and with him the feds and cops. Champagne usually dressed conservatively, but every now and then she tramped it up with a short skirt, black fishnets, and do-me stilettos.

"I'm in a hotel, and I don't want to draw attention. How are you dressed?"

"I don't look like I'm working, if that's what you mean. I look respectable."

"I'm at the Vista," I said. I gave her my room number.

Champagne arrived wearing a black trench coat and spiked heels. She stepped into the room and unbuttoned the coat, revealing a short, formfitting black cotton dress with a plunging neckline and a high slit.

She settled onto the edge of the bed and removed the rocks from her purse. I sat next to her and watched the nonstop Barry news. Champagne glanced at the TV and quickly returned her attention to the task at hand. Carefully, she cut a rock in half with a sharp red fingernail.

"I guess you've heard about the mayor," I said.

She shrugged. "Yeah, I heard they got him here in the hotel. He should've known they were watching him. He should've known better than to try anything in some place he couldn't control."

Champagne loaded half of the rock onto her pipe.

Her analysis made sense—enough sense to make me nervous. We were in a room over which we had no control. The cops or the feds would need a warrant to get into my home; I wasn't sure the same rules applied to a hotel room. I jumped off the bed and pressed my face against the door, staring out the peephole.

"No one's coming," Champagne said calmly.

I took a couple of steps back and stared at the small space between the bottom of the door and the carpeted floor. Crack smoke didn't produce any particular odor, at least none that I'd ever noticed. But suddenly I was fixated on the possibility that smoke would seep out and someone would notice and call the guy at the front desk, who would call the cops ...

Champagne seemed to read my mind. She placed her pipe and lighter on the bed, walked to the bathroom, and came out with a thick white towel. She folded it into a rectangle, went to the door, bent down, and pressed it into the space between the carpet and the bottom of the door.

I crouched to get a good look. It appeared to be a perfect seal.

I followed Champagne to the bed, undid my pants, and slid down my boxers. She handed me the pipe and lighter.

As I resumed watching the coverage of the Barry arrest, I lit up and inhaled.

Champagne went down on me.

Lou was at his desk doing paperwork when news of the bust broke on the little TV set atop a nearby filing cabinet.

No shock there. Lou made it a practice to debrief every witness or suspect, no matter how minor the charge. It was a good way of compiling street intelligence, and Lou had informants in every quadrant of the city. The people on the street knew Barry had been using.

Lou picked up the phone and called Gary Abrecht, the inspector in command of the First District. Abrecht was smart, hardworking, and straight-arrow honest. He had an economics degree from Yale. His wife served as a city judge.

"Have you heard the news?" Lou said.

"What news?"

"The mayor just got busted for drugs."

"Oh my God!" Abrecht replied. "Who got him?"

Unlike Lou, Abrecht cared about police department and city politics. He wasn't aligned with any particular faction of commanders, but he was careful not to offend any elected official who could affect his career—such as, say, Barry.

Lou couldn't resist the opportunity to needle his boss.

"One-D vice arrested him," Lou replied. Charlie Miller was the lieutenant in charge of the First District vice detectives—and a beast of a cop. The detectives in his squad were wearing out their handcuffs locking up slingers and users. It was within the realm of possibility that Miller's people had busted Abrecht's ultimate boss, the mayor.

Five seconds of silence turned into ten. *My God*, Lou thought, *Abrecht's about to have a heart attack*. Lou broke the silence and clued him in that the FBI, not 1D, had nabbed Barry.

Abrecht let out a sigh of relief. Lou allowed himself a brief grin and resumed his paperwork.

A few miles away, Jim and Grace sat on the couch in their living room in the Mount Pleasant section of Northwest and watched the unfolding news about Barry in near silence.

"It's not a surprise," Grace said.

"That's true, but it's a shame," Jim replied. He wasn't in denial about the mayor. Jim believed that Barry at times looked out for his political fortunes at the expense of the city. But he saw Barry as more than a self-centered demagogue.

In 1982, just before he launched his church on S Street, Jim had founded Manna Inc., a nonprofit that renovated homes and apartment buildings for use as low-income housing. It relied on tens of thousands of dollars in loans from the D.C. Department of Housing and Community Development. Manna paid back every dime.

Barry had a reputation for leaning on people and organizations that did business with the city, asking such individuals and groups for campaign cash, but he never asked Jim for anything in return for the city loans. Manna had never donated a nickel to Barry, and neither had Jim. The mayor was a junkie and a liar and at times a racial provocateur, Jim thought, but for all his flaws, Barry genuinely cared about poor people.

The news showed dumbfounded D.C. Council members and high-ranking city administrators walking into and out of the Reeves Municipal Center, the mayoral command post on 14th Street Northwest. Asked what he knew about Barry's arrest, Chief Fulwood said, "When I figure it out, I'll let you know."

"It's just sort of shattering," said D.C. Council member H. R. Crawford, who represented a section of the city, in far Southeast, where Barry was popular. "I'm devastated."

Reactions broke largely along lines of race and class. Three days after the bust, the *Post* reported that a poll showed that 57 percent of respondents believed Barry should resign as mayor. But half of the poll's respondents also believed that federal authorities were "out to get Marion Barry any way they could." Blacks were three times more likely than non-blacks to believe that race had played a major role in the decision to investigate Barry.

Across the country and around the world, the bust quickly became a symbol for the national drug crisis. "We've all been buzzing about the mayor of Washington," Colorado's top drug-prevention official told the *Post*. "Three different meetings, and everyone was talking about how amazing it is. I mean, the mayor of the capital videotaped by the FBI smoking crack! I think what it shows is we have a national social problem here that doesn't respect position or authority or anything."

French newspaper *Le Quotidien* editorialized that the United States would finally have to admit that cocaine use was rampant in high places. In Spain, prosecutors and other officials who'd gathered for an anti-drug conference applauded when Colombian representatives said that the U.S. government needed to address the problem of demand at home before it turned its attention to problems in drug-producing countries abroad.

Jim and Grace watched the news for a couple of hours. Before he turned in for the night, Jim got on his knees and said a silent prayer for Barry, for the city, for Manna, for Baldie and his slingers, for all the suffering addicts who bought crack on S Street.

A few days after the mayor was arrested, I was on a plane headed back to Los Angeles. The FBI, it turned out, had used Barry's former girlfriend Rasheeda Moore to lure him to the Vista. She'd provided the crack and the pipe that the mayor had used. The *Post* was putting together a profile of Moore, whose last known address was in Los Angeles. Phil Dixon, an assistant city editor, threw me the assignment. Phil had worked at the *Los Angeles Times* in the eighties and liked my *Herald Examiner* work. The *Post*'s West Coast bureau chief was new to L.A., and the paper needed someone who wouldn't get lost on the freeways, Phil told me.

A lot of reporters wouldn't have considered it a plum assignment. My job was to find out whatever I could and hand over my notes to the staffer who was writing the story. But I was excited to be going home on the company dime.

From my window seat I gazed down at the ribbons of freeway and rows of neatly ordered subdivisions. After having held out for most of the flight, I'd ordered my first rum and Coke somewhere over the Grand Canyon. I nursed it until we crossed into California airspace, then ordered another. I quickly killed my second drink, reached into the inside pocket of my sport coat, and checked for the envelope with the $1,000 worth of *Post*-issued traveler's checks inside.

As the airplane neared LAX, I gazed out the window at the Forum, home of the Los Angeles Lakers. I could still barely believe that I, an unconnected kid whose family had started out in gang-infested Boyle Heights, was working at the *Washington Post*. There was nothing I would rather be doing. Well, almost nothing—the only job I would rather have was shooting guard for the Los Angeles Lakers. Journalism was my passion, but basketball was my first love.

As a kid, under a merciless Southern California sun, I would shoot jumpers alone on the asphalt court at my middle school. I loved the distinctive, gritty music of an accurate shot falling through a metal-chain schoolyard net. Other kids who played on the blacktop during recess were taller, quicker, stronger. But I had a limitless supply of *ganas*—desire.

When I was in the first grade, my family moved to South El Monte, a little San Gabriel Valley city about ten miles east of downtown. When I was twelve, I convinced Pop to mount a basket and backboard over the garage door. I quickly made him regret it.

The first Saturday the hoop was up, I was out at first light, before 7:00 A.M., dribbling and shooting. The sound of the ball smacking against the cement driveway echoed throughout our quiet neighborhood. I was up and at it again on Sunday. I'd taken only a few shots when Pop leaned out the front door.

"Your mom is trying to sleep," he said, an edge in his voice. "And so are the neighbors." He gave me a *look*.

I grabbed the ball and didn't say a word.

I adapted. Ball under my arm, I walked a few blocks to my middle school. I played like a junkie on a ferocious binge. For nearly four hours at a time, on a court with no shade, I'd dribble and shoot, dribble and shoot, pausing once or twice to hit the water fountain.

One morning, I was following through on a jump shot when I felt a wet sensation on my shooting hand. The inside of my right middle finger, where the joint bends, was bleeding. The constant repetition of rolling the pebbled ball off my fingertips had created a nasty little red canal. I started taping my finger with Band-Aids before heading to the court. I didn't get any quicker or stronger, but I made myself a deadeye shooter.

Though I didn't know it at the time, I was developing the kind of relentlessness I would need to make it in journalism. I joined the high school newspaper as a freshman because it looked like fun. It was.

When I was a senior, a vice principal shut down a photographer for the school paper who was trying to take shots of a campus demonstration. The vice principal agreed to an interview in his office to talk about the skirmish. I was a skinny teenager who was painfully shy around girls. Sitting across from the administrator, pen and notebook in hand, I asked a series of questions about the incident with the photographer. To my amazement, the vice principal hemmed and hawed. This adult authority figure was *nervous*.

It was thrilling.

I was hooked.

From that point on, every move I made was designed to give me the best chance possible to make it with a big-time newspaper. Nothing came easy to me, yet I always seemed to find a way. I applied to USC because it had a good journalism program. My grades weren't stellar, but I aced the essay portion of the application and got in. Near the end of the last semester of my senior year of college, I landed an unpaid internship at the *Herald Examiner*. I worked my tail off and was offered a permanent position a couple of weeks before I graduated.

As the plane descended, I pulled a small address book from my shirt pocket. I planned on seeing some of my old *Herald Examiner* pals during my downtime. It would be good for my soul.

I was pleasantly drunk when I picked up my rental car and maneuvered out of the airport and onto the eastbound Santa Monica Freeway. I had a room reserved at the downtown Westin Bonaventure Hotel. As I approached the downtown exits, I wondered whether Raven was still working the motel off Olympic Boulevard.

The motel was only a few minutes from the Bonaventure. Maybe I'd cruise by just to say hello.

Raven was in her usual spot. I eased the car to the curb, leaned over, and rolled down the passenger-side window. She approached warily, then smiled broadly when she recognized me behind the wheel. Raven leaned against the passenger door.

"Hi, stranger. Haven't seen you in a minute. What have you been up to? When did you get the new ride?"

"I moved—to D.C. This is a rental. I'm in town for business."

Raven brushed away a stray strand of hair. She looked *good*. I'd planned on calling some of my old contacts to ask about Rasheeda Moore as soon as I got to my hotel. That could wait.

"So," I said. "Are you holding?"

"Not at the moment, but you know my connect is just around the corner. One thing, though: I don't have a room right now. Could you pay for that, too?"

I'm on my own time right now. It's not like I'd be violating any Post *policies prohibiting smoking crack on company time.*

"I've got a place nearby," I said. After quickly checking the rearview and sideview mirrors to confirm no cops were around, I handed Raven a pair of twenties. She walked around one corner of the motel, then returned less than a minute later and jumped into my car. Five minutes later, I drove into the underground parking structure of the Bonaventure. Raven gawked at the gleaming lobby of the hotel as we ascended in the circular glass elevators.

"Nice view," she said.

The elevator felt like a giant fishbowl. Good thing it was a cool night—Raven was covered up and dressed like a civilian.

We sat on the bed inside my room. Raven slipped off her jacket and broke out the party kit: two rocks, a pipe, a lighter. She cut one of the rocks in half with her fingernail and handed it to me. I grabbed it and hesitated.

"Wait a second," I said. I stepped into the bathroom and grabbed a bath towel.

Carefully, I folded it into a thick white rectangle, then bent down and patted it into the space between the floor and the bottom of the room door. I rejoined Raven and lit up.

Three days blew by.

By day, I worked hard. I rode out to Moore's last known L.A. address and knocked on neighbors' doors. I called every LAPD detective and street cop I knew. I rang up county prosecutors, defense attorneys, federal agents, private eyes—anyone who might be familiar with the woman who'd lured Barry to the Vista. Nobody knew anything about her.

My intentions were good. Every day, I thought about calling one of my friends and visiting my family. But my need to get high took precedence. At the end of each workday, I knocked back a few drinks at the hotel bar and ended up at the cheap motel off Olympic with Raven and a couple of rocks.

I compartmentalized. I kept my advance money and traveler's checks in a plain white envelope. I paid Raven from my own money, which I kept in my wallet. Since my assignations with her were on my dime, I was fine, I convinced myself.

My return flight was a red-eye. The airplane was filled to capacity with Salvadorans, mostly young men and women, with a few kids sprinkled in. It was obviously some kind of aerial version of an Underground Railroad for immigrants. A great story—maybe even one that would have landed on the front page. And maybe one that would have led to an immigration bust.

I kept my notebook holstered. These folks were heading east to work very hard for little pay at jobs most Americans would consider beneath them. Their lives were hard enough; they didn't need me adding to their struggles.

I was feeling bad enough about the L.A. trip as it was. I hadn't shirked my job, but the frequency with which I'd hooked up with Raven was unsettling. Getting high once or twice a week was manageable. In L.A., I'd done it four nights in a row.

I spent my first couple of days back in D.C. brooding.

A brazen shooting got me back on track.

Three nights after I returned, I headed to Northeast Washington for a homicide that was announced over the scanner. The victim was inside an SUV at the intersection of 5th and K Streets Northeast. Uniforms cordoned off the intersection. A couple of detectives in suits and overcoats peeked into the SUV. The victim, a young black man, was slumped in the front passenger seat.

I stood dutifully behind the yellow tape. We were in a residential neighborhood of brick row houses with small porches and small front yards. It was a cold night. Though it was only 8:00 P.M., there were just a few civilian bystanders.

A white shirt provided a brief narrative: Witnesses said the victim had been shot in the street. His pals had tried to load him into the SUV, maybe to take him to a hospital. A squad car rolled up. The buddies ran away, leaving the victim inside the vehicle in the intersection.

It was unlikely this murder would become a story. I was just grinding, putting in the time necessary to develop sources. Showing up at late-night crime scenes in combat zones helped me build credibility with white shirts, detectives, and street cops. At this scene, I was waiting to talk to a detective, hoping he would be helpful, or at least cordial. If a detective was friendly at a crime scene, I'd ask for a phone number, or simply call the homicide office some night down the road and ask for that investigator. That's how a night crime reporter develops police sources.

I blew out white breath and rocked side to side, trying to keep warm. My trench coat, gloves, and fedora were no match for the bone-chilling cold.

Bam! Bam! Bam! Bam! Bam! Bam!

Six gunshots, ear-splittingly loud, maybe thirty yards away. The onlookers ducked and ran in the other direction. Three uniformed cops drew their guns and sprinted toward the source of the sound. I pulled out my notebook and ran with them.

A block south, a middle-aged man was lying on a patch of snow on the sidewalk, writhing in pain. His forehead was bleeding; it looked like a graze. The uniforms and I arrived together.

Two cops stood over the wounded man. The third paused and

resumed sprinting down the street, looking for the gunman. One of the cops bent down to talk to the victim. I tore off my right glove, grabbed my pen, and began furiously taking notes.

The standing cop seemed to notice me for the first time. "Hey, who are you?"

"*Washington Post.*"

"You can't be here."

I ignored him and kept writing.

"You have to leave. *Now.*"

I backed away, disappointed at being shooed away, giddy that I was lucky enough to be there when a shooting broke out within yards of a half-dozen cops working a crime scene. I raced back to the car and called my editor. He told me to work the scene for another fifteen minutes, then get back and write it.

About ten minutes later, I buttonholed a detective who'd been working the murder and who was now helping investigate the second shooting. He provided a quick rundown: The new victim and his attacker were in a group of men who were talking when an argument broke out, the investigator said. Someone pulled a gun and started firing. I began writing the piece in my head as I drove back to the office. Once I was in front of my computer, I knocked it out in twenty minutes.

The following night, there was an envelope on my keyboard when I came to work. It bore the *Washington Post* seal and address in the upper left-hand corner.

Inside was a handwritten note: "Amazing story in today's paper, a shooting a block from a crime scene in full view of the police. Keep up the good work on the police beat." It was signed by Don Graham, the paper's publisher.

I showed the note to Carlos Sanchez, the daytime police reporter. "You got a Donnygram," he said. "He sends notes to people when he likes their stories. Congratulations."

All right then. How bad could things be if I'd just received a Donnygram?

CHAPTER 5

"NO ONE'S OUT THERE, BABE"

In the wake of the Barry bust, many people had wondered: *Knowing that the feds were watching him, how could the mayor have put himself in that situation?*

I knew how. An addict doesn't weigh risks and rewards the way other people do. When the drug of choice is offered, an active addict is powerless to resist. Taking the drug is as necessary as breathing. I became a regular drinker when I joined the *Herald Examiner*. Then I met Raven and took up crack. During those first months on the drug, my mind became more alert, and I had more energy than ever. It was a blast—until it wasn't.

My tolerance for alcohol and crack increased—slowly at first, then exponentially. By the time Marion Barry was arrested, I was on the downward slope of my alcoholism and drug addiction. I needed more drinks to get buzzed. I needed more crack to achieve not quite the same high.

Nonaddicts don't understand the deep sense of denial that's an integral part of being a junkie. Barry surrounded himself with sycophants who enabled his addiction. I convinced myself that I was fine because I was doing my job well. But in fact, my carefully compartmentalized double life was collapsing.

Three weeks after receiving my Donnygram, in February 1990,

I struggled to stay awake near the end of an unusually quiet Friday-night/Saturday-morning shift. As I leaned back in my chair, David Lindsey, the weekend-night city editor, sat at his desk ten feet away and aimed a remote at the TV suspended from the newsroom ceiling. He channel surfed and settled on a comedy show. The police scanners on both our desks were as quiet as big paperweights. Maybe it was the weather. Several inches of snow had fallen earlier in the week, and it was a brutally cold night.

A little before 2:00 A.M., a familiar screech blared from the scanners. A woman's dispassionate voice recited, "Attention. Units paged. Third District units at the scene of a shooting, the corner of 7th and S Streets Northwest." The location got my attention. I leaned in, waiting for the dispatcher to provide further details. None came.

David shrugged. We could slam stories into the same day's paper as late as 2:00 A.M. Whatever this was, it was too late to get the story into Saturday's paper.

"Up to you," David said as he glanced at the newsroom clock.

Something in my gut told me this was worth a ride. And I wasn't too worried about being recognized. The S Street slingers knew my Escort, but they'd never seen me in the company car, a Chevy Caprice. The dealers had probably scattered the moment the cops showed up anyway. If it looked dicey, I could simply drive past, come back to the office, and work the phones.

"I'll check it out," I said.

Less than ten minutes later, as I had dozens of times with Champagne riding shotgun, I turned left on Rhode Island Avenue and approached the corner of 7th and S. As soon as I made the turn, I saw four marked squad cars and an unmarked detective's sedan parked directly in front of John's Place. The streets were clean, but banks of snow lined the curbs on both sides. There were no slingers or spectators in sight.

Sirens filled the air. Ambulances and more squad cars roared onto the scene. A patrol cop broke out yellow crime-scene tape and attached one end to a light pole near the club. He was taping off the entire corner.

A friendly lieutenant was standing by one of the squad cars.

"How many down?" I asked.

He gestured with his fingers: six victims.

Six people shot? *Hello, front page.*

I called David. Work as long as it takes, he said. This would be for the Sunday paper. I stayed at the scene until 5:00 A.M., interviewing street cops and detectives, watching as workers from the medical examiner's office carried two bodies from the club.

After a few hours of sleep, I went back to the office and double-teamed the story with another reporter. Three men had been killed inside the club, and a fourth had died on the way to the hospital. The other two victims would probably survive, a white shirt said. We wrote it up, and I stayed in the newsroom through my Saturday-night shift. At about 1:00 A.M. Sunday, a news aide dropped a copy of the early edition on my desk.

Finally, there it was: my first page 1 byline.

I made a little victory fist.

Nine hours after I got my early edition, Jim drove past John's Place as he headed to church to prepare for the Sunday service. Fragments of yellow tape were scattered across the sidewalk.

All the kids in the Sunday-school program and their parents had to walk past the crime-scene detritus on the way to the church. The quadruple killing was all over the local TV and radio news and, thanks in part to me, was splashed across the front page of the *Post*. Only a couple of the victims had been identified. Jim didn't recognize their names. He figured they weren't S Street slingers. Baldie didn't frequent the nightclub, and the neighborhood grapevine would have gone into overdrive if one of his guys had been killed.

Inside the church, a little boy asked Jim what the tape was for. Jim crouched so he and the kid were face-to-face.

"Unfortunately," Jim said, "some people don't know how to solve disagreements peacefully. They use guns and hurt other people. That's what happened at the club. Instead of talking, someone used a gun, and four young men were killed. It's sad, but you're safe in here."

The boy nodded.

Jim's daughter, Rachel, helped out with the Sunday school. She was fourteen, a few years older than the dozen kids in the group. "We should do something to remember the victims," one of them said. Rachel asked the children what they wanted to do, and they came up with a plan.

In the church basement, Rachel, Jim, and Grace foraged some pieces of wood and a roll of twine. Rachel helped the kids tie the wood together into four crosses. Everyone put on their coats and gloves, and Jim led the kids and the rest of his flock outside. Four kids volunteered to carry the crosses. They marched to John's Place.

The morning was bright and freezing. The kids placed the crosses against the wall of the nightclub. Jim led the shivering group in a prayer.

"Dear God, we pray for the young men who lost their lives as they make their transition, and for the two who were wounded. We pray their souls find peace. We pray for those who use guns to settle disputes, that they may find nonviolent solutions. We pray for those who are caught up in the drug trade, that they may find another path. And we pray for those who are imprisoned by their addiction, that they, too, find a different way of life.

"Amen," Jim said.

"Amen," the group responded.

They trudged back to the church.

The following night was the beginning of my weekend. I downed three rum and Cokes with my TV dinner. The buzz amplified my good mood. On Sunday, I'd knocked out a follow-up story for the front page of the Metro section. That entire shift qualified as overtime. My next paycheck would be substantial. A celebration was in order.

I picked up the phone and paged Champagne. Fifteen minutes later, with Champagne riding shotgun, I turned right onto S Street and pulled over next to John's Place.

A little more than forty-eight hours after the quadruple killing inside the nightclub, it was business as usual on the block. Slingers dressed in heavy coats, boots, and knit hats stood at their usual spots on both sides of the street. I handed the cash to Champagne. She stepped out of the car and was quickly surrounded by dealers.

Champagne made the buy and strolled back to the car. As I watched her return, I noticed something odd a few feet behind her: four makeshift wooden crosses resting against the wall of John's Place.

Well, I thought, *that's different*. The usual street-killing memorial consisted of a pile of flowers and teddy bears.

Champagne plopped into the passenger seat. I pulled away from the curb and drove past the crosses, the slingers, and the church.

Copping crack on the same corner where I'd covered a quadruple killing less than seventy-two hours earlier was brazen, even reckless—maybe as reckless as going into a hotel room to smoke crack when you know the FBI is watching you.

I viewed my encounters with strawberries in purely transactional terms. In exchange for cash, which they used to buy crack for both of us, the women made the buy and provided sex. Most of the strawberries working in my neighborhood were white, but a handful of blacks and Latinas also roamed the streets, exchanging sex for crack. I didn't think much about them as people until I saw Stacy on the front page of the *Post*. She had gorgeous eyes and a nice smile. But she wasn't Stacy. Her real name was Sherry K. Larman.

The headline read, "Fateful Links of Seven Slain Women."

Sherry was twenty-six, the story said, and one of several

prostitutes who'd been murdered in D.C. or nearby Arlington, Virginia, over the previous fourteen months. Most of them had used drugs. The story appeared on the first day of June 1990. Sherry's mother, Sandra Johnson, was quoted at length.

Sherry had grown up in suburban Maryland. She'd had a decent life before she got hooked on crack, her mom said. Sherry's father was a retired D.C. cop. In high school, she won trophies for track.

Johnson said she'd warned Sherry that she was living dangerously and pleaded with her to give up drugs and prostitution. "She got caught up in this street life and it had a hold of her," Johnson said. "She knew what she was doing was wrong, and she wanted to get out, but the pull was just too strong."

Sherry's body had been found a few days earlier on the top deck of a parking garage in Arlington. She'd been suffocated, as had one of the other victims. All the others had been shot.

I absorbed the details of Sherry's life. I hadn't physically harmed this woman, and I'd never intended to hurt her. But there was no way around it: I'd helped destroy her.

The Sherry described in the article was a nice suburban girl who was loved by her parents. The Stacy I knew rented out her body to strange men in exchange for crack. I'd helped put her in a place where a man with bad intentions could place his hands around her throat and squeeze the life out of her.

Until I read about Sherry, I thought that my habit affected no one but me. But the details of her crack-addicted life seemed like an indictment. I dropped the paper and sank to the floor.

By now I'd covered hundreds of homicides for the *Post*, but I hadn't known any of those killed. I usually thought about the victims as long as it took to report and write my stories or news briefs. For most of them, that amounted to no more than a couple of hours. I hadn't had any of them into my home. I hadn't asked any of them to buy crack for me.

Stacy was different. I'd picked her up a couple of times when I couldn't find or reach Champagne.

My thoughts turned from self-recrimination to self-preservation: Did Stacy have a pager? I couldn't remember. If she did, and the cops recovered it, would my number be in it? Would a detective knock on my door? Suddenly I felt nauseated.

I rushed to the bathroom and vomited.

It wasn't the first time the sight of Stacy had prompted me to worry that my double life would be exposed. Six months earlier, just before Christmas, I'd almost run into her while on a reporting assignment.

I'd volunteered to work a double shift on a Saturday, a couple of days before the holiday. It meant a fat, overtime-enhanced paycheck and a guaranteed byline. I'd be covering a holiday party at Lorton Correctional Complex. Through a prison fellowship program, 150 female inmates would be visiting with their kids in the gymnasium. It would be an easy, heartwarming feature.

I walked into the building and froze the moment I spotted Stacy underneath the basketball goal at the opposite side of the gym. She was striking, with long legs and hazel eyes. Like Champagne, she worked the edge of downtown. But I hadn't seen her in weeks. Now I knew why.

She was with three other inmates. The other women were all holding little kids. Stacy was talking to one of the children.

I wouldn't have been so alarmed if I'd spotted Champagne in the gym. Champagne was a pro. I'd never told her or Stacy what I did for a living, but I was confident that if I ever ran into Champagne in the real world, she wouldn't expose me as a fellow user.

Stacy was a wild card. What would she say if she saw me? Would she blurt something out in surprise? Would she try to leverage what she knew about me to her advantage?

The inmates and kids were clustered in different parts of the gym. I made for a small group gathered near the goal opposite Stacy's. I turned my back and started interviewing.

Quickly, efficiently, I obtained quotes from three inmates and the fellowship director. Each of the women was locked up on a drug charge.

Without looking behind me, I nearly ran out of the gym and drove back to the *Post*.

The close call was unnerving, but I quickly regained my bearings. And learning from a front-page *Post* story that Stacy/Sherry had been murdered rattled me far more, but not to the point that I changed my behavior. Things could be worse. At least I hadn't been videotaped smoking crack by the FBI.

Barry went down—barely. On August 10, 1990, a jury convicted the mayor of one count of cocaine possession. The jury didn't convict him in connection with the Vista Hotel bust, which he'd been lured to by Rasheeda Moore. Instead it found him guilty of using cocaine at the Mayflower Hotel, in downtown Washington, with another woman, two months before the Vista episode. The jury acquitted the mayor of a second drug possession charge, and was unable to reach a verdict on twelve counts.

On the night of the verdict, my editors had me drive through the eastern part of the city looking for signs of civil unrest. It was business as usual. There were no riots. Drug corners continued to do a brisk business.

On my way back to the office, I drove through S Street, where the slingers were out in force.

As long as I was holding it together at work, I told myself, I was fine.

For about a year, I held it together at work, more or less. I showed up for my shifts and knocked out news stories and longer feature articles, which often ran in the Sunday edition. On my days off, I'd pick up Champagne and smoke crack. Instead of using two rocks at a time, Champagne and I began ingesting three, sometimes four rocks per encounter.

In June 1991, one year after the story of Sherry Larman's death was on the front page of the *Post*, I went to Los Angeles for a family dinner. I was getting worried about my increasing crack usage and figured the visit would be a good chance to clear my head and regroup.

On the day of the dinner, I joined some old pals at the Hollenbeck Youth Center, in Boyle Heights, for a few pickup basketball games. Then I cruised over to one of my favorite burger stands on Olympic Boulevard for lunch. I had less than $20 in my pocket and no intention of seeing Raven. But her motel was so close. I could at least say hi.

It was a warm day. Raven was rocking tight shorts and a sheer, plunging short-sleeved top. She sauntered toward my rental car and smiled broadly when she saw me.

"Hey, stranger. Good to see you again. I'm holding, if you want to party."

The family dinner wouldn't start for five hours. Plenty of time. I hit a nearby ATM and met Raven in her room. Fifteen minutes later, I exhaled the last of the residue as Raven worked on me. I wasn't anywhere close to getting off.

"Can you get a couple more rocks?"

Raven's head popped up.

"You know I can, babe."

I handed Raven the cash. Her dealer was camped out in another room. We went at it again. I failed to launch. I went back to the ATM. We did no better on the next try. We kept going. Three, four, five times I hit the ATM and returned to the room. I found a pay phone and called home to say I was running late but would be at the dinner. Night fell.

Raven said she needed to clear out of the motel.

"But I haven't finished," I whined. I was *this* close.

Raven slipped on her bra. "I know another place nearby where we could get a room by the hour," she said.

I handed her $50 for three more rocks.

The other place was a few blocks east on Olympic, on the western edge of downtown. I almost laughed when I saw the sign: EXPERIENCE MOTEL. It was an L-shaped, two-story hot-sheet joint with a faded pink paint job and a small parking lot. Flashing neon spelling out the motel's name was mounted above the tiny first-floor office. The O was burned out.

Twenty bucks got us an hour. We could have the room until the morning for an additional ten, Raven said. I handed her a twenty and a ten, just in case we needed more than an hour. She paid the clerk and we headed up the stairs. A Latino gangster in a white wifebeater, khakis, and pointy black dress shoes leaned over the second-floor railing, eyeballing us.

The gangbanger was about my height but stocky, with broad shoulders and thickly muscled arms, which were covered with tattoos. He looked to be in his early twenties. He was either MS-13 or 18th Street. He stood between us and our room.

We reached the top of the stairs. The gangster pushed off the rail and turned toward us. The walkway was narrow; there was no room to slip by. Homeboy stared at me. I glanced at Raven, hoping she would register recognition. If she knew the gangster, she could ask him to stand down. Raven returned my glance with a look that said I was on my own.

The *vato* stepped up and crowded my space. He smelled of beer and cheap cologne. The gangster pointed at my wrist.

"Nice watch, homes."

"Thanks," I replied warily. The timepiece was simple and probably cost no more than $25. But it had been a gift from my uncle Victor, my pop's oldest brother.

"Give me the watch," the gangster said as he reached for it.

I didn't think. I slapped his hand away and shouted, "No!"

It was a stupid, potentially suicidal move. If it had come to a fistfight, the *vato* would have pummeled me. He was probably carrying—if not a pistol, then a knife. And he no doubt had fellow gangsters nearby to provide backup.

Raven's jaw dropped. Homeboy's eyes went big.

I curled my fingers into fists, preparing to defend myself against an onslaught of blows. Instead, to my relief, the gangster snickered, waved dismissively, turned his back, and resumed leaning on the rail. Maybe he thought I was too crazy to mess with.

"That was stupid," Raven said when we got to the room.

We sat on the bed. She broke out her pipe, her lighter, and the three rocks. I grabbed the pipe and reached for one of the rocks.

About ten hours later, I pulled into the driveway of my parents' house in the last moments of predawn darkness. Raven and I had smoked our way through the night. Over and over, I'd driven from the motel to the ATM and back. At around 5:00 A.M., Raven said she had to go. The rocks were gone. She let me keep the pipe, the lighter, and a six-inch piece of coat hanger wire.

I drove home horrified at what I'd done. I parked and staggered to the side of the garage, near a wooden gate that led to the backyard. I turned my back to the street. Using the wire, I scraped the last of the res from the inside of the pipe, onto the bottom of the copper filter. Carefully, I used the wire to push the filter to the other end of the glass stem. I lit up and greedily inhaled the last hit. It barely registered.

The sun started to rise.

The dinner I'd missed wasn't just a family gathering. It was a wedding-rehearsal dinner. I was supposed to be my brother Javier's best man, and I'd gone AWOL. I looked at my watch: The wedding was in less than three hours. I was twitchy and sweaty—all that crack had bumped up my body temperature. I'd fucked up, monumentally, decisively, spectacularly, unforgivably.

Some birds chirped. The cloudless sky became bluer by the moment. It was going to be a gorgeous June day.

Shame and remorse overwhelmed me. If I could have flipped a switch and erased myself, I would have. Exhausted, I fell to my knees and wept.

"What happened?" Javier asked, plaintively, when I stumbled into the house. I had no answer.

"It was humiliating not having you at the dress rehearsal," he said. Javier spoke matter-of-factly, without anger, but each word stung.

After the ceremony, I joined Javier and dozens of other relatives at a backyard-barbecue reception.

The bar was open. I quickly killed three beers. I wanted to get numb. It didn't work. My tolerance was gargantuan. The beers barely got me buzzed.

My two-year-old niece Nastasia appeared. She toddled onto the back porch, dressed all in white, looking cuter than a box of kittens and puppies.

I stepped toward her, knelt, and opened my arms.

Nastasia looked right through me. She turned her back and walked away. She might as well have reached into my chest with her tiny hand and ripped my heart out.

A couple of days later, I flew back to Washington. I'd be okay once I got back to my routine, I thought. And a big day in the history of the *Post*, of American journalism, was imminent. I was looking forward to being a small part of it.

A little more than a month after I returned from Los Angeles, on the last day of July 1991, Ben Bradlee stood in front of his glassed-in office along the North Wall, the most prestigious part of the newsroom. An all-star cast flanked him: Bob Woodward, publisher Katharine Graham, her son Donald.

Bradlee was retiring as executive editor. Len Downie Jr. would take over as newsroom boss, effective September 1. Bradlee was taking August off before getting kicked upstairs to a VP post.

The room was packed. Hundreds of staffers stood shoulder to shoulder, crammed into the spaces between work cubicles. Some people stood on desks. Woodward and the Grahams delivered speeches.

In a prearranged tribute, dozens of male reporters and editors wore striped dress shirts with white collars, the kind Bradlee favored. I joined in the fun, rocking a casual, short-sleeve light-blue polo shirt with a white collar.

The ceremony was in the late afternoon, a couple of hours before the start of my shift. I arrived just before it started and stood way in the back, not far from a bank of elevators.

This is history, I thought as the speeches wound down. Bradlee wrapped it up with a brief, heartfelt oration, which was met with sustained applause.

Bradlee told someone to cut the big cake sitting on a nearby desk. The handshakes and hugs commenced. Staffers surrounded the journalistic lion to say good bye.

Though I'd been working at the *Post* for nearly two years, I'd never met the man. He was on vacation when I interviewed for my job. We'd shared an elevator a handful of times, but I hadn't even tried to make small talk. What could I have said to him that wouldn't have sounded fanboyish? "Nice work on that Watergate thing"?

But now he was happily greeting everyone. *What the hell?* It wasn't like I would run into him at the Y, or at 7th and S. I wasn't likely to get another chance like this.

I began to maneuver my way toward the North Wall.

A few feet in, I bumped into a copy editor. She worked nights, too. During slow shifts, we talked about books or city politics. We were casual work friends.

"Hi, Ruben. Are you okay?" Her face registered genuine concern. "Are you coming in to work tonight?"

"Sure. Why not?"

"You don't look so good. If you have a fever, you should just call in and stay home. We'll get by."

I doubled back, slipped into the men's room, and stood in front of the mirror.

A sheen of sweat covered my face and neck. A patch of perspiration marred the chest of my blue polo. I looked as if I'd just run a series of sprints. Or, maybe, I looked wired.

In fact, I *was* wired. A couple of hours earlier, I'd run into Champagne as I was walking home from my lunchtime hoops game. I hadn't planned on picking her or anyone else up, but she looked good, and I had a few hours before my shift. I took her to 7th and S and handed her fifty bucks for three rocks, which we split. I didn't even bother trying to get off. I figured I'd be fine for my night shift. But the rock intake had spiked my body temperature. I was like a car that was running hot because of a busted radiator.

"Damn," I muttered as I splashed cold water on my face and wiped myself down with a paper towel. I stepped out of the restroom and lingered on the south side of the room, watching Bradlee from a safe distance.

The famous editor smiled broadly. He serial-hugged staffers.

I pivoted toward the elevators and headed home.

The envelope appeared in my work mail slot in early October, a little more than two months after Bradlee's newsroom retirement bash. My eyes lit up: *Washington Post* stationery. I ripped the envelope open, hoping, hoping, hoping . . .

Yes! I clenched my fist, more in relief than in triumph. A reprieve from financial doom.

The envelope contained a check for $730. The money covered additional hours that I'd worked during the previous quarter. The *Post* gave staffers a choice: time off or cash. I always opted for the cash.

The payout covered June, July, and August. I needed the scratch.

I was now picking up Champagne or Carrie, a pretty blonde strawberry I'd met that spring, two or three times a week. And I was using more, dropping $50 to $100 for rock instead of $35.

Part of me realized that I was sliding fast. I tried to slow myself down. That summer, I'd walked into my bank and signed a document limiting the amount I could withdraw from the ATM to $100 every twenty-four hours. When that didn't work, I cut my ATM card in half. Every week, I wrote checks for cash, just enough for food and other legitimate expenses.

I quickly found a way around that. When I picked up Champagne or Carrie and ran out of cash after buying and smoking a couple of rocks, I'd hit up friends from the Y or co-workers from the *Post* for short-term loans—forty bucks here, twenty bucks there, sums not high enough to arouse suspicion. So I thought.

It took about three weeks to run through everyone I knew. I developed a new system: I'd call friends and relatives on the West Coast with a lame story about losing my wallet and get them to wire me money, usually $50 a pop.

My salary had shot up when I started working at the *Post* in 1989, from $33,000 to $45,000 a year. I had no mortgage, no child support or alimony, and hardly any credit card debt—and now I was barely scraping by. I always paid back the money I borrowed, but I was on a financial hamster wheel, and the pace was accelerating.

The fat check would help. I slipped it into the inside pocket of my sport coat and headed to the elevator.

Every other Tuesday, I got to pull a day shift, to get a breather from the run-and-gun and work on longer pieces. The "float" day was rotated between me and the other night reporter.

This was good timing: I'd walk home, have an early dinner, watch some TV, get to bed early, and hit the bank first thing in the morning.

Two blocks from my apartment, I ran into Champagne. It was a mild evening, on the cusp of fall. She was sitting on a bus bench, wearing black leather pants and a tight, low-cut red sweater. She was on her game.

I walked over to say hello. Champagne smiled broadly. She reached into her V-neck and adjusted her bra. I saw a flash of black lace on soft white flesh.

"So," she said. "Are you just here to make conversation?"

I had $30 in my wallet. But there was a check-cashing joint in Adams Morgan. Two percentage points for each check cashed. I could party a little and still drop nearly seven hundred bucks into my bank account.

"Let's go," I said.

I drove us to the check-cashing place, then straight to S Street.

Six hours later, I crouched at the bay window of my apartment, peeking through the blinds for the men in black I was certain were coming for me.

My fingers splayed the slats just enough to create a small opening. I twitched and sweated as I spied the cars parked on the dimly lit street outside.

Phantom figures in dark clothes darted from behind one car to the next. Did one of them have a walkie-talkie in his hand? Did another have handcuffs on his waistband? Were they D.C. narcotics? FBI? DEA? A federal-police task force?

Champagne sat on the chair at my desk, calmly scraping the res from her pipe with a piece of hanger wire. The res fell onto a small mirror. She worked by candlelight. I'd turned off all the lights, hoping that a dark apartment wouldn't draw the attention of the men outside.

"You've got to chill out," she said. "No one's after you or me. All this smoking is making you paranoid."

It was an hour or so before dawn. I'd given up on getting off after our fourth or fifth foray to 7th and S. I'd been straight-up hitting the pipe, getting more anxious by the hour, by the minute, by the hit.

Champagne remained cool. Her mood never wavered. She had an amazing tolerance for rock. She scraped out the last of the res and used a razor blade to gather the gray powder into a neat pile. As I'd seen her do dozens of times, Champagne put the pipe in her mouth, leaned down, and expertly sucked the res onto the filter.

She tapped the end of the pipe to make sure the res was secure, then lit up and took an enormous blast. Champagne gestured for me to come over. I took a nervous glance out the window, then crab-walked to her. She leaned down and shotgunned me.

It was a monster hit. I held it for seven, eight seconds, then exhaled and crab-walked back to the window to resume my vigil.

That was when the whispers started.

The voices emanated from behind the parked cars, too distant to be intelligible. I moved the blinds to the side and pressed my face to the window. The whispers glided through the night air, moved above the stairs of my front porch, slipped under my door. I heard snippets of dark schemes: *He's in there. The squad's in place. We can take him now.*

I shuddered and turned to Champagne, panic in my eyes. "They're coming," I murmured.

Champagne waved her hand dismissively. "No one's out there, babe. You've had too much."

I could see her words. They floated out of her mouth in big black-and-white letters and hung in the air, lining up next to one another to form her sentences.

Champagne put her pipe, her lighter, and her section of wire hanger into her purse and stood up.

"I think I should go now. Get some rest, okay?"

I heard and read her words simultaneously.

From my spot at the window, I watched Champagne sashay confidently down the steps and onto the sidewalk, certain that cops or feds were about to swoop down on her. She walked, undisturbed, around the nearest corner.

My face remained glued to the window until dawn. As the sun rose, I collapsed onto my back and stared at the ceiling.

I wanted to stop smoking forever. I needed another hit.

I awakened at dawn. I couldn't believe what I'd done. How many runs had we made to 7th and S? At least ten, for sure. We started out getting two for $35, and before long we were up to three for $50.

My God, had I blown through the entire comp check? I looked inside my wallet: It contained a solitary $10 bill.

Ten bucks. Maybe that was enough for a dime. I pulled myself up and headed out the door.

A lone slinger prowled the sidewalk in front of the bakery at 7th and S. Early-morning traffic was light. The neighborhood wasn't quite awake.

I pulled over to the curb in front of John's Place. The dealer's eyes lit up when he saw my car. He made a beeline for me. I motioned toward the passenger seat while I leaned across the console and unlocked the door. The slinger settled in. I drove into the alley parallel to New Community Church and cut the ignition. I didn't want to make the buy on the street in daylight.

"What you need, amigo?"

I checked the side- and rearview mirrors. "Can I get a dime?"

The dealer snickered and shook his head in disdain. "Nah, can't do that. Can't break up a twenty."

Sunlight gleamed off my watch. It was the same timepiece I'd defended from the *vato* at the Experience Motel. The watch my uncle had given me.

I held up my wrist. "Ten bucks and the watch?"

The dope boy studied the timepiece. I checked the rearview. The slinger nodded yes. I slipped off the watch and handed it over, along with my last $10.

He handed me a $20 rock and hopped out of the car. I drove home and quickly killed the rock.

I remained at the window, looking for cops or feds who never came, until I passed out from exhaustion.

In early November 1991, Milton Coleman, the Metro section boss who'd hired me, and Phil Dixon, the assistant city editor who'd sent me to L.A. for the Rasheeda Moore profile, intercepted me as I walked to my desk to start my shift. The looks on their faces told me I wasn't about to get a raise. Milton uttered the four words no one ever wants to hear from a boss or a lover: "We need to talk."

We walked down the stairs to the second-floor cafeteria in silence. My double life was falling apart. I was not only using more frequently, but also more unpredictably. More and more, I was using before my shift started. That fall, I'd called in sick at least a half-dozen times to cover up my bingeing.

We reached the second floor. We had the dining area to ourselves. Milton led us to a corner table. Milton and Phil sat across from me.

"We're worried about you, man," Milton said. "You've called in sick a lot lately, and some of your co-workers think you've shown up for work drunk more than once. If there's something going on, we'd like to help."

"You've been borrowing money from co-workers, including some people you barely know," Phil added. *So much for borrowing under the radar.* Ouch. My gaze turned from Milton to Phil. Quickly, Phil gestured with his hand, as if acknowledging that my borrowing, by itself, didn't prove anything, and added, "You *always* pay it back. But if you're in trouble, we want to help you."

Whew. They knew, but they didn't *know.*

Milton and Phil didn't know the awful details. They didn't know I picked up strawberries on the regular. They didn't know I was a crack fiend. Hell, they were throwing me a lifeline.

I looked down at the table for a moment, processing, strategizing. Denying everything would be stupid. Admitting everything? Well, I figured I'd be unemployed if I did that. I decided on something in between.

My eyes came up to meet Milton's. As I spoke, I shifted eye contact from him to Phil and back: "I have been drinking too much, I realize that. And now and then I've done some powder cocaine. I've had a rough time worrying about my father's health. I'm a little over my head with credit card debt, which is why I've been borrowing money. But I'm starting to get that under control."

I felt a limited sense of relief. I'd admitted my problem. Well, half-admitted.

Milton nodded. His expression softened, and his body seemed to relax as he leaned back in his chair. Phil leaned forward, his eyes locked on mine.

Reading my mind, Phil said, "Your job's not in jeopardy."

"As far as the company is concerned, this is a health issue, and will be treated as such," Milton said. "For starters, we want you to see someone with our employee-assistance program. We have a counselor who has an office here, in the building. Whatever you say to her is confidential. This meeting is confidential. This is nobody else's business. You're not the first *Post* staffer who's dealt with this kind of problem."

Milton and Phil looked at me. I looked at them.

"Do you have any questions?" Milton asked.

"No."

We walked back up to the fifth-floor newsroom in silence.

Milton headed to his office. Phil walked to his desk.

I settled in at my desk and turned on the police scanner, wondering how closely I was being watched.

CHAPTER 6

UNRAVELING

Lou had set a trap, and now the two gun-toting bandits were walking right into it.

They strolled toward the entrance to the Safeway grocery store in Capitol Hill just before closing time. A handful of plainclothes cops were inside the store. Another group watched from an unmarked van in the parking lot. Lou was in an unmarked sedan about a block away, in contact with the officers in the parking lot by radio.

The robbers had *always* gone straight to a checkout clerk. They'd show their guns, force the clerk to empty the register, and quietly slip away. Lou was ready for that. His people had placed devices on the floor at the checkout stations. If the bandits appeared, a clerk could tap the device with his or her foot. Two officers stationed inside the manager's office would see an alert. They'd radio the cops in the parking lot, who'd confront the bandits in the small vestibule that separated the store from the street.

It was the night of October 23, 1992. Police had briefed the clerks. Lou's people were ready. The two men walked into the vestibule, then into the main store. They were fifteen feet from the nearest checkout station. But they didn't head for it. Instead they brandished their handguns, grabbed an assistant manager, and forced him toward the manager's office.

The robbers were going for a bigger score. They wanted the contents of the safe inside the office. They had no idea there were two cops waiting for them behind the locked door.

At gunpoint, the manager fumbled for his keys. He found the one for the office, slipped it into the doorknob, and started to turn it.

The Safeway robbers were on a spree. Over thirty-one days, they'd taken down nineteen stores, in every quadrant of the city. But they were wearing out the one on 14th Street Southeast in Capitol Hill. Between late September and mid-October, the pair had hit the store four times.

The jobs weren't sophisticated, well-planned heists. Lou, by then the captain in charge of detectives in the Metropolitan Police Department's First District, where the store was located, suspected the bandits were drug addicts. The fact that they were hitting stores so often meant they needed a steady flow of cash. The fact that they hit them so brazenly meant they needed it desperately.

In those days, many grocery-store customers still paid in cash. If the bandits hit at the right time, a Safeway register could give up tens of thousands of dollars. And a grocery store was a much lower-risk target than a bank. The 14th Street Safeway was particularly inviting: Located in a residential area dominated by row houses, it was open at night, and nearby Pennsylvania Avenue led to several quick escape routes over the D.C. boundary into Maryland or Virginia.

"It was," Lou said, "a great place to commit a robbery."

After the store had been hit for the fourth time, Lou developed his warning-device plan. He also had detectives and officers ask their informants in 1D if they knew who might be knocking off the grocery stores. A street source mentioned a man who'd been seen running from one of the robberies. His name caught Lou's attention: Theodore "Teddy" Fulwood.

Teddy lived and hung out near the Safeway, and he was a known cocaine user. He'd been released from Lorton Correctional Complex in 1990 after serving a year for trying to sell the drug. But he wasn't just any ex-convict.

He was the brother of MPD chief Isaac Fulwood Jr.

After Teddy was released from prison, he lived in an Oxford House in Northwest D.C. Oxford Houses are similar to group homes, except everyone living in them is in recovery. Housemates are expected to help one another stay sober and hold one another accountable.

For a while, Teddy seemed to be doing well. He joined a drug-treatment program at St. Elizabeths Hospital, the city's psychiatric medical center, and worked here and there as a painting contractor. In 1991, the chief accompanied Teddy to an Alcoholics Anonymous meeting in the basement chapel of St. Elizabeths, where his brother was among a group of alcoholics and addicts celebrating their one-year anniversaries of being alcohol- and drug-free. Chief Fulwood spoke of the power of God to heal and presented Teddy with a bronze one-year AA chip. The two brothers teared up as they embraced.

Lou decided he'd better get word to the chief about Teddy's possible involvement in the robbery spree. He discreetly told a supervisor, Assistant Chief Addison Davis, that Theodore Fulwood was a possible suspect in the Safeway holdups. Lou didn't want his boss to be caught by surprise if his brother walked into a police trap.

The assistant manager opened the door. The two cops inside the office saw the bandits with their guns out and pulled their service weapons.

Gunfire blazed in both directions.

"It was like the gunfight at the O.K. Corral," one witness told the *Post*.

The cops prevailed, killing one of the robbers and capturing his accomplice. Officer Jonathan Fuller took a round in the leg, and the assistant manager caught one in the buttocks.

Chief Fulwood arrived quickly—faster than Lou had ever seen him get to any crime scene.

Neither of the bandits was Teddy. Lou's detectives later determined that he hadn't been involved in any of the previous grocery-store robberies, either. He was cleared.

But less than a month later, Teddy ended up in much worse trouble than being a possible armed robbery suspect.

At about 3:00 A.M. on November 19, a police officer on patrol near the 14th Street Safeway heard a series of gunshots. He raced toward the gunfire in his patrol car.

The officer found the body of a man sprawled on the sidewalk on 16th Street Southeast, two blocks from the grocery store and a short walk from Robert F. Kennedy Stadium. The victim was Teddy. He'd been shot multiple times in the head and torso. He was forty-three, and the 401st homicide victim in the District that year.

Detectives would determine that Teddy had been killed over a drug deal that had gone bad.

In an interview about a year before Teddy was gunned down, Chief Fulwood spoke of how much he'd encouraged his brother to stay clean. Still, the chief said, he knew that drugs were "like a huge monster that grabs a person and won't let go."

Like the vast majority of addicts, Teddy had been unable to break free.

The shootout at the Safeway capped a day during which MPD officers shot and wounded two other suspects in separate incidents and at least six other people in the District were shot, two fatally. At the time, about seven years into the crack epidemic, a night like that was "routine," Lou said.

Working as a police officer in the eastern half of the city was "like being in a war zone," Lou recalled. "And it was so concentrated in certain areas. West of 16th Street Northwest, you didn't have anything going on. East of 16th Street, there were a lot of dangerous areas. In those neighborhoods, it seemed that everyone had a gun."

Within the span of a few years, the drug gangsters had acquired so much firepower—semiautomatic handguns, AK-47s, machine guns—that by the early nineties Lou was concerned that they would graduate to even more effective ways of killing.

"I worried that they'd start to use explosives," he said. "Then you'd have a lot of collateral damage. A lot of people not involved in drugs or gangs could have been killed."

There seemed to be no end to the bloodshed. And the number of killings kept rising: In 1989, 1990, and 1991, the city clocked 434, 472, and 479 murders, respectively. Almost all of the deaths were east of 16th Street Northwest. The police department seemed powerless to do anything about the violence. About half of the city seemed to be flaring out of control.

In 1D, Lou handled a wide array of cases that weren't homicides: nonfatal assaults, break-ins, armed robberies like the Safeway holdups. A decade before, when he was a detective, he had gone after killers. But the MPD required officers to change assignments whenever they were promoted. After his stint as a homicide detective in the early eighties, Lou made sergeant and went to internal affairs. When he made lieutenant, he was assigned to patrol in 3D. In 1988, when he made captain, he was sent to 1D, where he worked as a patrol commander for a year or two before being assigned to lead the district's team of detectives.

Lou had long wanted the homicide command. He had some new ideas and believed he could do some good there. And he didn't need the chief and the mayor to bless him with a promotion in rank to get the position: Homicide was led by a captain. But it was a high-profile assignment, and he didn't lobby or politick for it. Lou was all about doing the job. He was *po-lice*.

"I knew I could have an impact in homicide, but there was nothing I could do about it," Lou recalled. "All I could do was the best job I could in my assignment, and I enjoyed working in 1D. There was always something to do, if you wanted to work. It may sound strange, but it was fun."

Believing that his police career was probably maxed out, Lou was already preparing for life beyond the MPD. In 1988, he'd begun taking courses at Prince George's Community College, in a Maryland suburb just outside D.C. He planned on finally obtaining his undergraduate degree and, eventually, a law degree.

If he never got the chance to return to homicide, he'd have something to fall back on.

In the meantime, Lou watched large swaths of the city fall apart. When he'd joined the police force, in the seventies, the situation in dozens of neighborhoods in the eastern half of the city was already dire. In some public housing complexes, the heat never worked in the winter and the air-conditioning never worked in the summer. Too many teenage girls became mothers. Too many young, able-bodied men loitered their days and nights away.

Beginning in the mid-eighties, crack made everything worse. Addiction to the new drug ripped through the neighborhoods east of 16th. It was different from the drug dependency Lou had seen in the seventies.

"Before, it was mostly men who were getting hooked on heroin and other drugs," he recalled. "The moms were left to raise their kids by themselves. But with crack, lots of women became addicted, too. You began to see a lot of grandmothers taking care of young kids because their moms were addicted."

Some of the children left in the care of grandmothers—or the city—were infants. During the late eighties, "boarder babies"—newborns abandoned by mothers strung out on crack—were left by the dozens in D.C. hospitals. During the first eight months of 1989, forty-one such infants were born at Howard University Hospital, five blocks north of S Street. Those infants represented 15 percent of all babies born in the hospital during that period.

Between the violence sparked by the drug trade and the social chaos wrought by crack addiction, it seemed to Lou that some sections of the city were on the edge of unraveling. "I felt really bad for the hardworking people who lived in those neighborhoods," he said. "Some of them had their kids sleeping on mattresses on the floor to avoid stray gunfire. A lot of the parents wouldn't let their kids go outside to play."

One night, he responded to a street where multiple gunshots had been reported. Lou and other officers found the body of a man in the backyard of a row house. Lou asked the homeowner, a woman, if she'd seen or heard anything unusual.

No, the woman said.

Lou pointed out that a man had been shot numerous times in her backyard.

"Oh, we heard gunshots," the woman replied. "But that's not unusual around here."

Lou was sitting in an unmarked squad car near Potomac Gardens, the same treacherous public housing complex where, on Halloween 1989, I had seen Marion Barry do his ramshackle "I can do anything in the whole wide world!" rap with the project's youngest residents. It was a mild night, and a big crowd was hanging out just outside the black iron bars surrounding the complex. Most of them were teenagers or young men.

On this night, Lou had company: his pal Father Tony, a priest with the Oblates of Saint Francis de Sales. When Lou was a young officer in 5D, Tony had been interested in a career in law enforcement and joined the MPD's reserves. He was assigned to 5D with Lou.

But instead of becoming a cop, Tony became a priest and earned a doctorate in forensic psychology. He worked for the FBI in the behavioral sciences unit and carried a handgun. Father Tony remained friends with Lou and had been riding with him on occasion for years.

Once, back when Lou worked in 3D, Father Tony was with him when he pulled up to the scene of a shooting. That night, Father Tony was wearing his collar. Lou and the clergyman stepped out of the car. Some kid took one look at Father Tony and said, "Man, don't mess with that cop. He goes around with his own priest!"

On this night, Father Tony wasn't wearing his collar. Lou was in uniform, though, working as the night supervisor for 1D.

A knot of four or five teenagers walked toward Lou's car. He was parked with the driver's side near the sidewalk, with the window down.

Lou always kept the window down when he was on the street, so he could listen—and smell. He wanted to be able to hear if there was a commotion or gunfire. And he wanted to be able to smell gunpowder, marijuana, or PCP.

The group of teenagers slowed as they got near Lou. None of them looked his way. They didn't want to be seen talking to a cop. That could be fatal in this neighborhood.

Just above a whisper, one said, "The nigga's got a machine gun."

Without looking at the teens, Lou said, "Could you be more specific?"

"The guy walking down the street with a hoodie," one replied.

"You should do something," another said.

Lou looked across the street and saw a kid in a hoodie, sixteen or seventeen, walking. The group of teenagers strolled past his sedan. Lou called for backup, hit the ignition, and rolled up on the sidewalk next to the hoodie kid. Then he jumped out of the car to confront him.

The kid turned toward Lou, a big gun in his hand. Lou saw the barrel pointed at him. He drew his own weapon and fired.

The nearby crowd scattered.

The kid with the gun sprinted into an alley. Lou raced after him.

The kid ran, turning toward Lou two, three times. Lou fired each time. The shots missed.

The alley got dark. Lou lost sight of the kid but kept sprinting. Suddenly, he heard footsteps behind him.

Oh, no, he thought. *The dude.*

Lou believed the teenager had hidden in the alley, that he'd run past him, and that the gunman now had the drop on him.

Quickly, Lou turned, ready to shoot it out. A wave of relief washed over him: It was Father Tony. The priest had followed him and the gunman into the alley. The kid was gone. But at least he hadn't shot anyone.

"If anything had happened to Father Tony," Lou remembered, "I would have had some explaining to do."

Backup arrived. An officer found a large gun in the alley—not a machine gun, but a .38 or a .44 Magnum.

Another routine night.

One of my best sources, a detective in 4D, called me on the night of July 9, 1991. It had been a slow night. It may sound sick, but the truth is, for a crime reporter, life is boring unless something terrible has happened. I wasn't just hooked on crack and booze—I was also an adrenaline junkie. On this night, I was about to get a big hit.

"I got a story for you," the source said. He told me that a woman had been shot in the head and killed while driving on North Capitol Street. Her eight-year-old boy, who was riding in the car, had been grazed by a bullet but wasn't seriously injured.

"How'd this happen?" I asked.

"Damn gangster thugs," my source replied. He'd always been even-keeled, but now he was angry. Two local gangs had been feuding. The woman and her son had almost certainly been hit by stray bullets fired by the neighborhood gangsters, the detective said.

The woman's name was Marcia Williams. She had been driving to her home in suburban Prince George's County when she was killed. She had three kids.

By the early nineties, Lou had spent most of his career policing streets in the eastern half of the city, in such combat zones as Potomac Gardens, the corner of 18th and D Streets Northeast in Capitol Hill, and the corner of 5th and O Streets Northwest in Shaw.

The vast majority of killings and nonfatal shootings in those areas didn't get much, if any, press attention, unless multiple people were murdered or the victims were very young. Most attacks garnered a minute or two on the local news or a brief in the *Post*.

Now and then, the killing of a "civilian" like Williams generated a flurry of press attention. I wrote a story for the next day's paper, and local TV news covered the killing. The uproar over Williams's death was such that Chief Fulwood held a news conference a day or two after the shooting.

A reporter told the chief that merchants in the area where Williams was shot had praised the chief's anti-crime efforts but wondered whether the tragedy might have been averted if there had been a more "persistent" police presence. An exasperated Fulwood noted that Williams was shot on a busy street, that young men nearby "had their firearms and decided to use them." The police, Fulwood maintained, are not "Houdinis."

"We're not miracle workers," Fulwood said. "I wish we were."

Killings like that, in which the victim was a law-abiding person who had nothing to do with drugs or gangs, briefly generated public outrage. The vast majority of the city's crack-era homicide victims lived lives that put them in harm's way: They sold drugs or ran with a gang or stole from a drug dealer.

Or they smoked crack and picked up strawberries.

*

On a warm spring afternoon in 1991, I knocked back a few drinks and woozily paged Champagne. She didn't answer, so I got into my car and cruised the neighborhood.

Three blocks from my apartment, on the edge of downtown, I saw a young woman sitting on the concrete steps leading to the side entrance of a hotel bar on Thomas Circle. She was wearing running shorts and a tube top. The young woman had blue eyes, shiny blonde hair, and perfectly toned legs. She was licking an ice cream cone.

The girl was in the badlands inhabited by Champagne and other strawberries. I didn't think that was a coincidence. I was drunk and looking for action. I pulled over, jumped out of my car, and sat next to her.

"Hi. What's your name?" I asked.

The girl licked a glaze of ice cream from her upper lip.

"Carrie," she said with a smile.

"Nice to meet you. What are you up to today?"

Carrie licked her cone. "Working at the moment. You want some company?"

"Do you party?"

"Sure."

"I know a place to get three rocks for fifty. If we split them, would you do me?"

Carrie stood and tossed the cone into a nearby trash can.

"Let's go," she said.

I drove us to S Street and handed her the cash. Carrie got out and calmly made the buy.

For a few weeks, I hooked up with her as often as I did with Champagne. Carrie had a sweet demeanor. She said she was from Arkansas. I missed her when she disappeared late that summer.

Two days before Thanksgiving 1991, I was walking home from my late shift when I ran into Carrie for the first time in months. She was wearing tight jeans and a black leather jacket. Carrie looked as if she'd put on a couple of pounds, which had gone mostly to her boobs and butt. She looked great. The sight of her snapped my libido to attention.

"Hi, Carrie. Good to see you again. Where have you been?"

"Went away for a minute, but now I'm back. How have you been?"

Pretty miserable, actually. But things are looking up now. "Wanna go?" I asked.

She smiled. "I'd love to, but right now I'm waiting on my ride. It'll be here any minute."

"When can I see you?"

A sedan rolled up and stopped at the curb.

"My ride's here," Carrie said. "How about tomorrow? I've got my own place now—you can come by whenever."

She gave me an address on 9th Street Northwest and hopped into the car. Her place was just two blocks from my copping zone on S Street. Convenient.

A few hours after I ran into Carrie, I walked to the newspaper to work a day shift, which the other night reporter and I got to do every other Tuesday. After work I went home and quickly knocked down two rum and Cokes. As I poured a third, I thought about Carrie. I'd volunteered to work on Thanksgiving. That would mean a nice holiday bonus. I could afford to see her. And she had her own place, which meant I wouldn't have to bring her to my apartment. That was good; lately, every time I lit up my crack pipe, I became paranoid that the cops or feds were watching me.

I reached into my bag and grabbed the notebook with Carrie's address in it. Minutes later, I pulled over and sized up the building: brick, three stories, black iron bars on the ground-floor windows, a heavy steel door, two blocks west of S Street.

Someone had tampered the lock to the steel door. One strong tug opened it. I stepped into a grim-looking three-story apartment building and hesitated at the foot of the stairs. I reached into my pocket and double-checked the notebook page. Carrie had scribbled "Apt. 32." She was on the top floor.

The scent of urine hit me just before I reached the first landing. A rat the size of a small raccoon appeared at the edge of the second. It jumped down and scurried by me, slaloming past the discarded condoms and hypodermic needles littering the stairs. I soldiered on.

Apartment 32 was a few feet to the right of the staircase. I raised my fist and hesitated.

Bad things happened in joints like this.

An image popped into my head: Carrie smiling, taking her top off, then leaning toward me as I lit up a crack pipe and moved it to my lips.

Aw, the hell with it. I gave the door two quick, firm knocks.

Nothing.

Come on, Carrie.

I gave the door another rap.

The door swung open. For a heartbeat, the doorway was empty. Suddenly a large man with a wild, uncombed Afro popped out from behind the door. He was wearing a wifebeater and old jeans.

"What you want?" His eyes were bloodshot. His expression was suspicious. He was north of six feet tall and weighed at least 220 pounds. I was five feet eight, 150.

My eyes went to the plastic number on the door.

"Maybe I'm in the wrong place," I said. "I'm looking for Carrie."

Big Man's expression softened.

"Oh, you know Carrie? She inside, in the bathroom. Come on in." He stepped back and waved his arm like a used-car salesman beckoning a mark.

The apartment was empty save for a wooden desk against the near wall, to my right, and a worn beige sofa in the middle of the living room, fifteen feet in. The hardwood floor was scuffed and dirty. The place smelled of takeout french fries.

My gut told me something was wrong. But my mental image of Carrie overruled my instinct. I stepped forward.

With lightning quickness, Big Man grabbed my shirt collar,

yanked me into the apartment, and slammed the door shut. He gripped the epaulets of my trench coat and pinned me against the door while calling out, "Slick!"

Like an apparition, a thin older man with short salt-and-pepper hair silently rose from behind the sofa.

"Get the thing, Slick, get the *thing*!" Big Man called out. The thing—a gun or a knife. A gun would be quick. A knife could mean torture.

"You don't have to do this," I croaked.

Big Man didn't respond. Slick shuffled toward the desk.

"You don't have to do this," I repeated, my voice cracking. "It's not worth it. *I'm* not worth it."

Big Man remained silent. Slick closed in on the desk. My eyes swept the apartment.

There was a window five feet behind the sofa. If I could break free, I could sprint to the window and . . . what? Crash through the glass and swan-dive three stories to the asphalt?

Slick opened the desk drawer, reached in, and pulled out a handgun. It looked small; it might have been a .22.

Slick turned and stepped toward Big Man and me.

My fear flipped to panic. I went from pleasantly drunk to sober in a heartbeat. I had to get away *now*.

I rotated my right shoulder backwards, wrested my right arm free, and balled my hand into a fist. As best I could, I reared my arm back and slugged Big Man squarely on the chin. But I had no leverage, I was unable to move my body forward to generate power; the punch was all arm.

Big Man took it like a pro. He didn't budge. He didn't blink. *Uh-oh*.

His beefy left hand went to my throat. The viselike grip said, *That's enough*. I realized he could snap my windpipe without breaking a sweat.

Slick shuffled behind Big Man, who took his right hand off my shoulder and reached behind his back, like a relay runner getting ready for the handoff of the baton. Slick placed the gun in Big Man's palm.

Big Man raised the gun and pointed it between my eyes, two inches from my face.

I thought of my parents, my sister, and my brothers in California getting the news. Would one of my homicide detective sources catch my case? Would Phil Dixon let my death be noted by a news brief buried inside the Metro section, or would he assemble a squad of reporters to find out how I ended up dead inside a combat-zone apartment building? Phil was a consummate pro. He would go after the story, bless him. Damn him.

My will to fight left like an exhaled breath. I was exhausted, defeated. I hung my head, stared at the floor, and waited for the darkness.

Whack!

Big Man slammed the gun against my left ear. Shock waves of pain radiated through my skull. I looked up. The pistol was back in my face. "I want answers—*now*! Who are you?" Big Man demanded, fury in his eyes.

A light went on inside my throbbing head: *Here I am in my work getup—decent trousers, dress shirt, trench coat. Big Man's probably high and paranoid; he must think I'm a cop or a fed.*

I had to kill those suspicions.

"Carrie cops rock for me on S Street," I said. "Check my shirt pocket."

As he kept the gun pointed at my head, Big Man released his left hand and reached into my pocket. He fished out my crack pipe, held it close to his face, and eyeballed the gray residue caked inside the cylindrical stem. The res was confirmation of previous use. Crackhead credibility.

His face relaxed. Casually, he stuck the pipe behind his ear. He kept the gun pointed at my face. He needed a nudge.

"I've got money," I said. "You can have it."

Big Man nodded.

Slowly, I pulled out my wallet and opened it. He removed the two $20 bills inside, stepped back, lowered the gun, and pointed it at the door.

I was turning to leave when Big Man said something that stopped me cold.

"Say, you have a car?"

Without thinking, I nodded. *Nice response. Here comes the carjacking.*

"I know a place we can score good weight, but I got no way to get there. If you give me a ride, I'll split it with you."

It was an absurd invitation. For a heartbeat, I considered it.

"No, thanks," I said.

I pivoted and raced down the stairs. By the time I hit the ignition and roared away from the curb, terror was morphing into elation.

The worst was over. It had to be. I was done with crack. I would stay away from it—and S Street—for good.

I stayed away from S Street for two days after my run-in with Big Man.

The Friday after Thanksgiving was the beginning of my weekend. By midafternoon I'd knocked back four rum and Cokes. I stood at my bay window and watched a gentle snowfall. I had $20 in my wallet. I was determined to make it last the entire weekend.

But I was drunk, on autopilot. I put on my coat and drove straight to S Street. The slingers were out in force, undeterred by the snow. I didn't bother to check the street for cops. I lowered my window and made the buy from the first dealer to reach my car.

I'd met with my employee-assistance program counselor for the first time the day after Phil and Milton confronted me, a couple of weeks earlier. The counselor, a kindly middle-aged woman, had handed me a pamphlet with a list of support-group meetings throughout the Washington area.

I needed to attend the meetings; it was the only way to get sober, she said. Any further drinking or cocaine use would risk disaster.

"You've been going to meetings?" she asked when we met a week later.

"Yes," I lied.

"That's excellent, Ruben!" the counselor said. She seemed genuinely pleased. "And how are you doing with the drinking and the cocaine?"

"I haven't had any cocaine for nearly two weeks. I did have one drink a few nights ago, a rum and Coke."

Her face registered alarm. I wondered how she'd react if I told her the truth: Three nights earlier, I'd gotten drunk and picked up Champagne. We'd split three rocks. It wasn't even about sex anymore; I was just chasing a high I could no longer capture.

"Slips like that are common," she said. "Do you feel you're on solid ground now?"

"Yes. I don't have any desire to drink or use cocaine right now." A lie, in essence: I didn't want to light up or drink at that moment, in the counselor's office, but I couldn't imagine stopping and staying stopped.

"Good," she said warily. She was clearly bothered by my "slip." She said I should tell her right away if I slipped again. I wasn't sure she bought my assertion that I didn't want to use cocaine or drink anymore. I wouldn't have if I were her.

"You have a lot to live for. You're healthy, intelligent. You have a good job," she said. "See you next week."

Big Man had taken my crack pipe, but that wasn't going to stop me. When I got back home from making my solo buy on S Street, I snapped off a six-inch piece of metal from an umbrella handle. It was a trick Champagne had shown me. I went into the bathroom, where I stuffed some copper mesh into one end of the metal tube, loaded it with the entire rock, and lit up. I smoked the crack in less than a minute. It barely registered.

I walked to the mirror and stared at my face. My eyes were bloodshot, my forehead sweaty. I'd never uttered the A-word to Phil or Milton or my EAP counselor, but now, as I stared at the anguish in my eyes, there was no denying it.

I'm an addict.

This thing has got me.

I'm looking at a dead man.

Three weeks crawled by.

Every night felt like an eternity. On weekends, I got drunk, drove to S Street, bought a couple of rocks, and lit up by myself, to little effect.

On work nights, I battled the urge to keep smoking. Each shooting announced on the police scanner provided a tiny reprieve. Saddling up and racing to a crime scene kept me focused and occupied, more or less, for an hour or so.

I continued lying to my EAP counselor. I told her I was going to support-group meetings and staying clean. I felt bad deceiving her, but admitting that I was lighting up every weekend and that I'd almost gotten shot while trying to meet a strawberry didn't seem like the way to go. Our sessions were supposed to be confidential, though I wasn't sure whether that covered illegal activity, such as crack possession. Of course, the counselor was not there to bust me; the confidentiality I had with her was as sacrosanct in that regard as a doctor-patient relationship, I would realize later. But at the time, all the crack I'd ingested made me paranoid, even on days when I wasn't using.

Five nights before Christmas, Phil wandered to my desk shortly after I settled in for my shift and sized me up.

My eyes were bloodshot and glazed. My clothes were wrinkled and disheveled. My face was covered with a full day's worth of stubble. My breath reeked of alcohol. That afternoon, I'd run into Champagne as I was walking home from my noontime pickup basketball game at the downtown YMCA. At my apartment, we split three rocks from S Street.

The crack didn't get me high, but it made me wired, edgy, sweaty. To even myself out before going to work, I knocked back two rum and Cokes and chomped a pack of breath mints. I thought I could get through my shift.

As he stood by my desk, Phil made no effort to hide his disappointment. It was written on his face with all the subtlety of a front-page banner headline. Later I learned that a news aide who was worried about me had alerted Phil to my condition.

"You're in no shape to work, Ruben."

"I'm all right," I protested. "I can work."

"I can't let you work."

"I'm fine, really."

Phil shook his head.

"What if you have to go out on a story? I can't let you check out a company car. Not tonight."

He was right. I was in no condition to drive. I looked straight down at my desk, humiliated.

"What now?" I said, my eyes on the Formica desktop.

"Take the night off. Go home. Get a good night's rest and we'll regroup tomorrow."

I straggled home, thinking, *If I can just stay clean for a week or so . . .*

The following night, Milton made for my desk the moment I sat down. "Come with me," he said as he led me toward the stairs.

"Where are we going?"

"We're going to see your EAP counselor."

She was standing behind her desk, waiting. Milton closed the door behind us. The counselor got to it: "We've made arrangements for you to be admitted to the rehabilitation unit of Suburban Hospital. There's a bed waiting for you now. Milton will take you and make sure you check in."

I looked at Milton, stunned. His expression was neutral. He was focused on the EAP woman. He was deferring to her. I turned back to the counselor.

"Why do I have to go to a hospital? Can't I do an outpatient program?"

"That won't be enough," she said. "Your behavior right now is unpredictable and dangerous. You don't know when or where you're going to use or where it may lead you."

Everything she said was true, and she didn't even know about my Big Man encounter and my strawberry habit.

"You're addicted at the *cellular* level," she continued. "You can't help but drink and use. And there's no telling what might happen the next time you go out drinking or using."

I looked at Milton, hoping for support. He was looking at the counselor, nodding in agreement. They were putting me away.

"How long will I be in for?" I asked.

"Three weeks," the counselor said. "It's an excellent program. I've worked with a number of people who have gone through there and gotten sober."

I didn't ask what happened to the ones who failed. I didn't want to know. "What now?" I asked.

"Milton will take you to your home so you can get your toothbrush and some clothes. Then he'll drive you to the hospital."

I sat dumbstruck in Milton's black Toyota SUV, staring out the window at the patches of snow on the ground as my boss drove north on Connecticut Avenue toward the hospital in Bethesda.

I had no idea what rehab was, other than expensive. A strange thought popped into my head: *This can't be good for my career.*

As we approached the hospital, I asked Milton who would cover my shift.

"Don't worry about that," he said. "We'll get volunteers."

"Will people know that I'm in rehab?"

"Absolutely not. That's nobody's business."

"How much will this cost?" I fretted.

A three-week stay clocked in at about twenty grand, Milton said. Before my heart could stop, he added, "Don't worry about it. The *Post*'s insurance has got this. Just focus on getting better."

We pulled into the hospital parking lot. Milton walked me to the front desk, made sure I signed in, and shook my hand.

"Good luck," he said. He looked as though he couldn't wait to get out of there.

I couldn't blame him.

CHAPTER 7

THE LEAST AND THE LOST

One afternoon in the summer of 1991, Billy Hart was sweeping the kitchen floor inside New Community. Billy was the resident manager at the church. The Sunday service had ended a couple of hours earlier, and Jim and the congregation were long gone.

Billy heard a loud bump upstairs. It sounded as if it was coming from the room used for the after-school program. Billy leaned the broom against a table and walked upstairs to check. He wasn't alarmed. *Probably a stray cat*, he thought.

He stepped into the classroom. Three men were loading boxes of crackers, cartons of juice, and bags of cookies into cardboard boxes. They were dressed in jeans or shorts and T-shirts. The invaders looked surprised to see him.

"What're you doing?" Billy challenged.

The men looked at him, then at one another.

"White man told us to come by and pick this stuff up," one of the men said.

The ringleader, Billy thought.

The white man would be Jim. He was well known in the neighborhood as the pastor. But Jim hadn't told Billy anything about three guys coming by to raid the after-school program's supplies. How dumb did these mopes think he was?

"He didn't tell *me*," Billy said.

The ringleader squared his shoulders.

"You get the fuck out of here," he snarled. "I told you what we're doing."

Billy began to curl his right hand into a fist. He was no Bambi: He'd done a few years in jail and prison for nonviolent offenses before he got his life together and met Jim, who hired him as New Community's resident manager in the late eighties.

Billy made the three raiders as junkies looking to swipe anything they could sell or trade to finance their next hits. He took a deep breath and did the math. Billy was five-eight, 170 pounds, in his late thirties. Each of the men was about his size and age, give or take a few pounds or years. Billy reckoned he could take any one of the three individually. But three on one?

This was no time to be a hero. Billy uncurled his fingers and backed out of the room.

"That's right, get on out of here," the ringleader taunted.

Jim had told Billy that if he ever had any trouble when he was at the church by himself, he should not call the police—he should get Baldie. Billy raced down the stairs, zipped right past the phone in the hallway near the kitchen, stepped out into the sunshine, and made the short trip to Baldie's house. The kingpin of S Street answered the door.

"Three guys are robbing the church," Billy said. "They're taking snacks from the after-school classroom." Baldie didn't say anything. He just nodded and followed Billy toward New Community.

Billy and Baldie were heading toward the side entrance when they saw the three men loading their loot into the back of a van parked in the alley behind the church.

Billy and Baldie walked toward them. The three bandits froze at the sight of Baldie. Two of them had boxes in their arms. The ringleader had already dumped his into the van. They knew who Baldie was. *Everybody* in the neighborhood knew who Baldie was.

"Hey, Baldie. What's up?" the ringleader said, all friendly.

Baldie turned to Billy.

"That's them," Billy said.

The three men seemed to go pale. The ringleader put his palms up. "Our bad, Baldie. We didn't know."

Billy almost felt sorry for them. They had no idea Baldie had two little girls in the after-school program. They might as well have been walking up to Baldie's kids and their little friends and taking their snacks away.

"Y'all need to take that shit back upstairs," Baldie said evenly.

There was no argument. The three would-be thieves picked up the boxes and marched back into the church. Baldie gave Billy a little nod; he wanted Billy to keep an eye on them. Billy followed the three men into the church and upstairs.

The three men and Billy returned. Baldie was waiting for them near the van.

"*All* of it," Baldie said.

The men picked up some more boxes from the van and carried them into the church. Billy followed, to keep an eye on the intruders.

Again the would-be bandits and Billy returned to the van.

"They bring back everything?" Baldie asked.

"Far as I can see, yeah," Billy said.

Baldie turned to the three men.

"Now, y'all need to get out," he said. "If I catch you in this neighborhood, me and my boys will break your fuckin' backs."

The men hustled into their van and zoomed off.

The following day, Billy ran it all down for Jim. Weeks passed. Jim heard rumors that Baldie and his boys had tracked down the intruders and inflicted an epic beat-down. Jim never asked Baldie about the rumor. If it was true, he would never admit it anyway.

The three men were never seen on S Street again.

After nearly a decade on S Street, Jim was comfortable coexisting with Baldie and his crew of slingers. He continued his ministry, preparing and delivering sermons, organizing and participating in mission groups, helping people get jobs and find affordable housing. Baldie doled out product to his slingers, paid them, and collected the profits. He kept sending his two young girls, Angie and Nicole, to the church's after-school program. Every summer, it seemed, Baldie fired up the grill and threw a party for the neighborhood.

Jim saw Baldie yell at his wife more than a few times, usually when the drug dealer was drunk. But he never saw Baldie physically harm anyone, and the big man's street slingers remained respectful of the church and its members.

Jim often talked to Baldie, trying to cajole him to change his life, to give up drug dealing, to come to church just once. Baldie never did. Nor did he refrain from violence entirely. One morning in 1993, Angie was outside the house waiting for her father to take her to swimming class. A man wandered by. Baldie started talking to him. From the conversation, she guessed that the man owed him some money.

The girl watched as her father picked up a piece of lumber and whacked the man on the head, knocking him to the ground. Angie ran back into the house, crying.

"Baldie was a complicated person," Jim said. "He believed in what we were doing. But I think he had no hope, that he couldn't imagine having a different life."

Most of Baldie's slingers couldn't, either. One Sunday morning, in the middle of a service, Jim answered a knock at the front door. A slinger held up a Styrofoam cup stuffed with cash—mostly ones, but also a couple of fives.

"This is for the church," the slinger said.

"Thank you," Jim replied. "Would you like to come in?"

The drug dealer waved him off and walked away.

Most of the slingers never accepted Jim's standing invitation to attend a church service. But a couple did join some members of New Community on a weekend retreat to the Maryland countryside. And Jim managed to help some of the slingers leave the drug trade.

One afternoon around 1989, Jim went out to the street and summoned about a dozen S Street slingers. Some of them were dealing drugs primarily to support their own addictions, Jim suspected.

"How many of you would get off the street if you could get a real job?" he asked.

Eight hands shot up.

Jim made a few calls to his D.C. government contacts and got each of the slingers a job in the Department of Public Works as a temporary garbage collector or street sweeper. Some of the dealers stuck with the city jobs; some didn't. But Jim didn't see any of them return to S Street to sell drugs. Eventually, one of the former slingers rose to a high position in the department. Jim didn't worry about offending Baldie, he didn't tell him about his effort to get some of the slingers off the street. Jim had told Baldie he was there to try to change people's lives. Besides, Baldie would have no problem finding replacements for street slingers.

It was part of the church's mission to embrace the "least and the lost, those rejected by society," Jim said. On S Street, that included not only Baldie's slingers but also their customers.

Whenever he had the opportunity, Jim showed the neighborhood addicts that he believed they could turn their lives around—even though he knew most of them wouldn't.

A commercial truck hauling building materials pulled up to the curb in front of the church. Jim stepped out to greet the driver. About four years after the church's inaugural service, on Easter Sunday 1984, the church looked much better, but there was still plenty of refurbishing to do. The truck was delivering supplies for the ongoing renovations.

Jim was expecting the truck. He wasn't anticipating the motorcyclist who pulled up right behind it.

The biker was a young, good-looking black man in his mid- to late twenties. He was wearing shorts, boots, and a do-rag beneath his helmet—and no shirt. That was a show-off move, Jim thought: The guy had the huge, cartoonish muscles of a professional bodybuilder.

The biker took off his helmet. Jim wandered over to talk to him.

The motorcyclist said his name was Diamond Jimmy. He said he'd followed the truck hoping to pick up some work. He had construction skills, he claimed—he could lay Sheetrock and do carpentry.

Diamond Jimmy was easygoing, charismatic, and confident without being cocky. The gangly white preacher and the ripped black motorcyclist couldn't have looked more dissimilar. But they turned out to have something in common: Both were world-class talkers.

Jim liked Diamond Jimmy straight off. On the spot, he hired the motorcyclist to do work for Manna Inc. He figured Jimmy could help fix up the run-down row houses and apartment buildings Manna bought to sell to people with low to moderate incomes.

Diamond Jimmy did good work, and he and Jim became friends. The biker and the pastor exercised together at a gym in suburban Maryland, near where Diamond Jimmy lived with his mom. Diamond Jimmy pumped prodigious amounts of iron; Jim lifted more modest quantities.

Diamond Jimmy revealed that he'd spent some time in jail on misdemeanor drug charges. He also said that he was a crack addict but that he was now clean. Diamond Jimmy's personal history didn't scare off Jim. In fact, he saw some of himself in the buff biker.

Jim had turned his life around after he'd given up booze, and part of his mission was to help others do the same. "The addicts around the church were no different from me," he recalled. "Different color. They lived in the city; I grew up in the South. But otherwise, we were the same."

Jim felt a little different about the more well-to-do people who drove onto the block from the Maryland and Virginia suburbs to buy drugs. "I did not like it that they came from outside to spend money to fuel the fire here. It was a desperate place," he said. "But they were addicts as well, so I had compassion for them."

After Diamond Jimmy had been working for Manna for a few weeks, Jim offered him the job of resident manager at New Community. The manager would maintain the building and keep an eye out for intruders, living in a spare room on one of the building's upper floors.

The motorcyclist accepted and moved into the church.

Hiring a crack addict, even one who was clean at the moment, to live and work in the middle of a crack emporium was a risk, Jim knew. The slingers were out in force every day and night. Diamond Jimmy would face almost nonstop temptation.

But the young biker was worth the gamble, Jim believed. "I saw the potential in him," he recalled. If Diamond Jimmy succeeded as the resident manager, he could be an example for other neighborhood addicts. He might help others get clean and sober.

Diamond Jimmy did well—for a while. He kept the church clean and helped with the ongoing renovations. Jim kept a close eye on him. But after about four months, he noticed that the biker was starting to slack off on his duties around the church.

Jim heard that Diamond Jimmy's girlfriend had been seen at the church late at night or early in the morning. Jim had told Diamond Jimmy that sleepovers were prohibited. The pastor also noticed a change in Diamond Jimmy's eyes—a slight glaze, the kind he'd seen in countless active addicts.

Jim told Diamond Jimmy that he had to let him go. Diamond Jimmy didn't get upset or try to cajole Jim into letting him keep his job. He seemed to accept that he had messed up, Jim thought.

"He tried," Jim said. "[Crack] was just too overpowering for him."

*

A couple of months after Jim had dismissed Diamond Jimmy, someone told him about another guy who might make a good resident manager, a man named Robert.

Robert was preparing to leave Lazarus House, a transitional housing center for alcoholics and addicts in recovery. Jim met with Robert at the church and asked if he'd like to be New Community's resident manager. No, thank you, Robert said politely. He knew he couldn't live and work in a crack zone. "He wasn't that strong, that dedicated to his recovery program," Jim said.

Instead Robert recommended a fellow addict he'd met at Lazarus House: Billy Hart.

Like Diamond Jimmy, Billy had been brought down by crack. In the mid-eighties, D.C. police caught Billy with a wallet that had been taken in a burglary. Years later, Billy said that he hadn't committed the break-in—but that he knew who had. Abiding by the code of the streets, he kept his mouth shut and took the charge. He pleaded guilty to burglary and receiving stolen property and did two years at the Lorton Correctional Complex.

Billy had already done some time for offenses related to his addictions to powder cocaine and bam and just about any kind of illegal pills he could get his hands on. While he was locked up in Lorton, he heard other inmates talking about an amazing drug that was new to D.C.: crack.

After he was released, Billy lit up a rock and was hooked. With one hit, he went from run-of-the-mill addict to desperate crack fiend. His run didn't last long, though—just a few weeks. It ended one night when Billy copped a dime from four teenage slingers a few blocks north of S Street.

Billy handed over his money. One of the dealers gave him the crack. Billy looked at the puny amount inside the little plastic baggie. It wasn't even a dime, half of the standard $20 rock.

"Sir, this is not what I paid for," Billy told the slinger. He asked for a bigger piece.

"Nigga, what you paid for is in your hand," one of the dealers said dismissively.

In that moment, something inside Billy broke. He refused to leave until the slingers gave him a bigger rock or his money back.

"Today, you'll have to kill me," Billy told the dealers.

Billy didn't know if any of the slingers were strapped. He didn't care. He was going to get his ten bucks back or take a bullet, and he didn't care how it played out. "I was ready to die," Billy recalled.

The lead slinger considered Billy for a moment, then said, "Give that nigga his money back." One of the dealers gave Billy his $10.

"Don't ever come back here again," the alpha dealer said.

That was Billy's lowest point. "I was sick and tired of being sick and tired," he said, reciting a phrase often used in recovery programs. It means that a junkie or alcoholic has had enough of the self-destructive cycle of addiction and feels defeated enough to try a new path.

In that moment, when the drug dealers let him go with his life, "I believe God stepped in," Billy said.

Billy had no money and no insurance. But he wanted to get clean. He checked himself into a twenty-eight-day treatment program at D.C. General Hospital, the city's public medical facility, and started attending support-group meetings. When his four weeks were up, Billy went into a transitional group home, then to Lazarus House, where he met Robert.

Jim could tell that Billy was serious about staying sober. He sensed that Billy and his sobriety could withstand living and working in a crack zone. He gave Billy the job.

Billy was great at maintaining the church, and though he often attended other churches on Sunday, he quickly became an integral part of the New Community family, developing close friendships with Jim and many members of the congregation.

Shortly after he was hired, Billy did something on his own that made Jim's spirit soar: He launched a weekly support-group meeting at the church, open to anyone from anywhere. He called it the No Exclusions, Everyone's Welcome group. As of 2014, twenty-five years after he launched it, the meeting was still going, every Tuesday night.

"Billy was the answer to my prayers," Jim said. The fact that Billy made it and Diamond Jimmy didn't demonstrates that for an addict to sustain his or her recovery, "two things have to be working," Jim added. "The individual has to come to a decision to take personal responsibility in his own life, to surrender his life to God. There also has to be a good support system in place."

Providing a support system was part of the church's mission. The rest was up to the addict.

"I didn't have a strategy to change one person at a time," Jim said. "My goal was to be faithful to God's call to come here, establish a church, be with the people, offer an alternative, and see what happens."

If that alternative wasn't embraced by everyone on S Street, it didn't mean that New Community had failed. "We didn't have the idealistic idea that we'd change the neighborhood or that we were the answer to everyone's problems," Jim explained. "We were joining with the people who were here, who were besieged by drugs, violence, crime, disinvestment by banks and businesses, and, to a degree, neglect by the city."

Jim never felt discouraged that most dealers and addicts he reached out to never reached back, never turned their lives around.

"My expectation was always that a few would get it, but most wouldn't," he said. "I don't care about numbers. We're not in control. We believe in a power greater than ourselves. You never know who's going to make it."

It was past 9:00 P.M. when I checked into the rehab unit on the third floor of Suburban Hospital. Most of the staff was gone for the day, and the patients were in their rooms. A nurse told me I'd have to spend the night in the detox unit, even if I was sober at the moment. "Procedure," she said.

I shared the detox room with a middle-aged man who was fresh off a hellacious bender. He muttered something about being a college professor. He said his name was Tom.

It had started with a park picnic with a pretty woman, Tom told me. It was a beautiful fall day. She brought a bottle of wine. After being sober for eleven years, Tom said, he figured one glass of wine wouldn't hurt. The drink sparked a two-month binge. Tom said he'd been slamming down booze nonstop for a week before he checked into the hospital.

Tom tossed and turned and moaned. I closed my eyes and eventually drifted off to sleep to the sounds of his agony.

My misery was compounded the next morning. As I sat inside a small office, filling out insurance forms, a nurse said I had to contact a family member, whoever would be considered next of kin, to let him or her know where I was.

"Is there any way around this?" I asked.

"No exceptions."

My head dropped. I brought my hand to my forehead and started rubbing the spot between my eyes where Big Man had pointed his gun.

Calling Mom was out of the question. She'd broken down crying when I told her I was moving to Washington to work for the *Post*, and they weren't tears of joy. She hated to see any of her kids leave home, let alone move across the country. I wasn't up for telling her I was in a drug-and-alcohol rehab unit.

The idea of calling Pop was equally unappealing. In almost every way, he was a great role model. He was short but strong, barrel-chested and robust. He'd enlisted in the Army as a teenager, become a paratrooper, and served in Germany during the occupation. He no doubt saw some awful things, which he never talked about, at least not to his kids. While I was growing up, he was a supervisor at the Southern California Gas Company, maintaining and repairing gas lines. He must have been ill from time to time, but until he suffered a heart attack in his fifties, I don't remember him calling in sick to work—not even once. I believe my father would have done great in college, but he never got the chance to go. He started working as soon as he was out of the Army.

When I was in seventh grade, my science teacher challenged the class to explain an experiment involving how air and water behaved in a beaker. She might as well have asked me to recite *Hamlet* in Farsi. That night, as usual, Pop was in his chair, reading the paper. I described the experiment and asked if he had any idea what it might be about.

"Partial vacuum," he said, without looking up from the paper. The next day, after class, I approached the teacher, Mrs. Powell. "That beaker experiment—is it a partial vacuum?"

Mrs. Powell broke into a big smile. "You got it. Only a couple of other people in the class got it. Great job."

But my father and I never had a conversation that involved any emotional depth. When I was a teenager, I asked out a girl I'd met on my first job, going door-to-door to sign people up for a drawing to win an air-conditioning system. She agreed to a date. The next day, an angry guy called and said he'd kill me if I got near his girlfriend. I ran the issue past Pop, who was watering plants in the backyard. He just looked at me and didn't respond.

It could have been that my problems seemed insignificant compared with what he'd experienced at my age. Pop grew up in the 1930s and '40s in the dusty Arizona border town of Douglas. He and his brothers moved to California as young men, and Pop talked about his life before that only when he was around his brothers and Mauro, a boyhood friend who married one of Pop's sisters. During holiday gatherings, Pop would loosen up, becoming outgoing, charming, and funny. I'd sit quietly nearby, listening to stories about how the white kids would pick fights with Pop and his brothers and friends. Or about Pop's own father, who,

according to family lore, not only rode with Mexican revolution-
ary Pancho Villa but was one of Villa's officers—and once mercifully
and defiantly spared the rich townsfolk he'd been ordered to kill.

I was afraid to tell Pop that I'd been put away. I feared
he'd respond with either unyielding anger or overwhelming
disappointment.

I came up with an approach the nurse accepted: I'd call my
aunt Linda, Pop's youngest sister. She could talk to him like no
one else in the family. She was usually sunny and agreeable, but
I'd seen her push back at Pop during family discussions. If I or
Mom or any of my siblings had tried that, there would have been
hell to pay. But Pop never said a cross word to Aunt Linda.

I made the call. I told my aunt where I was. I said I'd been
drinking too much and left it at that. She agreed to call my parents.
An hour later, I was summoned to the front desk. Pop was on the
line.

As I took the phone, I braced for the worst.

"Hi, Chach," he said. My childhood nickname. I think it was
short for *muchacho*; no one ever explained it to me, and I never
asked. Pop's voice was relaxed. I could sense him smiling on the
other end of the line, three thousand miles away.

"Hi. I guess Tía Linda called."

"She did. She told me you're in the hospital. This is good," he
said. "You're in the right place. I've known a lot of guys at work
over the years who have dealt with this. If they can do it, you can
do it."

It was the first time Pop had ever told me he believed in me.
That handful of words, delivered in that optimistic fashion, was
precisely what I needed to hear. Maybe I could somehow parachute
off this rocket ship to self-destruction.

A complicated mixture of emotions welled up in me: relief,
gratitude, hope—and pride. I had a father who, even though he
didn't say much, knew exactly how to buck me up when I needed
him the most. If Pop believed in me, I had a chance.

Pop and I talked for a couple more minutes. I promised to call home every week. I hung up the phone and turned to the nurse.

"Let's get on with it," I said.

The rehab unit reminded me of a freshman dorm. Everyone was assigned a roommate. Each room contained two beds, two night-stands, a dresser, and a bathroom.

My fellow patients ranged from teenagers to senior citizens. A woman in her early sixties had skin that was as yellow as a ripe banana, from jaundice. Her doctor had told her that one more drink would kill her. A truck driver in his thirties was on his thir-teenth go-round in rehab.

I threw myself into the routine and listened. I tried to *get* it.

In lectures, counselors and doctors described alcoholism and addiction as a disease. It can't be cured, they said, but it can be managed. The disease never rested, they said. Even when we weren't using drugs or drinking, our addiction or alcoholism was doing push-ups, building strength, biding its time. It was a monster that could be driven into hiding—but never killed.

Phil visited me on Christmas Day. He brought me a present—a thick Los Angeles Raiders sweatshirt. He tried to encourage me.

"Think of this as something you have to go through to succeed," he said.

A few days later, one of the counselors, an easygoing man with dark, curly hair, summoned everyone into a meeting room. Most alcoholics and addicts never seek help, never try to get sober or clean, he said matter-of-factly. Of those who do, maybe 15 percent stay clean and sober for a year or more.

"Look around the room," the counselor said. "Chances are, only one of you will make it." That got my attention. I couldn't think of any reason he'd lowball the success rate of rehab. The title of an Elvis Costello song popped into my head: "Clowntime Is Over." I looked around the room at my fellow patients.

If only one of us is going to make it, I decided, *it's going to be me.*

I was sprung on Friday, January 10, 1992. Some of my fellow patients became reluctant to leave as their release dates approached. I understood: The unit was a safe, controlled environment. The outside world was dangerous—booze and drugs were there for the taking. I didn't know if I'd be able to stay away from crack. It was time to find out.

On a cold, sunny morning, *Post* colleague Courtland Milloy, at my request, picked me up from the hospital and drove me straight to a support-group meeting. Courtland had been through Suburban, was doing well, and had visited me about a week after Phil did. At the meeting, I raised my hand and reported to the group that I was fresh out of rehab. I was all in.

The first ninety days were crucial, all of the counselors had said. They'd hammered the message into us: Any addict or alcoholic who was serious about recovery should go to at least ninety support-group meetings in as many days. Addiction is cunning, baffling, and powerful, they'd said.

I attacked my recovery with the energy I'd expended chasing crack highs. Every facet of my routine was structured around recovery. I hit at least one meeting a day—two or three on my days off, Fridays and Saturdays. I resumed working my night shift, listening to the scanner and racing to crime scenes. A couple of friends, fellow reporters, asked me how I was doing. They had asked an editor about my sudden disappearance, and I'd given the editor the green light to let them know I was in rehab. My transition back into the real world was going better than I'd hoped.

I was floating on what support-group old-timers call the "pink cloud," a feeling of well-being some people experience early in recovery. When I was drinking and using crack, I'd been running on a cycle of highs and crashes. Now, as the toxins left my body, I felt a pleasant, almost constant low-level buzz. Addiction was my punk.

Then, on my seventy-seventh day clean, I ran into Carrie as I walked home from work. It was just after midnight on a bitter early-March night. I could have easily waved to her and gone on my way. Instead, I waved and strolled straight up to her.

"Hey, stranger," Carrie said. She was wearing a heavy parka and slacks. "Haven't seen you in a minute."

"Yeah, I was away for a while."

"I've got a twenty," Carrie said.

The magic words. Just like that, an internal switch was flipped. *A hit or two couldn't hurt. I'd been good, I'd earned it.* It was a form of temporary insanity that's difficult to explain to a non-addict. Intellectually, I knew that using crack again could have dire consequences. Maybe some part of me needed to test myself. But the fact was, and always will be, that, as a junkie, using drugs comes naturally to me; abstaining is out of the ordinary. Later, I would learn that it was not rare for people who had been sober ten, twenty, even thirty years to relapse, often with horrific consequences.

"Let's go," I said.

At my apartment, Carrie divided the rock in two with her fingernail, loaded her pipe with one half, lit up, and took a long hit. She leaned over and shotgunned me. I exhaled and quickly loaded my chunk into the pipe. It dissolved instantly. I inhaled.

I knew I was in trouble before I exhaled. My addiction was no longer a punk. *Cunning* and *baffling* had done their bit, and *powerful* was now stepping in. My addiction wanted *more*.

Carrie saw it in my eyes. "Are you okay?"

I looked at her, not caring that she was sexy and skilled and willing. My words came out in a low, tortured whisper: "We need to get more."

Carrie nodded. A few minutes later, I turned onto S Street and pulled up in front of John's Place. A lone slinger stood in front of the bakery. He jogged over.

I rolled down my window. "You got anything?" The dealer shook his head. "Out of product at the moment."

"This can't be right," I said as I pulled away from the curb. I made a series of right turns and returned to the spot in front of the nightclub where I'd made hundreds of buys.

S Street was dry.

"I know another spot," I said. I pulled away and headed east on Rhode Island Avenue, toward the corner of 1st and T Streets Northwest, my secondary copping zone. There were no dealers in sight.

It was a minor miracle—two of the busiest open-air rock markets in the city were shut down on the very night I relapsed.

I drove Carrie back to Thomas Circle, dropped her off, and went home. A monstrous sense of remorse kicked in. My seventy-seven days of sobriety were gone.

How could I have been so dumb? When I started over—*if I started over*—I'd be a newbie again.

I wanted to be clean. I wanted to smoke half the crack in the city. I stared at the ceiling for two hours, until finally I drifted off to a fitful sleep.

I woke up as dawn was breaking. I'd gone to sleep hoping I'd be fine when I awakened, but instead, my addiction goaded me. *More. Now.*

More would be available. The morning was cool, but brilliantly sunny. By now S Street or 1st and T or one of the dozens of other rock zones within a short driving distance would be open for business. All I had to do was get in the car.

No.

Yes.

Maybe.

More, more, more. Every cell in my body screamed for more crack. I peeked out my bay window. It was almost 8:00 A.M. The neighborhood was stirring to life.

I paced back and forth from my living room to my kitchen, considering my options: I could call a fellow alcoholic in the program, turn myself in, and start over. I could call Champagne—I still knew her pager number by heart—and go to town.

I could try to live. I could self-destruct.

I was paralyzed. I didn't have the courage to pick up the phone and call a fellow addict, to admit what I'd done and start over. I was terrified of where I'd end up if I took another hit. Back and forth I paced.

I slipped on my leather jacket and stepped outside. In a daze, I wandered west toward downtown. I didn't have a plan, but I knew that it was only a matter of time before I ran into a strawberry or a slinger. I was moving toward my next hit.

I'd gone only a couple of blocks when I ran into Roxanne. She was wedded to heroin, but she stepped out with crack now and then. I'd picked her up a couple of times when I couldn't find Champagne or Carrie.

She had greasy, light-brown hair, bad skin, and a missing front tooth. Roxanne could have been in her late twenties or her early forties—her prodigious heroin consumption made it hard to tell. She always wore long sleeves, even on blazing-hot days. But in the summer, she wore open-toed sandals, and I'd seen the track marks between her toes.

Roxanne was sitting on the curb.

"Hey there," she said as I approached. She got a better look at my face and added, "What's wrong?"

I sat down next to her, confused, ashamed, afraid. For a long moment I stared at my feet, fighting back tears.

"It's all right," Roxanne said. "You can tell me."

I turned and looked into her brown eyes.

"I screwed up," I blurted out. "I went to rehab right before Christmas and I stayed for three weeks and I got clean and was released and I was doing great and I had seventy-seven days and last night I screwed up and I used again and now I just want to keep going."

My addiction crouched, waiting. Roxanne probably knew every slinger in the neighborhood.

If Roxanne had offered to hook me up, I would have handed her cash on the spot. I would have walked into the darkest crack house in the toughest combat zone in the city.

Roxanne put her hand on my shoulder.

"It's okay, sweetie. Take it easy," she said softly. "There's no need to kill yourself. You just need to start over. I know—I've been there. I was clean once."

I was sobbing freely now. I looked into Roxanne's face and knew she was telling the truth.

"Are you sure?"

"Just own up to what you did and you'll be okay. Go to a meeting, tell what happened, and take it from there. You don't want to go back to using."

I wiped away my tears, leaned over, and kissed Roxanne on the cheek.

"Thank you."

"You can do it," Roxanne said.

I wobbled back to my apartment. For nearly three hours, I paced. Then I drove to a club in Dupont Circle that hosted noontime meetings. I raised my hand and turned myself in.

"I relapsed last night," I said. "I'd been clean for seventy-seven days and I took another hit of crack."

The twenty people in the room listened, dead silent. A few looked straight down at the floor. I could sense what they were thinking: *Better him than me.*

I didn't care. The second I finished talking, my urge to use evaporated like so much crack smoke.

I wasn't cured—I knew the monster could reappear at any moment, commanding me to drink or smoke crack. But in that crucial instant, I also knew that I wasn't going to use that day.

I wanted to live.

A few days later, on a Saturday afternoon in early April, someone knocked on my door. I looked through the peephole and saw Carrie. She was in tight jeans and a formfitting cotton polo shirt.

I didn't think about it. I opened the door and let her in. She smiled.

"Hi, stranger. I've been wondering where you've been. Haven't seen you around the way. I was worried that something happened to you."

I'd been avoiding Carrie's usual spots. Something *had* happened: The relapse had scared the hell out of me.

"I've been around," I shrugged.

"I've got a couple of rocks, if you want to party," she said.

Should have seen that coming. My pulse quickened. I was thrilled. I was terrified. I should have asked her to leave.

Instead I said, "Can I see?"

Carrie reached into her inside coat pocket and pulled out two twenty rocks, each wrapped in a small plastic baggie. I stared at the rocks in her palm. She'd scored good weight.

"You have a stem and a lighter?"

She nodded, patted her coat pocket.

Carrie slipped off her coat. She started unbuttoning her blouse.

I thought about the consequences. Even though my addiction had been dormant since that terrifying night of my relapse, it would now be ferocious, twenty feet tall with ripped muscles.

It would win.

I would die.

Carrie was working on the second button of her blouse. I reached out and touched her hands.

"No, Carrie. I can't do this. Believe me, I'd love to. But I can't. I've been clean, and I'm trying to stay that way. I've relapsed once. It was pretty bad, and I can't do that again."

"You go to meetings? You're in the program?"

"Yeah."

Carrie nodded. She buttoned up and put her coat back on.

A crazy thought popped into my head. I went with it: "Listen, if you want to go to a meeting, I'll take you. If I can get clean, you can, too."

A wistful smile crossed her face.

"I was clean for a while. I was in the program. I had a few twenty-four hours built up. Then . . ." her voice trailed off. "Maybe someday."

Carrie walked out the door.

I slumped onto the sofa and waited for my heart to stop pounding.

CHAPTER 8

DRIVE-BY PROMOTION

On the morning of January 20, 1993, Lou stood at his post at the corner of 3rd Street and Constitution Avenue Northwest, three blocks from the Capitol. Like almost every other Metropolitan Police Department officer, he was on the street to provide security for Bill Clinton's presidential inauguration. As the captain in charge of detectives for 1D, Lou typically wore suits. But inauguration duty was all about visibility, so he'd broken out his white shirt, blue jacket, and MPD hat for the first time in a couple of years.

It was a beautiful morning, Lou thought—sunny and brisk, but not too cold for January. He had a perfect view of the west side of the Capitol, where presidents are sworn in. The crowds behind the barriers set up along the street were growing by the minute.

An unmarked car pulled up to the curb. Inspector William O. Ritchie was behind the wheel. He and Lou had worked together in homicide in the early eighties, when Lou was a detective and Ritchie a lieutenant. Before that, when Lou was just a young street officer, they'd both been in the Fifth District.

Ritchie was one of the few white shirts at the time who was college educated. In 1971, he'd gotten a bachelor's in physical education from Howard University, which he attended on a track scholarship. He later earned a degree in mortuary science from the

University of the District of Columbia. He was smart and hard-working and didn't like to engage in departmental politics. He and Lou knew each other, but they weren't drinking buddies or cronies.

People kept streaming toward the parade route. The crowd was two, three, four deep. It would be a sea of humanity by midmorning. Everyone seemed to be in a good mood.

Ritchie rolled down his window.

"How's your back?" he asked.

"Doing better, thanks," Lou said. His lower back was balky. He'd started going to a chiropractor and doing exercises to strengthen it.

Like Lou, Ritchie wasn't much for small talk. He got right to it: "I'm about to become chief of detectives," he said. "How would you like to be my homicide commander?"

"Yeah, I'd do that job," Lou replied almost instantly.

Ritchie wasn't surprised.

"I'll be in touch," he said, then rolled up his window and drove off.

Lou had aspired to command homicide since the early eighties. He knew that morale was bad in the squad, that detectives were overrun with unsolved killings. But he felt confident that he could improve its collective spirit and make it more effective. He had great street sources, including an ex-cop. Those sources alone would be good for an additional fifteen to twenty closures on homicide cases every year, Lou figured. He wasn't afraid of the demands of assuming the command at a time when D.C. was the nation's murder capital. In fact, he relished the prospect. He thought the plan he'd developed over the past few years could revolutionize the way cases were investigated, if only he could get an opportunity to put it into action.

But first things first. Lou returned to his parade-route duties. Many people in the crowd were smiling, excited that they were about to witness a piece of history and welcome a new, young president. An hour or so after Ritchie drove off, a pair of girls, about twelve or thirteen, approached Lou: They'd come to D.C. for the inaugural and gotten separated from their party. They were supposed to meet with the rest of their group at the corner of 12th Street and Independence Avenue Northwest to board a bus that would take them home after the parade.

They were old enough and close enough to their meeting spot that Lou could have given them directions. Instead he told them not to worry and drove them to the intersection in his marked squad car.

On the way, Lou thought about Ritchie's offer and what he'd do if he were in charge of homicide.

Ritchie knew better than most the demands of the homicide command. He'd served as the captain in charge of the branch from 1988 to 1990, when the number of killings in D.C. had spiraled toward five hundred per year. In 1992, the city had clocked 443, and the police department seemed to have no real strategy for quelling the violence.

Many killers were, in fact, getting away with murder: The homicide squad's closure rate was somewhere in the range of 35 to 40 percent. That didn't mean that all those suspects were eventually convicted of homicide, though. With drug gangs killing people who cooperated with police and prosecutors, many witnesses were afraid to testify, making it impossible to go forward with a prosecution. Some cases were dropped, and some suspects pleaded guilty to lesser charges.

The situation clearly weighed heavily on MPD chief Isaac Fulwood Jr., who in September 1992 had announced that he would be making good on his oft-repeated promise to resign if the bloodshed didn't stop. Talking about his tenure as chief to a *Post* reporter, Fulwood said, "The number one low has been the record number of homicides, the record number of young black men killed needlessly."

Three months after Fulwood's announcement, Marion Barry successor Sharon Pratt Kelly introduced the new chief: Fred Thomas, a former deputy chief who'd retired in 1985 and had been working as the vice president of the Metropolitan Police Boys and Girls Club.

Shortly after his appointment, Thomas met with all police department division commanders to get up to speed on how the white shirts were running their respective shops. Ritchie headed MPD's medical services division, overseeing the facility that treated D.C. cops and firefighters, as well as some members of the Park Police and uniformed Secret Service officers. He told Thomas that he'd saved the department as much as $350,000 annually by setting up a fee schedule for the private physicians who treated injured officers. Before, it had been paying whatever the doctors charged.

"Is there anything else you would like to say?" Thomas asked Ritchie as their meeting wound down.

Ritchie saw an opportunity: The white shirt who was in charge of the criminal investigations division at the time was preparing to transfer to another assignment. Ritchie made his move.

"I think I'm the best person to command the criminal investigations division," he told Thomas.

For weeks, Ritchie didn't hear from Thomas. Then, on January 19, 1993, the day before the inauguration, Thomas called to tell him he would be the new chief of detectives, effective the following day. Thomas said he was going to promote the current homicide captain, Wyndell Watkins, to the rank of inspector. That meant there would be an opening for a homicide commander.

"I only have one person in mind," Ritchie told Thomas. "Lou Hennessy."

Thomas told Ritchie he'd get back to him. The following day, on the inauguration route, Ritchie asked Lou whether he wanted the job.

But it was hardly a done deal. Thomas called Ritchie about a week later: "I've been getting some bad reports on Hennessy," he said. The chief had heard that Lou was "uncontrollable," that he'd had verbal skirmishes with fellow white shirts.

The second part, at least, was true. In the mid-eighties, when he was a lieutenant, Lou had discovered a patrol officer playing Russian roulette with his service revolver in the basement of the officer's home. The officer was distraught because his wife was having an affair with another cop—who happened to be close to Chief Maurice Turner. Lou relieved the man of his gun and badge and referred him to the Police and Fire Clinic for a mental health evaluation. Following procedure, he then wrote up a memo and sent it to the chief's office.

The memo was kicked back: The officer was to remain on the street, with his gun. Livid, Lou called Reggie Smith, the lieutenant in the chief's office who handled departmental memos.

"What the fuck is wrong with you?" Lou yelled at Smith, who was close not only to Turner but also to Fulwood, then an assistant chief. Smith didn't want a written record of the messy problem in the chief's office, Lou believed. Lou went over Smith's head, straight to Fulwood, who sided with Lou and arranged for the officer to be relieved of his duties while he was evaluated.

Ritchie wasn't going to let some badmouthing and exaggeration interfere with his plan to appoint Lou homicide commander. He was highly motivated to have Lou in that key post.

"Lou knew homicide," Ritchie recalled. "And we were getting our asses kicked."

The chief needed reassurance, Ritchie sensed. He provided it: "Chief, if you give me Lou Hennessy as my homicide captain, I will personally assume responsibility for his conduct."

Thomas signed off on Lou's appointment.

Lou took over the homicide command in mid-September, during a particularly violent stretch of time in the city. It wasn't just the usual gangsters who were getting killed; *civilians* were going down.

On Georgia Avenue Northwest, robbers gunned down a Vietnamese man in his family-owned jewelry store. A few blocks away, someone fatally shot a Korean woman inside her dry-cleaning shop. In Southeast, four gunmen emerged from the woods and methodically hunted and executed a spectator at a pickup football game. A stray bullet struck a four-year-old girl in the head. She lingered for four days and died in the hospital.

A feeling that the entire city was starting to veer out of control began to take hold. Mayor Kelly said publicly that she wished she had the authority to call in the National Guard.

Lou didn't get much rest during those first few weeks. He rode out to murder scenes with his detectives to get a feel for how they worked. He kept a change of clothes and a shaving kit at work and sometimes slept on the couch in the homicide office.

When he wasn't going out to crime scenes or meeting with detectives about the progress they were making, Lou sat at his desk and typed his plan to revolutionize the way homicide handled cases. As far back as anyone could remember, detectives had worked on a rotating basis. A detective who was "on the bubble"—first in line for the next homicide—would be responsible for that investigation, regardless of where in the city it occurred or under what circumstances. Then the next detective would be on the bubble.

That meant detectives were often investigating five or six killings at a time in different neighborhoods throughout the city, including homicides in places where they had no sources.

Lou's plan called for creating seven teams of homicide detectives, one for each police district. The detectives would be responsible for getting to know the players in their respective districts and developing contacts with street cops, merchants, and residents—as well as whichever local thugs were willing to play ball.

Victims and shooters almost always lived in the same neighborhood, Lou believed. Southeast D.C. gangsters generally weren't beefing with crews in Northeast or Northwest. They were waging battles on their home turf, killing people they'd grown up with. Assigning detectives to specific districts would give them the opportunity to build up a network of reliable informants, Lou reasoned. It was the same idea pressed upon him by his training officer, Skip Enoch: A good cop knows whom on his beat to call; a great cop has people in the neighborhood calling *him*.

To maximize the value of the intelligence that would be gathered and to foster collaboration, Lou proposed holding weekly meetings at which the representatives of each detective squad would talk about their cases and swap information. Other officers from police districts with high crime rates would take part in the meetings, too. If homicide detectives obtained a lead that a guy nicknamed Peanut or Black was involved in a killing, they may not know which of the dozens of young men with those handles they should look at. But narcotics detectives or street cops working that neighborhood probably would. Representatives from nearby police departments in Maryland and Virginia would also be invited to the meetings.

"The approach just made sense," Lou explained years later. "It really was the community-policing concept, only with detectives instead of patrol officers."

Executing his plan properly would require additional resources. When Lou took over the squad, about thirty detectives were assigned to homicide. Lou asked for that number to triple within a year. He proposed that all detectives receive intensive training from prosecutors with the U.S. Attorney's Office, representatives of the medical examiner's office, and retired investigators.

Lou wrote up a fifteen-page proposal. A couple of weeks after he assumed the homicide command, as the mayor spoke of bringing in the National Guard, Lou and Ritchie walked into Chief Thomas's office.

Lou handed Thomas a copy of his plan and described his vision. Thomas asked detailed, thoughtful questions. The meeting lasted ninety minutes. Lou told the chief that he was confident his plan would bring down the number of killings in the city, maybe even below four hundred a year. "If you do that, you'll be considered for a Nobel Peace Prize," Thomas said.

At the end, the chief looked at Lou and Ritchie and said evenly, "I'm going to give you everything you want. If I don't see some results in a year, I'm going to fire both of you."

*

In the summer of 1992, about two months after Carrie last offered me crack and sex, Phil Dixon gave me a chance to move to the day shift. There was an opening covering social issues, including public housing and homelessness. I'd hit the wall on the night shift. The late hours were taking a toll, and I'd felt myself burning out on all the shootings I was racing to. One crime scene blurred into the next.

Also, I'd been starting to wonder whether working the late shift was threatening my recovery from crack and booze. Social isolation is an inevitable component of addiction. When I'd started to drink heavily, during my *Herald Examiner* days, I routinely joined colleagues at Corky's after work. But as I drank more—and began using crack—I became more of a loner.

At first, I usually smoked crack with strawberries. But toward the end of my run, right before Milton Coleman drove me to rehab, I was smoking by myself. At that point I'd been drinking by myself for years. On most weekends, I would leave my apartment only to pick up strawberries and crack or to play pickup basketball.

After my relapse, I hadn't had any urges to resume smoking crack or drinking—at least not any conscious ones. But nightmares about using crack had begun to invade my sleep. In one, I'd be at my apartment with Carrie or Champagne. I'd light a loaded pipe, bring it to my lips, and inhale. I'd wake up in a panic, unsure for a few moments whether I'd actually used again and wrecked my recovery.

In another nightmare, I stood in the dark at the edge of a deep crevasse. Carrie or Champagne would be on the other side of the fissure, ten feet away, inhaling from a crack pipe. They'd smile and hold out the pipe, beckoning me to take a hit. I'd jump, anxious to be with them, eager for a hit. About halfway across, I'd start spiraling down into the dark. I always woke up before I crashed.

The dreams weren't subtle.

They weren't even the worst of my sleep problems. Around this time I'd also started grinding my teeth. My dentist fitted me with a guard made of supposedly unbreakable material. I'd chomped through it in a few months. Then I started snapping my left wrist as I slept—with such force that it would be sore when I awoke. I asked a couple of doctors about it; neither had an answer. I researched the problem and found nothing. I adapted: I started sleeping with a soft wrist brace, the kind people afflicted with carpal tunnel syndrome wear.

I took the job on the day shift.

For about eight months, I worked my new beat. I was energized, making new contacts, writing stories about overextended social workers and the horrors of the city's public housing stock. I was also going forward with my recovery, attending support-group meetings, staying in contact with fellow sober addicts and alcoholics.

One member of my informal support network, a man who'd been sober for about two decades, noticed that, unlike many newbies, I wasn't fighting constant urges to drink or use drugs again.

"You're one of the lucky ones," he said.

Then, in the spring of 1993, Phil took me to lunch and asked me to take over the daytime police beat.

I wasn't thrilled at the idea of jumping back into combat zones. But I was loyal to Phil, and it was supposed be a temporary assignment. Besides, working the beat during the daytime would mean I would get more of an opportunity to write real stories, instead of news briefs or overnight memos. I agreed to do it.

"How do you want me to handle the beat?" I asked.

"Follow the violence," Phil replied.

Sometime during Lou's first week on the job, I called his office to check on the status of the investigations into the spate of civilian killings. The captain had been cordial the one time I'd met him, at the scene of the drive-by at the intersection of 5th and O Streets Northwest, but I wasn't expecting much.

The previous homicide commander usually wouldn't take or return my calls. I had to work around his lack of cooperation as best I could.

The homicide secretary who answered the phone asked me to hold. *I'll just leave a message and . . .*

"Captain Hennessy."

The captain wasn't defensive or dismissive, like many white shirts. He didn't volunteer anything, but he answered my questions and provided basic information about where the cases stood.

It was a start.

During the first few months he was in charge of homicide, Lou made my life marginally easier. He was professional, which made him stand out among white shirts. When he declined to answer a question, he usually explained that doing so might compromise an investigation. I figured that the new homicide captain probably wouldn't become a source—but that he wouldn't become an obstacle, either.

Everything changed in late January 1994. I was sitting at my desk when a caller offered a bombshell tip about the homicide squad. The caller claimed that the office was embroiled in racial strife, and he blamed the new captain.

The tipster was a black detective named Rod Wheeler. He dropped a passel of accusations: Captain Hennessy was playing favorites, assigning high-profile cases to white detectives. He'd brought in some white cronies. He was shutting out veteran black investigators. The squad was fracturing along racial lines.

There had just been a contentious meeting to clear the air, he said. Each of the thirty-five homicide detectives, as well as another fifteen who worked with the feds on task forces, had confronted Hennessy and his lieutenants. Wheeler said he'd asked Hennessy during the meeting whether he was racially biased. The captain had declined to answer. The detective said all this on the record, which strengthened his credibility.

I took notes and put down the phone, my adrenaline surging. An accusation of racial bias in Chocolate City could blow up a white cop's career.

Lou didn't strike me as someone who carried any racial baggage, but that was a gut feeling. I didn't know him very well. On the other hand, the detective who'd called in the tip was a smart guy. He didn't seem the type to level such accusations lightly. But what if his agenda was strictly to stick it to the new captain? What better way to do that than accuse him of bigotry?

I thought of Phil's edict to follow the violence. It was crucial that I maintain a good working relationship with the homicide commander. He was the single most important contact I could have on the police force, more so than even the chief, who was as much a politician as a cop. How would the captain react to my doing a story on Wheeler's allegations? I could envision it poisoning our working relationship—if Lou even survived. If he didn't, I couldn't imagine that his replacement would be thrilled about talking to me.

There was something else to consider, too: The *Washington Times* had an aggressive police reporter. Wheeler might ring him up, too, especially if a story didn't appear in the *Post* within a couple of days. I didn't want to disappoint Phil. And I really didn't want to disappoint *Post* executive editor Len Downie, who would almost certainly read any potential *Times* story and then yell at Phil.

Phil was a rarity, the kind of editor who would take a bullet for his reporters if he could. He hadn't ever come down on me for missing a story. He appreciated how hard I worked. I didn't want to put Phil in the position of explaining how I hadn't picked up on racial tension in the homicide squad.

I stared at my notebook. There was no way around it: I had to pursue the story—and kick it out quickly, before the *Times* did.

I took a deep breath and called the homicide office. I identified myself to the receptionist, who put me through.

"Captain Hennessy."

"Hello, Captain. I have to ask you about something. Detective Wheeler said there's racial animosity in the homicide squad, that there's a perception you're not treating the black investigators fairly. He told me about the meeting. He said he asked you if you were racially biased and you declined to answer."

Silence for four, five counts.

"I'm not comfortable talking about that," he finally said. The discomfort was evident in his voice.

"I don't think it's as simple as all that," I said. "I'd really like your side."

"I'm sorry, I can't comment on that."

We hung up.

Under the rules of journalism, I was covered, technically: I'd given Lou a chance to respond. I could knock out the piece in good conscience. A story this explosive would have a shot at the front page.

But it didn't feel right. I didn't blame Lou for shutting down. Anything he said would make him look defensive. I drummed my pen on my desk. There was more to this, I sensed. I stood up and began pacing around my desk.

I needed to get the captain to talk.

An idea came to me. I picked up the phone, dialed the number to a pager, and punched in my phone number.

Trevor called five minutes later. He was a detective in the Fourth District. Each police district had its own contingent of detectives, which worked on nonfatal attacks, robberies, burglaries, and other crimes that weren't the responsibility of the investigative teams that worked out of headquarters, such as the homicide squad. Trevor was one of the best investigators on the force and about Lou's age. They might know each other.

"I need your help on something," I said. I laid out the accusations.

"That doesn't sound like Lou Hennessy," Trevor replied.

"Yeah, I know, but I have to do a story. Do you know him? Can you talk to him, persuade him that he's better off talking to me? Or at least convince him to give me names of other cops who will speak up for him? If he doesn't, this story may not turn out too well for him."

"Yeah, I know him. I'll call him. Hit you back in a few."

Trevor called back ten minutes later.

"Call him right now," he said.

The captain talked to me.

There had been some heartburn among some of the detectives, he acknowledged. But as he saw it, the issue was change, not race. He was shaking up the unit, and some of the big egos in the squad were getting bruised. He'd set up a team of detectives to focus on homicides in one specific police district, on the theory that most killings involved players from the same neighborhood. Eventually, Lou said, he planned on creating a team for each police district. He was holding sergeants accountable for the closure rates of their teams of detectives. Homicide cases were assigned based on a rotation; he hadn't been freezing anyone out of any big investigations. The captain didn't mention he was planning on radically changing the way investigations were assigned and conducted. Not yet. His tone was calm and measured.

I called Lieutenant Lowell Duckett, president of the Black Police Caucus, who was well known for speaking his mind on racial issues within the department. Duckett scoffed at the idea that Lou was racially biased. I interviewed a veteran black detective, who said he and Lou had talked after the tense meeting and agreed to work together "harmoniously" for the betterment of the unit.

Then I talked to William Ritchie, the inspector who'd hired Lou as homicide captain. He told me something Lou hadn't mentioned: Twice in the past seven years, Lou had taken troubled teenage boys from D.C. into his home to try to help them get on the right track. Both of the kids were black.

The background provided by the captain, the veteran detective, Duckett, and Ritchie put Wheeler's allegations in context. I wrote up the story, focusing on the changes Lou was bringing to the squad. Deep in the article, the racial question was brought up and knocked down by Duckett and others.

The story ran on the front page of the Metro section, not on the front page. I was good with that.

Around noon, a call for homicide came out over the police scanner. I rode out to Northeast, where a young man had been shot in the courtyard of an apartment complex. Outside the building, I ran into one of the lieutenants Lou had brought to homicide. This lieutenant always carried a book, pulling it out whenever he wasn't talking to detectives or witnesses. He was glued to a dog-eared paperback as I approached.

The lieutenant looked up from his reading.

"You wrote that story about the captain?"

"Yes, that was me."

"Good story," he said.

I called Lou the following day. I'd worked into the article a brief reference to the two kids he'd taken into his home. One of them was Kenny McFarland, a basketball star at Gonzaga College High School.

"Tell me about these kids you brought into your home," I said.

A week later, I sat next to Lou in the bleachers of the Gonzaga gym, watching Kenny play. The kid had game. He was six foot six, wiry, and strong, with quickness, speed, and skills. He dropped twenty-six points on the opposing team, delivering the final two with a thunderous two-handed dunk.

"He's going to get a Division I scholarship," Lou said.

The captain had met Kenny while working as a volunteer basketball coach at Gonzaga. Kenny lived in a tough section of Northeast. A lot of his contemporaries had ended up in the drug game. Kenny wasn't a bad kid, but he was impressionable, the captain said. His home life was chaotic. He was drifting in school. He was on the verge of tumbling into the drug world.

Lou talked to Kenny's mom and aunt, who gave their blessing to his taking the teenager temporarily under his wing. Then he simply brought Kenny home; he didn't ask Loraine, he just did it. Loraine wasn't thrilled about suddenly having a teenager, a stranger, in the house, but she didn't object.

Lou described how he'd taught Kenny to study with three-by-five flash cards. He told me how they worked out together with free weights.

I interviewed Kenny and Loraine and wrote up the story.

This one did hit the front page.

One evening in March, I was getting ready to go home for the day when a call came over the scanner for a shooting at the corner of 7th and O Streets Northwest, just three blocks from my apartment. The dispatcher said homicide had been requested but provided no details. I could have left it to the night reporter, but I was curious to see what had happened so close to where I lived.

"I'll check it out," I told Phil. "If it turns out to be nothing out of the ordinary, I'll brief the night reporter and go home."

The attack had occurred inside the O Street Market, a brick building filled with small stalls where merchants sold baked goods, meat, fish, candy, and other items. The entire building was surrounded by crime-scene tape. A crowd of spectators almost two dozen strong was gathered across the street from the market. One TV news crew was already on the scene.

I buttonholed a friendly sergeant and asked him what he knew.

"We're still sorting out the details," he said. "We've got nine down."

I wasn't sure I heard him right.

"Did you say nine victims?"

"That's right."

"How many dead?"

"One, so far. Someone from PIO is on the way."

I had no interest in dealing with the Public Information Office, but there was no sign of Lou. That was odd. He made it a point to respond to every high-profile crime scene. I was judicious about paging him. I wouldn't have necessarily tried to raise him for a double or even a triple shooting—but nine down was an easy call. I called his pager and punched in the numbers to my *Post* cell phone.

He called back almost immediately. His voice was weak.

"You don't sound so good, captain."

"I'm sick as a dog. Flu's kicking my ass."

"Sorry to hear that. I'm out here at 7th and O. Can you help me?"

"I can tell you on background there were multiple shooters, at least two, maybe more. They seemed to be going for specific people. We don't know who, not yet," he said.

The one victim who'd died, a fifteen-year-old boy, was the son of his secretary, he said. She was the woman I talked to every day when I called him.

"Geez, I'm sorry to hear that," I said.

"Yeah, it's a shame. She's a nice lady."

For about two weeks, detectives worked the case hard without getting traction. Then Detective Donald Bell, sitting at his desk in the homicide office, got a call.

Bell was part of a squad of investigators assigned to the Fifth District, in Northeast D.C. Lou had created the team a couple of months before the O Street Market attack. It was the pilot squad, the first district-based homicide team Lou had created. Some of his detectives were still skeptical about the district-squad concept, Lou knew. If the 5D unit succeeded, he believed, those detectives would see its value and be less likely to grumble about change.

Lou had appointed veteran investigator Sergeant Dan Wagner leader of the 5D squad. He let Wagner choose his own team. Bell was an obvious pick for the unit.

He'd joined the department in 1973, the same year as Lou. Like

Lou, he'd started out in 5D. Unlike Lou, he'd stayed there, working as a street cop and in the vice unit.

In the late eighties, while the MPD spent millions in overtime on mass arrests of low-level drug suspects in Operation Clean Sweep, Bell wasn't simply making busts and pocketing extra pay. Instead he was cajoling street dealers for information, sometimes using the threat of jail time to encourage cooperation. He eventually built a stable of reliable informants in 5D. Bell worked the way Lou believed the entire police department should be operating, establishing contacts among the low-level offenders to go after the bigger players.

In 1989, Bell worked in homicide on a three-month detail to help out on a spate of 5D killings. He did well and accepted an invitation to stay.

When his phone rang two weeks after the O Street Market incident, it was one of his 5D informants.

"He told me the information that was in the news about the O Street Market shooting was wrong," Bell recalled. Until the moment his source called, Bell hadn't been working the O Street Market shooting, which had taken place in the Third District.

TV news reports suggested that the attack had sprung from a conflict between rival crews battling to control the neighborhood surrounding the market. It was a highly plausible theory, given that many shootings broke out over drug turf. But in fact, the shooters were with a Northeast D.C. crew, the informant told Bell. The group's ringleader was nicknamed Heavy. He was a skinny guy, the informant related. A few weeks earlier, Heavy had been out near the market alone. Some local gangsters relieved him of his leather jacket and car. Heavy had organized a get-back attack.

Bell believed his mole. His information always panned out. He took notes and ran them down for Wagner. Wagner took the information to Lou.

Detectives obtained search warrants for the homes of four

Northeast D.C. gang members. They found a gun in every house and test-fired them. Each weapon was a match for shell casings from the O Street Market attack.

I'd completed my shift and was relaxing at home when my *Post* cell phone rang. It was Lou.

"We're getting ready to lock up some suspects in the O Street Market case," he said.

It was the first time the captain had called me with a tip. He explained that the suspected shooters had been out for revenge for a carjacking and asked me to keep the information to myself until they were in custody.

I held back. I didn't even tell my editors. I didn't want to take the chance that they would push me to publish the information. A day or two later, the police department held a press conference announcing the arrests.

I called Lou after the presser, knowing he would now be free to talk more about the case. He told me about the 5D pilot squad and about how he planned on creating similar units for each police district.

"This is exactly what we set up the squad for: to develop this kind of intelligence, which will help us combat the violence," he said. "This is a perfect example of what we need and what we hope will be a trend."

The detectives working the O Street Market shooting had had no reason to look at suspects in 5D. If Bell hadn't had such a great source there, the case might have stayed open for a long time, maybe forever.

It was exactly how Lou had envisioned the district-squad concept could work. He began to sense something happening in homicide. He could see it in his detectives' faces, in their body language. They'd seen how Lou's idea could help them get killers off the street.

And now, Lou believed, they were ready to change.

*

In September 1994, five months after the O Street Market arrests, homicide detectives locked up eight suspects in various murder cases over a span of four days. The arrests vaulted their closure rate to above 50 percent for the first time since 1991.

Lou tipped me off, and I co-wrote an article on the milestone with a *Post* courts reporter. The article noted that the homicide team was now reorganized, with squads of detectives assigned to each of the seven police districts. There had been 284 killings in the city up to that point, 54 fewer than at the same time the previous year, the story noted. I quoted Lou: "We've reversed two trends. The homicide rate is going down, and the closure rate is going up."

By this time, the homicide commander was no longer "Captain Hennessy" to me. That summer, he'd invited me to his house for the first time, to help construct a pigpen. We labored under a broiling sun for hours, then had dinner with Loraine. After dinner I thanked her for the meal and walked to my car.

"Thanks for the invite, Captain."

"Call me Lou," he replied.

By September, Lou and I were talking about ongoing homicide investigations at least once a day, often two or three times a day.

That month, Chief of Detectives William Ritchie retired from the police department to take a job at the Washington Hospital Center promoting organ donations. At his retirement lunch, Chief Thomas congratulated him on his long career and his new job, then added, "Thank you for persuading me to hire Lou Hennessy as homicide captain. He's making a difference."

CHAPTER 9

BALDIE GOES DOWN

About an hour before midnight on the last day of July 1993, Metropolitan Police Department officer Vernon Gudger walked into the alley on the west side of the abandoned Hostess bakery on S Street Northwest. Halfway down the alley, he stopped at a light pole three feet from the bakery wall.

Gudger looked south, toward S Street, then west, in the direction of 7th Street. No slingers were in his line of sight, and no one seemed to have spotted him in the alley. He adjusted the binoculars hung around his neck, moving them over his right shoulder, then checked his belt to make sure his handheld radio and gun were secure.

He grabbed the light pole with both hands and swung his legs toward the bakery wall. The soles of his boots grabbed brick. Gudger pressed his feet against the wall and moved one hand over the other up the pole. He was headed for the roof.

Gudger was wiry and strong, five-nine and 175 pounds. The other cops called him Tree Monkey. Trees, poles, walls, fences, buildings—whatever needed to be scaled, Gudger could do it.

He had developed his climbing skills while living in Southwest Washington as a child, playing at the big construction site of what would become the Environmental Protection Agency's headquarters. To little Vernon, exposed rebar was a playground.

The family living in the house next door included a boy about the same age as Vernon. They were friends as kids and young teenagers, shooting hoops together at the local Boys Club. But things changed when they got older. Gudger entered the police academy. His neighbor, Wayne Perry, broke the other way, becoming a feared drug-gang enforcer.

In the spring of 1988, Gudger, now a young officer, was playing in an outdoor pickup basketball game. Sides were chosen. Perry sauntered onto the court and said he'd be playing, too. Gudger told him to wait his turn. None of the other ballers dared back him up.

"Don't make me go to my trunk," Perry threatened.

"Go to your trunk," Gudger said as he patted the fanny pack secured around his waist that held his service revolver. "I'm authorized to carry this 24-7."

Perry huffed and puffed—but he didn't go to his trunk.

Now, at thirty-one, Gudger was a veteran cop tired of seeing young men in the drug game take their last breaths while bleeding on the street. He grabbed the edge of the bakery's roof with one hand, then another, and lifted himself up. He walked to a front corner of the building, crouched, broke out his binoculars, and looked down on S Street.

S Street was part of Gudger's Third District patrol beat. Climbing the bakery was strictly his idea. He'd used the roof as an observation post maybe twenty times before. He'd seen a handful of street deals and radioed to cops on the ground, who arrested the slingers and a few buyers. But those were all small-time collars for insignificant amounts of crack. Like every other cop in 3D, Gudger knew that Baldie ran S Street's crack trade.

He just needed to find a way to get to him.

*

It seemed like an unusually quiet night, with only a couple of dealers on each side of S. About an hour into his surveillance, Gudger watched as a white guy appeared on the street. A white guy on that street, at that hour, was likely to be either a cop or a buyer. Gudger zoomed in on the man's face. He wasn't a cop.

The man walked toward a slinger standing in front of the house next door to New Community Church. The white guy and the dealer talked. The slinger walked to the front door of the house and knocked.

Baldie stepped out of his house. He walked up to the white guy. They strolled down the sidewalk toward John's Place. They took a few steps into the alley separating the nightclub from a row house. Gudger watched.

The white guy pulled some cash out of his pocket and handed it to Baldie. The kingpin of S Street pulled something out of his pocket and handed it to the white guy. The buyer walked away. Baldie walked back into his house.

Gudger put down his binoculars and grabbed his radio. He told a cop in a nearby squad car to jam up the white guy as soon as he turned the corner. The radio call came back a couple of minutes later: The guy was holding—a single rock.

Gudger stared at Baldie's house. He couldn't go in and get Baldie without a warrant. Baldie's pickup truck, parked right in front of the house, inspired an idea. Gudger radioed the cop on the ground with instructions. He hustled to the nearest light pole and shimmied down to the ground.

A couple of minutes later, a uniformed cop stood next to Baldie's truck and slowly wrote up a parking ticket. The cop tucked it under one of the wipers on the front windshield. Baldie opened his door and stepped onto his porch.

"What are y'all doing?" he yelled. "You can't write me up! I park there all the time!"

Gudger walked over. He almost always wore his uniform when he climbed onto the bakery roof, but tonight he was in dark blue police utility coveralls. He looked like a tow truck driver.

"I got one more car to tow, then I can get this truck," Gudger told his fellow cop.

Baldie stormed off his porch toward the uniformed cop.

Gudger showed his badge.

"MPD. You're under arrest for selling a controlled substance, crack cocaine," he said.

The big man turned his attention toward Gudger.

"I didn't sell no goddamn cocaine!" he bellowed.

A third officer arrived. The other two cops stood on either side of Baldie as Gudger broke out his handcuffs. Baldie was no fool. He turned around and held out his thick wrists.

Word quickly spread through the Third District station: Baldie was locked up. The 3D narcotics squad had been after him forever, with scant success—a couple of minor charges over the years, but nothing serious enough to get him off the street for long.

A day or two later, with Baldie still in the 3D cellblock, Gudger and a handful of other cops went to his row house to execute a search warrant. The officers knocked on the front door. A young woman, probably one of Baldie's older daughters, answered and let them in. She and a little girl about five years old sat on a couch in the living room as the police swept the house. The girl was probably Baldie's grandchild, friends of the drug dealer would say years later.

The cops checked drawers, closets, everywhere. They found nothing. They met up in the living room, a couple of the officers shaking their heads in frustration and disbelief.

"Where's the money? Where's the drugs?" one asked to no one in particular.

"They're next door!" the little girl chirped.

The woman slapped the back of her head and said, "Shut up!"

"Touch her again and we're taking you in," Gudger warned.

Then he and the other cops looked at each other: *Next door*.

*

Baldie was a thug and a drug dealer, but he was old-school: He would rather intimidate someone than beat him, and he would rather beat someone than shoot him. He didn't like to use violence if he could avoid it, a philosophy that earned him a great deal of respect among the residents of S Street.

There were shootings on and near the block. The volunteers who came to the church to help renovate it and the kids in the after-school program often heard gunfire nearby. Billy Hart and other church workers trained the volunteers and children to hit the floor when they heard shots.

But S Street wasn't the killing zone that many crack markets were. Other parts of the city, some of them just a few blocks away, were ruled by young men who were quick to initiate bloodshed.

In combat zones throughout the eastern half of the city, the level of violence was high and steady. But now and then there were dramatic spikes. On a single week in June 1993, for example, sixteen people throughout the city were killed. The District would finish that year with 454 homicides, a scant improvement over the all-time record of 482 killings set two years before.

In the early nineties, Antone White and Eric Hicks, both in their early twenties, ran the First Street Crew, which operated just six blocks east of S. The crew's slingers sold crack on both sides of 1st Street Northwest, at all hours, in all kinds of weather. I knew first-hand: On a few occasions when Champagne didn't like the pickings on S Street, she'd directed me to 1st, where she'd make the buy.

The First Street Crew's reign would end in a torrent of blood. In August 1992, Arvell "Pork Chop" Williams walked into a U.S. Attorney's Office and offered to help law enforcement investigate the gang. Pork Chop was angry with the crew's leaders. He believed they had information about the murder of his uncle but wouldn't give it to him. Under the direction of police, Williams began making large drug buys from White and other crew leaders.

After his last buy, on October 2, 1992, Williams was obviously shaken. White had refused to talk to him, and he believed the gang suspected he was "hot" and working with the cops. On a crisp afternoon a few days later, Williams was sitting in a car, trying to set up a meeting between crew leaders and an undercover cop, when two gunmen pumped sixteen bullets into his body and head and ran away.

The brazen killing didn't derail the investigation. By the spring of 1993, White, Hicks, and two other crew leaders were indicted on federal racketeering charges under the Racketeer Influenced and Corrupt Organizations Act, commonly known as RICO. Federal prosecutors also charged White with killing Williams.

In October of that year, MPD homicide detective Joseph Schwartz testified in a routine pretrial hearing. In his testimony, Schwartz described what a handful of witnesses had said about Williams's killing. The detective didn't name any of the witnesses, whom police and prosecutors were determined to protect. He provided no ages or addresses or even genders.

Even so, two days after the detective's cautious testimony, Janellen Jones, forty-one, a former crew member, was gunned down as she walked home from a bus stop. She had a subpoena in her pocket. Jones was shot in the mouth—a message to other potential witnesses. A man who was nearby when Jones was killed, John P. Barton, fifty-three, was also shot to death. Police and prosecutors believed that Barton was killed because he'd witnessed the Jones hit.

The killing didn't begin or end there. By the time the RICO trial had concluded, in March 1994, nine witnesses connected to the case against the gang had been shot to death. Five, including Williams, were gunned down before Schwartz's testimony, four after. White and his fellow crew members denied that they'd killed anyone or ordered any hits.

The jury didn't convict White or any other gang members for killing Williams. But the jury did convict White of racketeering. During sentencing, U.S. District Judge Harold H. Greene cited the destruction caused by the gang's drug enterprise: "It is hard to know but easy to imagine how many persons had to rob, burglarize, even kill, to get money to buy the amount of drugs distributed by this organization," he thundered. White got life in prison. The other gang members all got long terms behind bars.

Greene noted the killing of the police informant, adding that many witnesses who did testify were obviously terrified. "The judicial systems of several countries [such as] Colombia and Italy at one time were paralyzed by witness killings and intimidations," the judge said. "We must prevent that kind of development [from happening] in the District of Columbia and in the federal courts at all costs, because if witnesses can be intimidated, injured, or killed, all the crime bills Congress may pass will be just illusions, limited in practical effect."

During the late eighties and early nineties, there were dozens of gangs like the First Street Crew in every quadrant of the city. Some were even more violent. About five miles from White's crew's turf, near the U.S. Capitol in Southeast, Alberto "Alpo" Martinez ran his drug operation with impunity. His enforcer was Vernon Gudger's childhood friend Wayne Perry.

D.C. police arrested Martinez in November 1991. He eventually pleaded guilty to federal drug-trafficking charges and gave up Perry. In March 1994, Perry pleaded guilty to five murders—though he admitted to FBI agents Dan Reilly and Vincent Lisi that he'd killed thirty-three people altogether. Perry said he had registered his first kill at age twelve, and he provided enough details to suggest that he was telling the truth about most, if not all, of the murders he claimed to have committed.

Compared with the likes of White, Martinez, Perry, and others, Baldie was a lovable teddy bear. But then, his was apparently a strictly mom-and-pop operation, selling drugs on S Street and nowhere else. Other, younger D.C. drug dealers moved large quantities of product all over the city. Baldie undoubtedly made a lot of money selling drugs—probably in the hundreds of thousands of dollars each year, maybe even north of a million. But there was no evidence that his drug-dealing operation extended beyond S Street. Baldie didn't make nearly the amount of coin that other local kingpins did.

According to federal investigators, between 1982 and 1990, the R Street Crew, which operated in Northwest, sold $50 million worth of drugs. Nearby, the P Street Crew sold $100 million worth of drugs during a handful of years in the late eighties and early nineties, federal authorities alleged. Both crews were taken down by federal investigations in the early nineties, with the leaders of both gangs convicted of offenses connected to drug trafficking.

Baldie didn't have any flash in his game. Younger neighborhood kingpins went on shopping sprees in Georgetown and jetted to big boxing matches in Las Vegas. They wore gold and diamonds and tooled around in fully loaded SUVs and luxury sedans. In the early nineties, Martinez and other drug dealers organized teams for pickup basketball games; the losing side would have to pony up $10,000 to the victors.

Baldie did none of that. He had his old truck and his row houses—the one he lived in and the one next door, which, police would discover, he used to run his drug enterprise. He never took part in a high-stakes hoops game. He splashed out by hosting annual barbecues for his neighbors.

If someone else had been running the drug traffic on S Street, the church and the after-school program probably never would have had a chance. Jim was grateful for Baldie's protection. But Jim didn't tolerate everything Baldie did.

In fact, Jim became so upset with Baldie once that he threatened to renege on his promise not to call the police on him.

A couple of weeks before Gudger's rooftop reconnaissance mission, Cynthia Barron had taken some of the kids from the after-school program out for an afternoon of fishing at Hains Point, a recreation area on the Potomac River in Southwest D.C. She parked her car across the street from New Community and retrieved a half-dozen bamboo fishing poles from the trunk, struggling to keep them from slipping out of her arms as she walked toward the church. Baldie got up from his porch and met her on the sidewalk.

"Let me help you with those," he offered.

In the five years she'd been running the church's after-school program, Cynthia had developed a cordial relationship with Baldie. He always waved and said hello when she and her kids walked past his house, heading to or from the after-school program. She knew that he had a soft spot for the program and the church—and for her. One evening, after she'd walked the kids to their homes, she was headed toward her car when Baldie approached her.

"You guys need some money?" he asked as he reached into his pocket and pulled out a thick wad of cash. Cynthia was making seventeen grand a year. She looked at the bills in Baldie's hand. She could see they were all hundreds. Cynthia thought about the art supplies and books she could buy for the after-school program. She thought about her own monthly bills. But she knew where Baldie's money came from.

"No, thank you, Baldie. But thanks for offering."

So Cynthia didn't hesitate when Baldie volunteered to help her carry the fishing poles—no harm in that. She led Baldie to the back of the church and down the steps to the basement. She opened the door and stepped inside.

Baldie was on her as soon as she was inside the door.

He pressed his big torso against her slender frame and hugged her. Cynthia tried to squirm out of Baldie's grasp. She smelled alcohol on his breath.

"No, Baldie. I think you've been drinking."

Baldie held her body tight against his and started pawing at her. Cynthia tried to struggle out of his grasp. He drew in for a kiss.

"No way!" Cynthia shouted. She wriggled her arms free and pushed Baldie as hard as she could. He could have easily overpowered her, but he backed off. He turned and lurched out of the basement. Cynthia put away the fishing poles and drove home.

The following day, as he parked his car outside the church, Jim saw Baldie sitting on his porch as usual. Cynthia had told him about her encounter with the drug dealer. Jim made straight for Baldie and got right in his grill.

"Listen to me, Baldie. I heard what you tried to do to Cynthia," Jim said sharply. He was visibly angry. "If I ever hear of you doing anything like that again, you're finished. Do you understand?"

Jim didn't say he would start cooperating with the police, but he didn't have to. Baldie understood.

The big drug dealer stared at his shoes. He looked sheepish— embarrassed, Jim thought.

"Yeah, okay," Baldie muttered.

The outburst from the little girl sitting on Baldie's couch had given Gudger and his fellow officers a second chance to find the evidence they needed. Gudger and a supervisor got into a squad car and drove to a judge's home in an upscale neighborhood in upper Northwest D.C. They recounted the girl's spontaneous statement. The judge issued an emergency search warrant for the house next door to Baldie's.

The police discovered a passageway that connected Baldie's home to its neighbor. The houses were narrow and deep; the passageway was near the back, hidden from view from the street by a wooden partition. The officers entered the house through the concealed side entrance. One videotaped the search.

The door was unlocked. The cops stepped inside and immediately found a sixteen-gauge pump-action shotgun.

They walked into the kitchen. There was a .357 Magnum on a mirrored table. Nearby were a strainer, a measuring spoon, loose razor blades, and some two-kilogram scales, all tools used for cutting crack—which was in the room in great abundance.

The officers started opening kitchen drawers. One held dozens of bags of huge chunks of crack, each the size of a small pancake and a couple of inches thick. They hadn't yet been cut for street sale.

In another drawer, the cops found dozens of $50 rocks wrapped in small plastic baggies. In a third, they found dozens of $20 rocks. In all, the crack was worth $43,000.

In other parts of the house, the officers found boxes of ammunition for the .357, for a .270 handgun, for .44s and .45s and .22s, for twenty- and twelve-gauge shotguns.

Gudger walked out of the stash house thinking, *Mother lode.*

Police and federal prosecutors still had to tie the guns and the drugs and the ammunition to Baldie. The little girl's utterance had provided probable cause, but she was too young to serve as a witness in a federal drug-conspiracy prosecution.

They questioned Robert Epps, the man renting the house, who was known as "Bama Rob." The night of the search, he acknowledged that he knew Baldie and even claimed that he was his brother. A fingerprint on the .357 matched his. The police scooped him up.

A federal grand jury indicted Baldie and Bama Rob for running a drug conspiracy. Baldie was scheduled to go on trial in late July 1994. Just before Baldie's trial began, Bama Rob cut a deal with the government. He pleaded guilty to one count of conspiracy with intent to distribute more than fifty grams of cocaine and using a firearm during a drug-trafficking offense, in exchange for a fifteen-year sentence.

He also gave up Baldie, agreeing to testify that he had begun renting the row house on behalf of the drug dealer in October 1991. The house was used to cook, cut, and stash crack, he said. The passageway between the two homes was constructed in 1992. Baldie used it to go between the two houses and gather crack, which he would provide to his street slingers, Bama Rob told investigators.

Baldie's trial lasted four days. His defense attorney argued that the crack in the stash house didn't belong to Baldie. The members of the jury didn't buy it. They convicted him of conspiracy to distribute crack cocaine, possession with intent to sell, carrying a firearm during drug trafficking, and a couple of other counts. Baldie had made his living off crack, and now nationwide fears over the crack epidemic assured he would never be a free man again.

In 1984, Congress had passed the Sentencing Reform Act, as part of the Comprehensive Crime Control Act. Among other provisions, the SRA abolished parole eligibility for those who committed a federal crime on or after November 1987. Before the passage of the reforms, the judge might have had some latitude in sentencing Baldie. The changes in sentencing, coupled with the crimes he'd been convicted of, guaranteed that Garnell "Baldie" Campbell would be spending the rest of his life in prison. He was fifty. His young daughters, who at that time were on the cusp of adolescence, would never see him as a free man again.

In October 1994, Baldie's attorney, Cynthia Lobo, stood to address U.S. District Judge Charles R. Richey before he sentenced her client.

"Well, Your Honor, I'm afraid that, after practicing law for fourteen years, this is the first time I have stood next to someone who is bound to be sentenced to life in prison with no possibility of parole," Lobo began. "This is also the first time in my life, therefore, that I have had very little that I could say, since I know there's nothing that I can say that can persuade the court, since the court is bound by the law in this case."

Lobo offered "profound thanks" to Richey for giving her and her client "probably one of the best criminal trials that I've had the pleasure of trying in fourteen years. It is rare, and it is becoming increasingly rare in the climate of drugs and violence in this country, unfortunately, to find such an honest judicial temperament in the face of very strong evidence."

Then it was Baldie's turn to speak.

"How you doing, Your Honor?" he began. "I wanted to thank you, because I think I got a fair trial, and I want to thank Ms. Lobo for handling my case, and I wanted to thank Mr. [Assistant U.S. Attorney John] Cox, because I don't think he treated me so bad, you know. I think he gave me a fair trial, and then it could have been an act of God, you know. In fifty years, I never picked up a Bible in my life, but since I've been locked up the last fourteen months, I have one in my hand every day. So it might have been an act of God. So I'm satisfied with what happens."

Richey then sentenced Baldie to life in prison. A couple of federal marshals quietly escorted the kingpin of S Street out of the courtroom.

Jim heard about Baldie's conviction from a couple of street slingers. During the fourteen months he was in jail before being sentenced, Baldie never reached out to the pastor, never asked him to write a letter to the judge or testify on his behalf. Baldie didn't ask Jim or anyone else from the church to visit him in jail. He didn't ask them to attend his trial or sentencing.

"I think he was embarrassed, being locked up," Jim told me, nearly twenty years after Baldie's conviction. "I kept praying for him. But he knew that I wasn't going to testify for him or write a letter to the judge saying what a great guy he was."

On S Street, the crack market was as bustling as ever in the immediate aftermath of Baldie's arrest, though it would begin to slow down by the time of his conviction a year later. Slingers still lined both sides of the block; users continued to drive onto the street day and night to make their buys. Maybe one of Baldie's lieutenants filled the power vacuum. Perhaps another drug dealer slid in and took over Baldie's street crew. It's even possible that more than one drug dealer did business on the block, in relative harmony. Jim didn't know who was running the street in Baldie's absence, and he didn't try to find out.

"I kept talking to the guys on the street, the dealers, trying to get them to leave that life," Jim said. "I never stopped trying, as I'd never stopped trying with Baldie before he was locked up."

The accommodation and friendship Jim had with Baldie had developed organically, over time. It occurred because Baldie, for all his faults, understood and supported what Jim and the church were trying to do, and because Jim reached out to Baldie and his dealers rather than turning them in to the cops. Their understanding couldn't simply be replicated.

Baldie was gone, but he'd left a legacy on the street: The church was off-limits. New Community remained safe, whoever was running the block.

While Baldie went down, Marion Barry rose up.

His political resurrection began on April 23, 1992, the day he was released from prison. Barry didn't merely return to the District with his head held high. He came home like a conquering hero.

About 250 supporters piled into a six-bus caravan in the predawn hours in D.C. and greeted the former mayor in the parking lot of a Days Inn forty miles from the low-security federal correctional institution in Loretto, Pennsylvania, where Barry had finished serving his six-month prison term for misdemeanor drug possession. (He'd originally been housed at a federal prison in Virginia but was moved after being accused of receiving oral sex from a female visitor. Barry denied the charge.) The caravan had been organized by the Reverend Willie F. Wilson of the Union Temple Baptist Church, in Southeast D.C. Many of the people who took part were middle-aged women. When Barry arrived, some were singing the hymn "Victory Is Mine."

Wearing a black suit, dress shirt, and tie, accented by a colorful kente cloth scarf and kufi, Barry was accompanied by his mother, Mattie Cummings, seventy-five. Barry basked in the crowd's adulation, speaking of his personal redemption and spiritual rejuvenation.

"I come out of prison better, not bitter," he said. "I gained the realization that I had come to experience a spiritual power outage. It caused me to get my life out of balance and out of control."

"Amen!" some in the crowd shouted.

"God does not require perfection of us, only progress," Barry said. The phrase is similar to one commonly heard within recovery groups, in which individuals are encouraged to seek "progress, not perfection."

Barry and his supporters had lunch in the motel ballroom. There, he sang "Happy Birthday" to Florence Smith, who'd come to Pennsylvania from Southeast on the day she turned fifty-four. "He is one of the greatest persons, one of the only people I know who can do something for us as poor blacks," she told the *Baltimore Sun*.

The former mayor then joined the caravan for the ride to the District. The buses arrived at Union Temple Baptist, where another large crowd of admirers was waiting, at around 8:00 P.M.

Barry stepped off the bus and proclaimed, "Free at last! Free at last!"

During a brief meeting with reporters at the Days Inn, Barry had talked about a possible return to D.C. politics. "I have a number of options," he said. "I cannot get involved ever again in my life-time, I can wait and run later, or I can get involved this year."

Few political observers in the District believed he would go for option three. But just two months after his release, Barry announced that he'd be running for the D.C. Council seat in Ward 8, which comprised the poor, violence-plagued neighborhoods east of the Anacostia River.

In the Democratic primary in September, he easily defeated four-term incumbent Wilhelmina Rolark. In the general election in

November, he trounced two candidates, a Republican and an independent, winning with 90 percent of the vote.

He was just getting started. In May 1994, he walked into the auditorium of Calvin Coolidge Senior High School, in Northwest. The school is located in Ward 4—then-mayor Sharon Pratt Kelly's home ward. There, Barry announced he was launching a campaign to return to the mayor's office. This time, he spoke in biblical terms of redemption: "The day they arrested me, I was blind, but now I can see," he said. "I was lost, but now I'm found."

Barry's timing was good: Kelly's administration was mired in a fiscal crisis. In March, Congress had voted to slash $150 million from the city's budget of $3.4 billion for fiscal year 1995. A report by the General Accounting Office had said the D.C. government could run out of money in less than two years if it made the $190 million in pension contributions it was required to.

In the eastern half of the city, where drug violence was still exacting a horrible toll, Barry campaigned relentlessly. He showed up at barbecues, at senior-citizen centers, at Sunday church services, missing no opportunity to talk about his personal transformation. One of his campaign strategists was Rhozier "Roach" Brown, a charismatic former con who courted and organized the city's ex-offender vote.

In 1965, when he was in his twenties, Brown was convicted of first-degree murder and sentenced to life in prison. He and three others had beaten and fatally shot another man during a robbery. Brown admitted he had been part of the attack but maintained that he didn't shoot the victim.

Brown was sent to the Lorton Correctional Complex, where he joined an inmate advisory council. Prison guards who weren't happy about his activism inflicted a beating so severe that for a while he lost feeling on his left side. Instead of being taken to a hospital, Brown was thrown into solitary for eight months. Years later, a civil jury would award him $300,000 in damages over his mistreatment.

At Lorton, Brown also became one of the leading members of the Inner Voices, a troupe of prisoners that was allowed to leave the facility to perform plays throughout the Washington area. Brown wrote plays about the difficulties and humorous absurdities of life as a prisoner. Because of his dramatic work, around Christmas 1975, Brown caught a big break: President Gerald Ford commuted his sentence from life to thirty years in prison. The sentence reduction made Brown immediately eligible for parole. He was released.

Brown worked a series of jobs, including production at a local TV news station. But everything fell apart for him again in 1987. He started smoking crack and was caught selling cocaine to an undercover law enforcement agent. About the same time, Brown stole $45,000 from the Hillcrest Children's Center, a charity that serves emotionally disturbed kids from poor homes. From a girlfriend who worked there, he learned how the charity invested its funds, convinced a bank official he was the organization's executive director, and had the money put into his own account. In federal court, Brown pleaded guilty to drug and embezzlement charges and was sentenced to ten years in prison. He was also ordered to pay $45,000 in restitution to Hillcrest.

Again, Brown caught a big break: In 1993, he was transferred from federal prison to the D.C. Department of Corrections to finish serving the thirty-year sentence for his murder conviction, which would have been an additional sixteen years behind bars. The D.C. parole board released Brown after he'd been in District custody only five months, most of which he spent in a halfway house. A year after his release, he was working hard on Barry's campaign. Just like the candidate, Brown often talked about redemption and second chances.

"A lot of people make mistakes," he said in an interview after the election. "Why do we keep on punishing them for the same act?"

*

In D.C., winning the Democratic primary for mayor was tantamount to winning the election. Barry was running against Kelly and six others. A few weeks before the early-September primary, I was talking to Lou on the phone about some homicide investigations when we turned to the subject of the mayoral race.

In the eighties, the *Washington City Paper* had dubbed Barry "Mayor for Life." But I didn't think he could overcome his conviction for crack possession and all the tawdry details about his life that had spilled out during his trial—not in a citywide election. The campaign was racially polarizing. From news reports, it was clear that Barry had virtually no support west of 16th Street Northwest, which divides the eastern and western halves of the District. The western half of the city was predominantly white. I expressed my doubts to Lou.

"He's going to win," Lou replied confidently. "He's a master politician, maybe the best I've ever seen. He's great at working crowds. He seems to know everyone's name. I'm telling you, he will be your next mayor."

"No way," I said. "Sure, he can win in Ward 8 forever, but he can't win another mayoral election. He won't get a vote west of 16th Street."

"He's going to win."

"I'll bet you dinner that he doesn't."

Lou was right. Barry easily won the primary, with 47 percent of the vote. D.C. Council member John Ray, endorsed by the *Post*, received 37 percent. Kelly lagged far behind with 13 percent.

Following Barry's primary victory, the *Post* published a poll showing that 81 percent of the city's black voters planned to vote for the former mayor in the November general election, while 74 percent of whites planned to support Carol Schwartz, the white Republican candidate, who was a member of the D.C. Council. With African Americans making up about 65 percent of the city's population, Barry was all but back in the mayor's office.

A few days after the primary, Lou and I were sitting in a booth at one of Lou's favorite Irish restaurants, near Union Station, when the waiter came over with the check. The waiter looked at Lou, then at me. I gestured for the bill.

"I told you," Lou said, laughing. "He's a great politician—'Get over it.' "

In a press conference after he'd won the primary, Barry had been asked what message he had for white voters wary of his return to power. He responded that he was the best person to handle the city's finances—and advised those who opposed him to "get over it."

I shook my head as I took the cash out of my wallet. "Unbelievable. I wonder what he would have to do to lose an election in this city."

Lou didn't seem particularly worried about Barry's imminent return to the mayor's office. During his first three terms as mayor, Barry had developed a reputation for meddling with the police department, often when officers were investigating his behavior. But the homicide team was a rare bright spot for MPD. There seemed to be no reason for Barry to mess with it.

I figured that there would probably be no shortage of Barry rumors for reporters to chase, and that I'd be called on to pitch in.

That November, Barry easily defeated Schwartz, winning 56 percent of the vote. It was impossible to predict how his return to office would play out.

The only sure thing was that it wouldn't be boring.

CHAPTER 10

"CAPTAIN HENNESSY MUST DIE!"

Two days before Thanksgiving 1994, Lou was sitting in front of a typewriter on his kitchen table, typing a law school paper on contracts. He'd started taking night classes at the University of Maryland School of Law, in Baltimore.

Lou didn't have a bachelor's degree. He'd gotten into school through a program that provided opportunities to people with atypical educational backgrounds, including those who'd worked in law enforcement. He'd earned the required ninety college credits by attending community college at night. He was following through on his plan to launch a legal career after his time in the police department ended.

The young Lou Hennessy wouldn't have aspired to a career practicing law. The people in the neighborhoods he grew up in became cops, firefighters, and bartenders. But spending time in courtrooms with high-powered attorneys from Ivy League law schools had given him confidence.

"I realized they were no smarter than me," Lou said. "I knew I could do it. And the fact I was going nowhere in the police department motivated me." He'd started law school in August, just after his son Billy was born.

This was the first workday Lou had taken off since he assumed the homicide command, fourteen months earlier. He had the house to himself. Loraine was out running errands with Billy and their toddler daughter, Megan.

In the middle of the afternoon, the phone rang. "There's been a shooting," one of Lou's detectives said.

"Okay," Lou said. There's *always* just been a shooting.

"No, you don't understand," the detective said. "The cold-case squad got hit. We don't know how bad it is. We don't know how many shooters there are, or if they're still in there. ERT's preparing to go in." ERT was the Emergency Response Team—the SWAT unit.

Made up of a team of Metropolitan Police Department homicide detectives and FBI agents, cold case was down the hall from Lou's office, which was connected to the main squad room.

"I'll be there as soon as I can," Lou said.

Lou put on a suit and tie, clipped his nine-millimeter Glock onto his belt, and strapped on his ankle holster. He opened the ankle holster and slipped his .38-caliber revolver in place, then began the forty-five-minute drive to the city from his home in Charles County, Maryland. With the holiday two days away, traffic was light, and Lou made good time.

His pager chirped over and over as he drove toward headquarters. It seemed as though every detective in homicide and every member of the police brass was trying to reach him. Cradling his department-issued cell phone on his shoulder, Lou returned as many of the calls as he could. No one knew anything beyond the awful fact that gunshots had been fired.

As he approached the 3rd Street Tunnel, leading to police headquarters, Lou punched in the numbers to the cold-case office.

The phone rang and rang and rang.

About ninety minutes earlier, FBI agent John David Kuchta had wandered into the cold-case office for work. He and the other members of the squad typically started their shifts in the afternoon, unless they had to be in court.

The squad room, nearly empty so close to the holiday, was small, containing only about a dozen old metal desks. The phone on the one belonging to Detective Mike Will rang. Kuchta picked it up. A teenage boy asked for Will, then asked if there was a voucher authorizing payment for an informant on the detective's desk. Kuchta found it. The teenager's name matched the one on the voucher. The kid said he'd come around to pick it up.

Sergeant Henry "Hank" Daly then invited Kuchta into his "office." Daly had set up some portable cork walls around his desk, near a six-foot-long sofa. Daly was a twenty-seven-year MPD veteran. Kuchta considered him a walking encyclopedia when it came to homicide investigations. When he wasn't chasing leads or interviewing witnesses, Kuchta liked to talk to Daly to soak up investigative wisdom. Kuchta settled into the sofa, to the left of Daly.

As the two chatted, FBI agents Mike Miller and Martha Dixon Martinez arrived and started in on paperwork at their desks.

A few minutes later, the main door opened again. Three young men walked in, striding past Martinez. They were in their late teens to early twenties. It was bright and cold outside, and each of the three was wearing a heavy coat. One of them looked like he was on his way to a job interview. He wore gray slacks, a tan shirt, and a red tie under a brown sweater.

The three stopped five feet in front of Kuchta.

"Is Mike Will in?" one asked. *The kid looking for the voucher*, Kuchta thought.

The teenager standing directly in front of Kuchta, the one in the red tie, reached inside his three-quarter-length blue coat and pulled out a Cobray M-11 assault weapon. The gunman turned toward Daly and squeezed the trigger.

Bam-bam-bam-bam-bam-bam-bam-bam-bam!

Daly's chest exploded in blood. The shooter slowly turned to his right as he fired, making a full 360-degree sweep. He wasn't pulling the trigger for each shot—the weapon had been modified so it was fully automatic. Cobrays were relatively cheap, the

Saturday-night specials of assault pistols. This one was a machine gun.

The two others scrammed. One took a round in the buttocks and fell to the floor.

Kuchta got tunnel vision. All he saw was the assault weapon.

Bam-bam-bam-bam-bam-bam!

Smoke filled the room. Kuchta rose from the sofa as he recited a silent Hail Mary.

Bam-bam-bam-bam-bam-bam-bam!

The kid was strafing every corner of the cold-case office. The booming sound of the fired rounds seemed to shake the room. Kuchta got to his feet.

Hail Mary, full of grace, the Lord is with thee. Blessed art thou—

One round slammed into the right side of Kuchta's chest. Another entered his left side and penetrated his heart. A round hit his right arm—his shooting arm. Bleeding, he grabbed the nine-millimeter Cobra from the holster on his hip and desperately started squeezing rounds at the gunman.

The shooter was now at one end of the sofa, Kuchta at the other. The agent and the attacker traded shots from a distance of seventy-two inches. Hopelessly outgunned, Kuchta backpedaled as he fired. He broke off the Hail Mary and started silently reciting Glory Be.

Glory be to the Father and to the Son and to the Holy Spirit. As it was in the beginning, is now, and ever shall be, world without end. Amen.

A bullet grazed his neck. Kuchta kept firing, knowing his chest wound was serious, fearing his life might be about to end. *I gotta get down, I gotta get down.*

Bam! Bam! Bam! Bam! Bam! Bam! Bam! Bam!

Three rounds slammed into Kuchta's lower right leg. He collapsed to the floor, his femur shattered.

Kuchta lay prone, lifted his wounded arm, and fired blindly toward the guy with the machine pistol.

Everything went blurry. Kuchta lost consciousness. He woke up. He saw Hank Daly slumped in his chair, his chest bloodied. Kuchta checked his gun and realized he had a few bullets left.

Gunfire boomed a few feet away. The shooter would probably come back to finish him off, Kuchta thought.

He tried to raise his weapon.

As Kuchta traded shots with the gunman, Neil Trugman, a 1D detective who at the time was detailed to homicide, was walking down the steps outside police headquarters heading toward his car. He'd worked his early shift and was going home.

He was thirty feet from his car when the screaming voice of homicide lieutenant Michelle Taylor blared from his handheld radio: "Emergency! Shots fired on the third floor!"

The third floor—the homicide office.

The detective pivoted, raced back into the building, and charged up a stairwell. He turned a corner and smelled gun smoke coming from the cold-case office down the hall. A group of detectives and uniforms was near the main cold-case entrance.

Trugman ran down the hall to the cold-case office. The detective pressed himself against a wall and eased his way in. Another step and he'd be exposed, without cover. Was the shooter waiting to ambush more cops? Were there multiple shooters? There was no way of knowing.

He backed out and saw two younger investigators, Chris Kauffman and Brian Callen, near a heavy wooden side door that led to Hank Daly's office.

Trugman joined them. Gun smoke was filtering out of the room through a horizontal vent near the bottom of the door. Other detectives and officers gathered near the door. Angry and anxious talk filled the hallway.

Trugman crouched and put his ear near the vent. Another

detective kept trying the doorknob. "Shut up!" someone ordered. The hallway went quiet.

Inside the office, the shooting had stopped. Kuchta heard voices from behind the door, on the other side of the sofa.

Cops!

"Officers down!" Kuchta cried. "Three black male unsubs"— FBI-speak for "unknown subjects."

Kuchta's life was draining away. He needed help—fast. He cried out, "I'm FBI agent John Kuchta." His voice faded with each syllable.

Kuchta heard a series of clicks at the door.

"We can't get in!" someone behind the door shouted. The other entrance, the one Trugman had backed out of, was too dangerous. Anyone who entered through there would be exposed if any attackers were lying in wait. But Trugman and the other officers knew that a wounded FBI agent wouldn't be crying out for help if a shooter was still in his immediate area.

Kuchta suddenly remembered: A few days earlier, a maintenance worker had changed the door's cipher locks.

The agent thought of his thirteen-month-old daughter, Anastasia, and his young wife, Helena, whom everyone called "Leni." They needed him. "I'm John Kuchta. I'm an FBI agent. I'm shot. Get me out of here," Kuchta croaked.

On the other side of the door, Trugman heard Kuchta's calls for help. The door was huge and solid and bolted from the inside. Kicking it in wasn't an option—it wasn't going down without a battering ram.

Trugman put his mouth close to the vent and yelled: "Reach up and slide the bolt!"

Kuchta heard Trugman's voice. The voice told him to open the bolt lock. Cordite and the coppery odor of fresh blood filled his nostrils.

Kuchta eyed the door, ten or twelve feet away. He vowed to himself, *I'm not dying in here.*

On his belly, Kuchta reached out and crawled toward the door, leaving a trail of blood on the tile floor. He slid past the sofa, past Daly, slumped in his chair. Slowly, he moved toward the voice. His shattered leg pulsed with otherworldly pain.

Kuchta reached the far end of the sofa. He crawled to the door. He looked up at the bolt. In his condition, he might as well have been peering at a sheer thousand-foot cliff. Kuchta thought of Anastasia and Leni.

The FBI agent struggled to his feet. He reached for the bolt—and fell onto his backside. The voice on the other side of the door pleaded with him to open the lock.

Kuchta was getting light-headed. Blood was gushing from his leg, leaking from his chest. Again he looked up and stared at the bolt. One more lunge.

I'm not dying in here.

His bleeding leg quivering, Kuchta struggled to his feet. He braced himself against the door. He reached for the bolt. He grabbed it. He slid it open and collapsed.

On the other side of the door, Trugman heard the bolt move. Someone tossed him a bulletproof vest.

Kauffman and Callen got on their hands and knees. Trugman unholstered his Glock. With one hand, Trugman held the vest in front of himself and his fellow cops like a shield; in the other hand, he held his gun.

Trugman opened the door. Together the three cops moved into the smoke-filled room. Kuchta was lying on his back, bleeding, screaming in pain. Kauffman and Callen grabbed him by his belt. Kauffman was a big man, and he wasn't gentle. He and Callen pulled Kuchta out of the room.

Kuchta was bone white. That was bad, Trugman thought. It meant he'd lost a tremendous amount of blood. Yet Kuchta was still screaming—that was good. It meant he had a fighting chance. Kauffman and Callen let go of Kuchta in the hallway, and a couple of paramedics grabbed the wounded agent.

Kuchta felt two sets of hands lift him from under his arms. He felt himself being dragged backwards through the hallway. He saw officers lined up on both sides of the corridor—uniforms, detectives, ERT cops in full battle gear.

The rescuers pulled Kuchta into an office. Cops and emergency medical technicians seemed to fill the small room. He saw two paramedics. One of them said, "We need a stretcher." Kuchta heard the voice of his dead father, who'd been a medic in the Navy: "You have to get him out of here now!" The paramedics suddenly seemed to respond to the voice Kuchta had hallucinated.

Someone wrapped him in a sheet and carried him to an elevator. The rescuers lowered Kuchta onto a stretcher on the elevator floor. When they reached the ground floor, they ran him out of the building, into an ambulance. A police sergeant rode with him. Kuchta knew he would never wake up if he lost consciousness.

The ambulance reached the Washington Hospital Center. Kuchta saw a hallway whiz by. He found himself on a bed in an operating room.

Kuchta shivered so fiercely that he thought he might die from the cold. Nurses placed hot towels on his bleeding body. A doctor moved a mask toward his face. The doctor was going to put him under.

He thought of Anastasia and Leni. *I'm not going to die.*

"Is it okay to fall asleep now?" Kuchta asked.

"Yes, it's okay to fall asleep now," the doctor replied.

Kuchta knew he would keep his vow. He would not leave Anastasia and Leni. The doctor placed the mask over Kuchta's face.

Less than an hour after Trugman and the others pulled Kuchta to safety, Lou and a handful of detectives and FBI agents stepped into the cold-case office. The room remained thick with gun smoke and the acrid smell of cordite. The walls were pocked with dozens of bullet holes. Paramedics had taken away the teenager who'd walked into the office with the shooter and caught a round in his butt as he ran away. Wounded and terrified, he'd hidden inside a small interview room connected to the main office until Trugman and the others rescued Kuchta. The other teenager had run out of the cold-case office as Kuchta and the invader traded shots.

The lawmen gazed at the aftermath of the massacre in silence. The bodies of Martinez and Miller lay on the floor. Martinez had engaged in a furious shootout with the killer. Investigators would learn that one of her shots had disabled his Cobray. But by then she was mortally wounded. The attacker grabbed her gun and fired a final shot into her head before turning the gun on himself. Lou's eyes settled on the shooter, whose body lay on the floor next to Martinez's. The assault weapon lay nearby.

In the moment, Lou didn't feel anger or a sense of violation or fear. He didn't have time to process his emotions. This was a crime scene, and he had a job to do. Forensics would have its hands full accounting for all the fired rounds. The feds would run down the source of the machine pistol. The crucial, immediate questions were: Who the hell did this? What was his beef? Was he working alone, or were there more attacks to come?

A crime-scene technician walked into the office with his fingerprint kit. He knelt next to the gunman's body and went to work. Lou and the others retreated to his office to start divvying up assignments.

As Lou and the FBI agents launched the investigation, I stood on the street outside police headquarters, rocking from side to side, trying to stay warm. Twilight was descending, and so was the temperature. A police spokesman had doled out the basics to me and the other reporters gathered outside headquarters: Two FBI agents were dead inside the homicide office, and a police sergeant had died on the way to the hospital. A third agent was seriously wounded, in the hospital, fighting for his life. The killer was dead, apparently by his own hand.

For what seemed like the hundredth time, I pulled out my *Post* cell phone and punched in the digits to Lou's office. The phone rang and rang. I paged him a dozen times, with no response.

The afternoon had begun with a routine press conference. Along with a handful of other reporters, I'd gone to a room around the corner from the homicide office where departmental brass would be trying to explain how an officer had apparently botched a kidnapping-and-child-prostitution case. Wyndell Watkins, the chief of detectives, had been assigned the task of damage control.

Watkins stepped to the podium at the front of the room. Notebooks were flipped open. TV cameras and tape recorders were activated. Still photographers moved into position. Watkins adjusted his tie and began to speak.

Sergeant Joe Gentile, MPD's main spokesperson, burst through the door.

"There's been a shooting in the building," he said. "Everyone needs to stay right here. The building's on lockdown. We don't know where the gunman is, or if there's more than one shooter. Stay here. You'll all be safe."

Gentile and Watkins flew out of the room. I called my editor, Keith Harriston; then Lou; then every other cop I knew. I knew that Lou had been planning to take the day off to work on a law school paper, but I also knew he would get to the office as soon as he heard about the attack. Lou didn't answer his cell phone or his home number, and he didn't respond to my pages.

An hour or so after Gentile had announced we were locked down, body-armored ERT officers began escorting us out of the building. We raced down the stairs and jogged out of the entrance.

For more than two hours I called Lou's direct office line, with no luck. Finally, he answered.

"Homicide."

"It's me. What the hell happened in there?"

"Some guy walked into cold case and shot it up," Lou answered calmly. I could hear excited voices in the background, but Lou was as composed as ever.

"Can you tell me anything about the shooter—who he is, why he did this?"

"Just some guy. Young black male, late teens, early twenties. We don't know who he is yet."

"Any idea why he picked cold case? Motive?"

The background commotion on Lou's end intensified. The voices were getting louder, more excited.

"Not yet. Listen, I'm up to my elbows in alligators right now. I'll have to call you later." Lou rang off.

Someone from the crime lab called Lou a couple of hours later. The shooter's prints were on file. His name was Bennie Lee Lawson, age twenty-five. A handful of detectives were in Lou's office. Lou hung up the phone and asked them if they'd ever heard of Lawson.

"Yeah, he's the guy you interrogated about a week back," said Willie Jefferson, a veteran detective. "On that home-invasion triple, remember?" Lou didn't. He usually had great recall of specific cases, but for some reason he couldn't bring Lawson to mind.

"You remember," Jefferson said. "Home invasion; an old man was killed."

Now Lou remembered: A couple of gunmen had burst into a home in Northwest, near the Maryland state line. An eighty-nine-year-old man struggled with one of them. He and two others were gunned down. It looked like a drug beef.

The night of the killings, a patrol cop had stopped Lawson and another guy as they drove near the triple-murder scene. The cop didn't have enough evidence to hold them. He wrote Lawson's name in a field report.

One of Lou's detectives paid Lawson a visit. Lawson agreed to come to homicide to answer some questions. Lou watched the beginning of the interrogation on a closed-circuit hookup. Then the detective had to go to court, so Lou stepped in for him.

"You've heard of DNA?" Lou asked.

Lawson nodded.

"We found blood on the floorboard of the car you were stopped in. DNA tests will be back in two weeks," Lou said. "If we find any of the victims' DNA, you're done. With three bodies, you're looking at a hundred years. That number could go down—if you help us."

It was a bluff. There was no blood, no DNA test.

Lawson squirmed. He stared at the table. He said nothing—until he said he wanted to go home. Lou forgot about Lawson the moment he walked out the door.

There was nothing memorable or unusual about him: Lawson was a garden-variety thug, a low-level member of a Northwest D.C. drug gang that operated about three miles north of downtown. Lou had hundreds of other cases on his plate. That had been nine days earlier.

An hour or so after Lou learned that Lawson was the shooter, a small army of shotgun-wielding FBI agents and black-clad ERT officers stormed the brick rambler where Lawson lived with his father. Lawson's room was in the basement.

Homicide detectives and FBI agents began going over every inch of the basement. *Carlito's Way* was in a VCR. In it, Al Pacino portrayed a doomed drug dealer. A detective saw a notebook on the nightstand. He picked it up and started reading.

Lou was in his office, talking over the investigation with Sergeant J. T. McCann, when the detective who found the notebook called. McCann answered.

"You won't believe this," the detective said. The cold-case shooter was after the captain. He wanted to kill Hennessy. McCann thought it was a bad joke.

"This is no time to screw around," he scolded.

"This is no joke," the detective said. "We found a notebook. The shooter wrote all these lines; they look like rap lyrics. Over and over, he wrote, 'Captain Hennessy must die!'"

McCann put down the phone and looked at Lou. "You're not going to believe this," he said.

He told Lou about the notebook.

Lou wasn't sure what to make of it.

After my brief conversation with Lou, I went back to the office to write the main story. Other reporters were contributing, but I was putting it together. One of the local TV news stations had reported that the shooter was a disgruntled cop, but no one else had anything specific about the gunman or his possible motive. It was after 8:00 P.M. I was crashing on deadline when my phone rang.

It was Lou. "We got the guy's name, and we think we know the motive," he said, his voice a near whisper. There were other voices in the background. He didn't want anyone to hear him.

I cradled the receiver on my shoulder and grabbed a pen and notebook.

"Who was he? Why did he do this?"

Lou told me Lawson's name, then added, "He was after *me*."

"What do you mean he was after you?"

Lou explained—how Lawson was identified through fingerprints, how Lou had interviewed him about a previous triple murder, about the search at the suspect's home, the notebook, and the lyrics directly threatening the commander of the homicide squad.

I was already wired, fueled by the adrenaline of working on a big breaking story. As I furiously took notes, I experienced a moment of pure journalistic joy. It was the feeling of having a monumentally great fucking story all to myself. Local and national reporters were covering the massacre, but none of them had *this*.

For an instant I thought of the TV reporters who made double, triple, maybe quadruple my salary. A few seemed to be mostly skilled at looking good. Some of them were legitimate, hardworking journalists. Like many print reporters, part of me resented the big money many of the TV people were paid for doing one- or two-minute stand-ups. *When you read the paper tomorrow, you can chew on this story, you overpaid, blow-dried—*

"You can't use it," Lou said.

I felt as if a 230-pound linebacker had just knocked the wind out of me.

"What? Why not?"

"We've got to track down as many of Lawson's associates tonight as we can. We'll probably be serving more search warrants tomorrow. We don't want to tip them off about how much we know. I'm asking you to hold it."

He might as well have told me that Thanksgiving, Christmas, and my birthday would be canceled for the rest of my days. I could actually feel the adrenaline recede. My joy at having a great exclusive evaporated. For a moment or two, I had envisioned breaking the news that the headquarters killer was gunning for the homicide chief. But I knew that if I agreed to Lou's request, news this juicy wouldn't stay under wraps for long, not with so many TV and radio journalists working on the story. Someone else would break the story.

For a couple of seconds, I thought about trying to figure out a way to use the information anyway. I had several detective sources—maybe one of them would confirm the incredible story that the headquarters shooter had been gunning for the commander of the homicide squad.

Lou might be momentarily upset if he saw the story in the paper the next day, but I could explain it by blaming my editors; that was a time-honored and usually reliable journalistic tactic. I could say that my bosses had heard about Lawson and ordered me to call every source I knew until I confirmed the story. Lou knew that I had bosses to answer to, and that I had other sources in the police department; he would no doubt accept such an explanation.

But Lou trusted me—which was precisely why I couldn't try to slide the story into print through a side door.

Lou was one of the fairest, most honorable men I'd ever known, and maybe the smartest. I considered myself a tenacious and resourceful reporter who always found a way, but I couldn't try to pull a fast one on him. And I didn't want to do anything to endanger the investigation. Lou had always been straight with me. He deserved the same in return.

"All right," I said. "I won't use it until you give me the green light."

I finished writing the story. I sat on the Lawson material. It would likely come out the following day, and one of the well-compensated TV people would be the first to report it. Which is exactly what happened.

I'd thought that losing the scoop would bother me, but it didn't.

Some things are more important than a story.

Metal detectors were installed at police headquarters the day after the attack. The building was also home to other city offices, including the Department of Motor Vehicles and the Board of Parole. For years, even people with criminal records had been free to go in and out without having to clear significant security. Those days were over.

Working together, Lou's detectives and FBI agents quickly determined that Lawson had been acting alone. By interviewing Lawson's friends and associates, the investigators put together a narrative: After Lawson had returned to his neighborhood following Lou's interrogation, some of his thug friends had taunted him, suggesting he'd been let go because the police had broken him. They'd teased him for being a "weak link."

Lawson had previously been imprisoned for a weapons violation. Investigators discovered strong evidence that he'd been raped while incarcerated. The sexual assault and the taunting had probably motivated Lawson's attack, investigators believed. FBI agents and police also discovered that the leader of Lawson's gang, Kobi Mowatt, had apparently planned to have Lawson killed. Lawson had learned about Mowatt's plan and preempted it by going on a suicide mission. It was a warped, violent way to show his fellow gangsters he wasn't weak. And by killing himself, Lawson had made sure he wouldn't face another sexual assault in prison.

It was happenstance that Lawson had ended up in the cold-case office instead of the much larger main homicide squad room, where he might have killed more people. When Lawson walked into police headquarters, he had run into two teenagers he didn't know. He had asked where the homicide office was located, and one or both of the teenagers had said they were headed that way. Lawson had simply tagged along as they walked him to the cold-case office.

Lawson might have wanted to prove something to his fellow gangsters, but his actions ended up getting many of them locked up. In the wake of the shooting, a team of MPD detectives and FBI agents took down Lawson's former crew. The task force arrested eight leaders of the gang, who were charged in federal court with offenses including murder, racketeering, kidnapping, and drug trafficking.

Understandably, the members of the task force took Lawson's attack personally, and they vowed to search every corner of the earth for the killer's compatriots. Almost all of Lawson's fellow thugs were tracked down in the neighborhood where they sold drugs and committed other crimes—around 1st and Kennedy Streets Northwest. FBI agents and police clamped down on the neighborhood, pulling over everyone who bought drugs from the crew and trying to flip them. Facing jail time, many of the drug buyers agreed to testify for the government. By early 1996 the task force had locked up about a dozen of the gang's most active members.

Collectively, the suspects were charged with seventeen homicides, including the triple murder that had led to the headquarters attack. Almost all of them eventually pleaded guilty.

Most D.C. gangsters who go on the lam get about as far as an aunt's house in another quadrant of the city. But the leader of Lawson's crew showed some enterprise in his efforts to evade justice. Kobi Mowatt was nowhere to be found in his neighborhood, in D.C., or anywhere else in the country.

FBI agent Mark Giuliano and D.C. homicide detective Anthony Brigidini teamed up to track down Mowatt. They were determined to get him.

"He's the king," Giuliano recalled. "And he needs to go down."

Giuliano and Brigidini interviewed everyone Mowatt knew—gang associates, girlfriends, relatives. The case was featured on *America's Most Wanted*. After about a year of painstaking investigation, Giuliano and Brigidini executed a search warrant at the home of Mowatt's mother, in Prince George's County, Maryland. They searched almost every inch of the house and discovered nothing suggesting where Mowatt might be hiding out.

On their way out, Brigidini tipped over a trash can and went through the contents. He found a phone bill. One number stood out. It had sixteen digits. They tracked it to a pay phone near the city of Arusha, in northern Tanzania—the only pay phone in a one-hundred-square-mile area.

Investigators sent photos of Mowatt and copies of his file to Tanzania. They told the police in Arusha that the guy they were looking for was responsible, indirectly, for the killings of three law enforcement officers in D.C. The locals went to work, standing at the phone in shifts and showing Mowatt's photo to everyone who came by to use it. Someone recognized the man in the photo. He pointed in the direction of Mount Kilimanjaro.

The investigation picked up speed.

Giuliano and Brigidini enlisted the help of a State Department security officer in neighboring Kenya, who did some sleuthing. The officer discovered that Mowatt had been renting a hotel room in Arusha. He'd left a few weeks earlier, skipping out on his bill and stealing a guard dog.

The Americans couldn't just snatch Mowatt. There hadn't been an extradition from Tanzania in a long time. Justice Department lawyers began researching what paperwork would need to be written up and filed. By stiffing the hotel and stealing the dog, however, Mowatt had provided Tanzanian police with two reasons to lock him up. Arusha cops went out in a squad car and drove in the direction in which the witness at the pay phone had pointed.

The cops entered an area of flat grassland and spotted a lone mud hut, maybe five miles from the base of Kilimanjaro. The hut's resident spotted them—and ran. The cops laughed: There was nowhere for Mowatt to flee, nowhere to hide.

The local cops watched as Mowatt sprinted until he got tired and stopped, then they drove over and arrested him. They held him in a tiny police precinct with no air-conditioning. When they took Mowatt's booking photo, he flipped both his middle fingers.

It was March 1996, nearly sixteen months after Lawson's rampage at police headquarters. Giuliano and Brigidini flew for nearly twenty-four hours to reach Tanzania. But they couldn't bring Mowatt back right away: A Tanzanian official insisted on a $25,000 payment before the prisoner would be handed over. Giuliano and Brigidini had to wait until someone from the FBI could fly over with the payment.

The two lawmen killed time. They saw lions and giraffes and hippos in the countryside. They also ate something they shouldn't have and got violently ill, with fevers and chills and diarrhea.

After several days, and more than 7,500 miles from D.C., Giuliano and Brigidini finally stepped into the little police station to arrest Mowatt. The gangster's face registered shock when he saw them.

"Man, y'all are pressed to lock a nigga up," he said.

It turned out that Mowatt had been in Tanzania for about a year. Before landing in Africa, he'd flown to Russia, where he wandered around Red Square during a layover that lasted a few hours. When he first arrived in Africa, the gangster had been living in a little community of Jamaicans in Rwanda. The Jamaicans expelled him because they didn't like his attitude. Mowatt struck out on his own.

Outside his little hut, Mowatt grew vegetables and marijuana. He had a pet baboon that he kept on a leash. Mowatt said he'd taught it how to slip cassettes into a battery-powered boom box and hit the Play button.

The temperature in Tanzania felt about a thousand degrees to Brigidini. But Mowatt was still dressed like a D.C. gangster, in jeans, a long-sleeved Polo shirt, and Timberland boots. For a minute, he tried to pretend he was someone else. He spoke some half-assed Jamaican. The two lawmen asked Mowatt to pose with them for a photo.

"Fuck you," he snarled.

Giuliano and Brigidini brought Mowatt back on a commercial flight. They got him a window seat and wrapped him up in a blanket to hide his handcuffs. Brigidini cut Mowatt's food and fed him during the trip.

After he landed at Dulles International Airport, outside Washington, the pilot came back to ask the two lawmen what was up with the guy in the blanket. Giuliano and Brigidini showed him their badges. Brigidini lifted the blanket to show Mowatt's handcuffs. They were bringing back a fugitive, they explained. The pilot wasn't happy.

Brigidini paid a steep price for the capture. At five foot five, Brigidini weighed close to 200 pounds when he went to Tanzania, though not because he was overweight. The detective was a power-lifter. For three years after he returned, he became repeatedly ill, about once every three months. At one point he was down to 130 pounds. Probably due to a parasite he'd picked up in Tanzania, doctors told him. It would work its way out of his system. Eventually it did, and Brigidini's health returned.

The detective never regretted the mission.

"I just couldn't fail," he said years later. "It was a responsibility we owed to the family members of those people who were killed just reading case jackets at their desks. I couldn't fail."

Most of Lawson's associates pleaded guilty to federal charges and received lengthy prison sentences, which they accepted quietly. Mowatt, however, went down with bravado.

A few months after he was captured, Mowatt pleaded guilty to participating in a racketeering conspiracy and agreed to a thirty-five-year prison sentence. At his sentencing hearing, in January 1997, Mowatt stood to speak moments before U.S. District Judge Royce C. Lamberth formally announced his punishment.

Mowatt pounded his chest with his right arm and, referring to Lawson, declared, "He represented to the fullest. And that's my man, my comrade for life."

On Thanksgiving Day, two days after Lawson's rampage in the cold-case office, a *Post* editor asked me to interview Lou. The news that Lawson was gunning for him had been reported on the local TV news the day before, and I'd written about it for that day's paper.

"It could be a good story—what is it like to be the intended target of the headquarters killer?" the editor said.

I was working the holiday anyway, and it was no secret that the homicide captain talked to me. I routinely quoted him by name in news stories. A few days before the attack, Lou had even invited me to his home for Thanksgiving dinner. I'd told him I would try to come over, if I could get away from work early enough. Lou and his family lived on a farm in southern Maryland, about twenty-five miles south of D.C.

That morning, I'd called Lou at home, not sure if the invitation was still open, given the chaos of the previous forty-eight hours. "Come on over," he'd said. He sounded tired.

Lou greeted me at the front door, welcomed me in, and immediately sank into his living room couch. He had raccoon eyes and looked as if he hadn't slept in days. I settled into a chair a few feet away. The smell of roasting turkey filled the room.

I felt queasy about my assignment. Lou knew I was far from my family in California. He had no agenda other than to assure me that I'd have a place to spend the holiday.

After some small talk about the football game, I said, "I'm supposed to interview you about what it was like to be Lawson's intended target."

Lou rubbed his eyes.

"I haven't had time to process it, to be honest. I've been working straight through. I don't think there's much I could tell you right now."

Maybe I could have chipped away at him, gotten a couple of usable quotes, and fashioned a story around them. I could have played on my editor's expectations, telling Lou I'd be in a jam if I didn't come up with something for the next day's paper.

Instead, I called the editor who'd asked me to interview Lou.

"I'm at his house," I said. "He didn't say no. He said he hasn't had time to process what happened. I think if I work on him, I can get him to start talking."

"Keep trying," the editor replied. "Call in if he starts talking, so we can budget a story for tomorrow's paper."

I rang off and returned to my chair. Lou and I watched the game in silence until it was time to eat. I didn't work on him.

I could always interview him some other time, I figured.

CHAPTER 11

D.C. CONFIDENTIAL

In September 1995, Lou and his detectives received recognition from the Justice Department for their effectiveness in locking up suspected killers. The homicide squad had continued to maintain a closure rate of a little more than 50 percent, the milestone it had first achieved under Lou twelve months earlier, eight weeks after he had detective teams in place in every police district.

Justice sent Lou a shiny plaque commemorating the achievement and announced that it was awarding a $200,000 grant to the scandal-plagued New Orleans Police Department to study and try to emulate Lou's district-squad concept. Lou appreciated the recognition, but he was focused on closing cases. He stuck the plaque inside a desk drawer. He figured he'd find a place to display it later.

Meanwhile, I spent the first half of the month in Durham, North Carolina, attending Duke University on an "academic fellowship." Duke had a deal with the *Post*, offering reporters and editors short fellowships that allowed them to audit any class, so long as the instructor approved. The university provided an off-campus apartment.

I sat in on a handful of journalism, psychology, and sociology courses, and faithfully attended two classes: basketball and tennis. I was back at my apartment every day by early afternoon, allowing me plenty of time to watch the final weeks of the O. J. Simpson trial on cable television, a luxury I didn't have at home in D.C.

Every year, dozens of *Post* staffers applied for six fellowship slots, spread out through the academic year. Executive editor Len Downie chose the recipients. I was being rewarded for doing a good job on the crime beat, a veteran editor told me.

By then I was going well beyond pro forma coverage of the most spectacular crimes of the moment. I had good police sources, but I was also interviewing gangsters and their friends. In March, I'd written a story about D.C. gang culture, describing the significance of various types of graffiti and discussing mourning rituals for fallen comrades. In D.C. combat zones, the sight of sneakers and boots hanging from power lines was as familiar as slingers on street corners, but their meaning remained a mystery to many. The suspended footwear honored the dead—friends and adversaries alike—gangsters told me.

At the corner of 1st and T Streets Northwest, once a backup corner for my crack buying, I interviewed a teenage gangster who called himself Dogg. He explained the graffiti on a nearby wall, the names of ten teenagers or young men who'd been killed. "It's in memory of the homies who died. We got to keep their memories alive," Dogg said as he thumped his arm against his chest.

As I wrote down his quote, I wondered if I'd ever copped crack from any of those homies whose names now adorned the wall.

Just before I drove to North Carolina for the fellowship, I filed a story for the *Post*'s Sunday magazine chronicling the extraordinary measures Lou and other white shirts and detectives had taken to keep the peace between white and black officers after a white cop had shot and killed a gun-wielding black man who was in street clothes in Southeast D.C. The cop thought the man was a bandit; it turned out he was a fellow officer from the white cop's own district. The black cop, it turned out, was trying to stop two men who were robbing a cabdriver.

I hadn't covered the shooting, which occurred in February, because I was out sick that week with the flu. But Lou had tipped me off to the story that summer, when I was at his house for a barbecue.

"We did a lot of unusual things to keep the lid on," he'd said. "It almost became a race riot within the department."

Many black officers, as well as some white ones, believed the shooting officer might have been quick on the trigger because he saw a black man with a gun. The district commander, Inspector Winston Robinson, held his shop together by keeping everyone informed and calm. Lou and Robinson arranged for the homicide detectives who were conducting the investigation to brief the officers in the station.

Reporting on a racially charged mistaken-identity police-on-police shooting was complicated, and Lou's cooperation was crucial. Many other white shirts, street cops, and detectives hedged when I first called them to talk about the tragedy—until I mentioned that I'd interviewed Lou. His name worked like a key card. Lou might not have been liked by everyone in the department, but he was universally respected.

The article became a cover story. Steve Coll, the magazine's editor, would later tell me that publisher Don Graham bear-hugged him in congratulations the day after the piece was published. Post editors would nominate it for a Pulitzer Prize.

By then, Phil Dixon had moved on. Earlier that year, Milton Coleman had been promoted, so Phil put in for the job of Metro editor. He was passed over in favor of another editor, Jo-Ann Armao. Phil worked for a couple of months in the sports department, but by the end of the summer he'd moved to Philadelphia to work for the *Inquirer*.

I missed Phil, but I kept churning out stories. Around the time I left for the fellowship, in August, my editor, Keith Harriston, told me how much he appreciated my work. "You're the best police reporter the *Post* has ever had," he said.

My fellowship ended in mid-September. I was given a nice certificate saying I'd completed the program. I stuck it in my duffel bag and drove back to D.C. I'd enjoyed my respite as a quasi college student, but I was looking forward to getting back to work.

Like Lou, I had every reason to feel optimistic about my career.

In mid-September, Lou received a strange phone call from a fellow white shirt he'd known for years. "I hear the mayor wants you out of homicide," the caller said. "What gives?"

"News to me," Lou said. He figured it was just the police rumor mill working overtime. Why would Marion Barry want him out? Lou and Barry didn't know each other and hadn't had any run-ins. Why mess with the one unit in the police department that was clearly succeeding?

A few days later, in the underground parking garage at police headquarters, Lou ran into Ron Linton, chief of the police reserves. Lou and Linton were friendly. Linton and Barry were tight. Lou buttonholed Linton and said, "I hear the mayor wants me out. Can you find anything out for me?"

"Get out of here," Linton said. "Why would he want to bounce you?"

"He probably doesn't," Lou replied. "But can you look into it?"

Two weeks later, Linton called Lou. He sounded perplexed. "You're right," Linton said. "The mayor wants you out. I don't know why."

Lou needed to know what was going on. Fred Thomas had retired as chief in July. Barry had named an assistant chief, Larry Soulsby, to step in as interim chief.

Lou went to see Soulsby in his office. "Am I being transferred?" he asked.

"No way," Soulsby said. "Everything's fine."

Lou kept working cases. Soulsby wasn't known as the most honest guy in the department—the rank and file called him Lyin'

Larry. But if Barry was going to make a move on him, Lou wondered, what could he do?

Lou told me about the rumors shortly after I returned to Washington. By early October we'd both verified that the talk was true. Worse, Lou was being transferred to night patrol. It was a slap. Traditionally, homicide captains were promoted to the rank of inspector once they'd finished their time in charge of the squad.

Lou had been arguably the most effective homicide commander in the department's history. He'd launched a bold and successful initiative under extraordinarily difficult circumstances. He'd turned things around. Homicide wasn't just holding its own—it was being lauded by the Justice Department.

Still, the transfer was a done deal, sources told Lou and me. All that was left was the formal announcement.

In late October, Barry called a press conference to announce that he was removing the "interim" from Soulsby's title. Soulsby would be the permanent chief. That meant he could appoint and transfer white shirts.

A couple of hours before the press conference, Lou was outside police headquarters, walking to a deli to get lunch. His pager went off. Lou checked the number—it was an informant. Not just any source—a friend, an ex-cop Lou had known since his patrol days.

Lou pulled out his cell phone and called back. "I need to see you *right now*," the informant said, his voice tense. They met outside a burger joint on New York Avenue, just east of downtown.

Lou arrived first and waited by an outdoor table. His source roared up in a rental car. He had a gig returning other people's rentals. He didn't bother with niceties: "What's this I hear about you getting kicked out of homicide?"

"It's true," Lou said. "Soulsby's announcing it today at a press conference. He's putting me on night patrol."

"Do you want me to kill him for you?"

Lou knew his informant was serious. He wasn't just running his mouth. And he was fully capable of hitting the chief.

The source's street skills were legendary. In the early eighties, when the entire police force was looking for a cop killer, he'd put on street clothes and found the guy within twenty-four hours, then taken him down in a shootout. The cop was a hero for a minute. But he met a woman who liked heroin and coke. Internal affairs got wind and busted him for supplying her with drugs. He went to trial and beat the charges, but the department fired him anyway.

Until then, Lou's friend didn't use. He loved the job—it gave him purpose. Without it, he fell down the rabbit hole. He started drinking, then using crack. He hung out at nightclubs and followed drug dealers home. The former cop would take them at gunpoint as they entered their apartments. He'd jack their money, their drugs, or both. He did a couple of jolts in federal prison for cocaine possession. By the early nineties he was back on the street. Other cops turned their backs on him after he was fired. Lou never did. He even slipped him money now and then.

Lou's friend was grateful. Through the years, he gave Lou enough good tips to close out two dozen felonies: armed robberies, attempted murders, a handful of homicides. His information always panned out. Lou figured he was probably still doing some dirt himself—his tips were *too* good; he was too close to the violence to not be part of it. Lou never pressed him, though. He didn't want to know.

The source was one of the toughest men Lou had ever known. And one of the most loyal. He was loyal enough to take out the chief or die trying.

"No!" Lou said. "Listen to me, I don't want you to go anywhere near Soulsby. Don't try to kill him. Don't hurt him. Don't scare him. I don't want you to do anything. I'll handle this myself, do you understand?"

"Whatever you say," Lou's ex-colleague said reluctantly. "But someone's got to do something about that motherfucker."

"Let me handle it," Lou pleaded.

The informant nodded. Then he got back in the rental and sped off.

Lou took a deep breath and went for a walk to clear his head.

About an hour after Lou met with his informant, I stepped into a city government building across the street from police headquarters and took an elevator to the fourth floor for the mayor's press conference.

Barry said he'd scoured the country and decided Soulsby was the best choice for the job of chief. He shook Soulsby's hand. The new chief, clad in his dress blues, smiled from the Potomac River to the Washington Monument.

Over and over, Soulsby thanked Barry. He giddily hugged the mayor. Then Soulsby announced a series of white-shirt transfers.

Oddly, he said nothing about Lou Hennessy or homicide. The presser broke up.

A TV guy, a radio guy, and I stepped up to Soulsby. The TV guy made small talk with the chief and asked a couple of questions. The radio guy asked a question, too.

"What about Captain Hennessy?" I asked. "What's happening in homicide?"

Soulsby's grin disappeared.

"Captain Hennessy is being transferred to night patrol," he said.

"That sounds like a demotion," I said. "Sounds punitive."

Soulsby pointed at the radio guy's tape recorder and barked, "Turn that thing off."

The radio guy complied.

Soulsby said he would tell us why Hennessy was being busted down to night patrol—but only if each of us agreed the information was off the record.

The TV guy nodded yes. The radio guy nodded yes. I should have said no. I should have demanded that Soulsby explain the transfer on the record. But I knew that if I didn't agree, Soulsby would ask me to leave and then tell the other two reporters.

Okay, I nodded.

"Hennessy's under a criminal grand jury investigation. I can't go into detail, but it's bad," Soulsby said. "It will all come out in a few weeks."

I went light-headed for a few moments. Lou the target of a grand jury investigation? No way. The new chief had just lied to me and two other reporters. Right to our off-the-record faces.

The three of us questioned Soulsby about the purported investigation: When had it started? What crime was Hennessy suspected of? Would he be indicted?

Soulsby parried. He provided no specifics. "The details will eventually be revealed," he said. "It will eventually come out."

Goddamn, I thought. *He's attacking the reputation of the best cop on the force, and one of the best men I've ever known. He's using the cover of "off the record" to smear a fellow cop. The lying motherfucker.*

After a couple of minutes, our little scrum broke up. I stepped into an elevator to leave the building. The doors started to close. A hand reached in; the doors spread open. Soulsby stepped into the elevator. I hit the Down button.

He gave me a stiff nod. I decided to give him a chance to step back from what I was certain was a lie.

"Chief, I think maybe you misspoke back there," I said. "You didn't really mean to say that Captain Hennessy is the target of a grand jury investigation, did you?"

Soulsby turned to me and squared his shoulders. "I did not misspeak," he said. "He is the target, and the details will come out in a few weeks or in a few months. You'll see."

We reached ground level. The elevator doors opened. I stepped out, rattled. How could Soulsby lie so easily, about something so important, with such conviction? The chief stepped out and marched away. He didn't look happy. I'd taken only a few steps when I realized I'd forgotten to pick up a copy of the press release.

It listed the names of all the white shirts Soulsby was promoting and transferring. I'd need it for my story.

The police department's Public Information Office was on the third floor of headquarters, across the street. The office would have copies. I walked over, went to the elevator, and hit the button.

A moment later, the elevator doors opened—and out stepped Lou. We exchanged hellos. Lou asked, "How'd the press conference go?"

"Soulsby's really happy about being named chief," I said. "He kept hugging Barry. I thought he was going to kiss him."

"What'd Soulsby say about me?"

It's a cardinal rule of journalism that off-the-record information is to be treated with extraordinary care. But ask ten journalists to define the term and they'll provide ten different definitions. Some definitions will be decisively dissimilar. Some will differ in nuance. Many journalists, including me, would say that unless there is an explicit agreement with the source that the information not be repeated, it's okay to try to confirm it with someone else, as long as the original source isn't revealed.

I was virtually positive Soulsby was lying.

But suppose he wasn't? If Lou was the target of a grand jury investigation and I didn't check it out and it got reported elsewhere, my editors would chew me out, for starters. One way or another, I had to check out the chief's statements.

I hadn't planned on telling Lou that Soulsby was assassinating his character. But he'd caught me by surprise.

I responded to his question with a question: "Do you know anything about being the target of a criminal grand jury investigation?"

Like that, Lou's face turned into a mask of rage. His teeth showed. His eyes got wide. His nostrils flared. He clenched his fists and rocked from side to side.

"That lying son of a bitch!" Lou snapped. "I knew he'd do something like that! I just knew it! That no-good, lying son of a bitch!"

Uh-oh. Lou had always been preternaturally calm, even as he led the investigation into the massacre at headquarters, even after he learned he was the intended target. I'd never seen him so much as mildly annoyed. Now he was enraged, maybe even dangerous.

Lou grunted.

I felt myself shrinking into my clothes.

Lou looked at me as if he didn't recognize me, then stormed off. I stepped into the elevator, sensing I'd stepped into something bad, hoping that Lou didn't run into the chief anytime soon.

In his state of mind, he'd tear Soulsby apart.

As soon as I returned to the office, I told my editor about Soulsby's statements and my encounter with Lou. Keith said he'd run it by our boss, Jo-Ann Armao.

Keith wandered back to my desk a few minutes later. He said he'd told Jo-Ann what happened. "You probably shouldn't have said anything to Hennessy," he said.

"Just be careful from now on," Keith added. He didn't seem alarmed.

I called Kevin Ohlson, the spokesman for the U.S. Attorney's Office, and asked whether Lou was targeted by a grand jury.

"Absolutely not," Ohlson said, his tone incredulous. Another reporter had already called to ask the same thing, he said.

"What's going on?" Ohlson asked.

"I don't know."

The next day, Lou ran into Soulsby in the basement parking lot at headquarters. He asked: "Are you telling people I'm the target of a grand jury? Lie to me all you want, but don't lie *about* me."

Soulsby put his palms up. "No, it's not like that. Come up to my office and I'll explain."

"Fine. I'll see you in a few minutes," Lou said.

The chief took an elevator to his fifth-floor office. Lou hustled up to the homicide squad room, on the third floor. The idea came to him as he marched up the stairs: He'd deal with the chief like a lying perp. He slipped a small recording device into his suit coat pocket and went up to see Soulsby.

A couple of minutes later, Lou sat in front of the chief's big desk and asked Soulsby if he'd told reporters he was the target of a grand jury.

"No, I never said that," Soulsby replied.

"I hear that's exactly what you said to some reporters," Lou shot back.

"No," Soulsby said. "They kept asking me questions about you, pressing me. It didn't come out the way I meant, but I didn't say the grand jury was after you."

"So why are you transferring me?" Lou asked.

"The unit's disorganized," Soulsby said. "You're not using the computer system to keep track of investigations."

What the hell, Lou thought. He'd *created* the tracking system.

Lou bore down: "Why did you lie about me?"

"I didn't lie," Soulsby insisted.

"Chief, you realize that if you did tell those reporters I was under a grand jury investigation, I'd have to arrest you. You understand that it's illegal to talk about an ongoing grand jury, don't you?"

Soulsby looked like he wanted to cry, Lou thought. For a heartbeat, he almost felt sorry for the chief.

Lou knew his time was limited. His rage was growing, but it was manageable, for the moment. It was time to put it to use.

"Stop lying about me," Lou said.

Soulsby looked down at his desk. Lou reached into his coat pocket and activated the tape recorder he'd brought with him.

"I'm not lying," the chief muttered.

Lou stood up, his anger surging like a tsunami. "If you ever lie on me again, I swear to God, I'll get you! If you ever lie on me again like that, Chief, you and I are going to have a problem! I'll tell you that right now!"

The chief stayed calm. He said he wasn't lying.

Lou wanted a confession.

"You're a goddamn liar! There's no grand jury investigating me anywhere! You call the U.S. Attorney's Office right now!"

Calmly, Soulsby said, "I did not say there was a grand jury—"

"Bullshit! Bullshit! Bullshit! You lying son of a bitch. Don't lie on me like that! Tell me what you said—"

"Sit down," Soulsby said, his voice barely audible.

Part of Lou wanted Soulsby to get up and come at him. The chief was a moose—six foot four and about three hundred pounds. Lou was six-one, two hundred pounds; he was in good physical condition. Fueled by rage, he likely would have pummeled the big chief, if they'd come to blows.

Lou screamed at the top of his lungs, "I ain't sitting down! You lie like shit! I'm going to tell you something: I knew you'd come up with some bullshit. I knew it!"

Soulsby denied lying once again.

"If you ever lie about me again, I swear to God, I'll get you!"

The office door flew open. Soulsby's administrative lieutenant and secretary ran into the room. The lieutenant looked at Soulsby and asked if he should call for backup. Soulsby waved him off.

Lou wheeled to face the lieutenant and the secretary.

"The two of you can stay! He's lying about me! I want you to hear what he's saying!"

The chief told his lieutenant and secretary to leave. They looked at each other, bewildered, a little scared. Soulsby told them again to leave. They did.

Lou resumed berating Soulsby. The chief sat there and took it. Lou screamed himself out and stormed from the office.

*

Lou listened to the tape in his car in the basement. The quality wasn't great. He could hear himself yelling and swearing and Soulsby making his weak denials. Why would he just sit there and take such a tongue-lashing from a subordinate? The chief had had no plausible defense. But he hadn't explicitly confessed.

Another idea came to Lou. He pulled out his cell phone and called Jeff Greene, a retired homicide detective working as an investigator for a K Street law firm. Jeff was tight with Soulsby. They'd golfed together back in the late eighties, when Jeff was a detective and Soulsby commanded homicide.

But Jeff was tighter with Lou. He'd helped train Lou as a detective.

Lou laid out his idea.

"Come on over," Jeff said.

Ten minutes later, Lou stepped into Jeff's office and closed the door. Jeff called the main police dispatch number. He told the officer in charge who he was and that he needed to raise Soulsby.

Soulsby called a few minutes later. Jeff put the call on speakerphone so Lou could hear the chief. Lou was hoping Soulsby would confess to his old friend.

"I'm really troubled that Lou, who's been a friend for more than twenty years, is being treated this way," Jeff said.

"I'm sorry that it happened," Soulsby said. "I didn't mean for it to come out the way it did, but the reporters kept throwing questions at me."

"What do you mean?" Jeff asked. "Did you say he's the target of a grand jury?"

"I'm sorry," Soulsby said. "What should I do?"

The chief's tone was apologetic. His words were slurred. Lou and Jeff both thought he'd been drinking.

"Maybe you can smooth this over, put Lou back in homicide," Jeff suggested.

"I can't do that," Soulsby said. The chief said he knew that Lou had taped their conversation.

Before taking the tape recorder into his meeting with Soulsby, Lou had asked a homicide lieutenant to plant a wire on him. The lieutenant had balked. The lieutenant must have told Soulsby of his plan, Lou realized. Well, he couldn't really blame the lieutenant—Soulsby was the chief, after all.

Soulsby said he had to go. He and Jeff hung up.

Jeff and Lou looked at each other.

"We should've taped that call," Lou said.

The next day, Lou went straight to the police medical clinic. "I'm under a lot of stress," he told a shrink. "The chief is slandering me, telling people a grand jury is investigating me. I want to rip his throat out. I'm afraid of what I'll do if I see him."

The shrink told Lou to go home, right away, on paid stress leave. The doctor wanted Lou *gone*. He didn't even ask Lou to turn in his gun.

A couple of nights after Lou taped himself confronting the chief, he called and invited me to join him and Jeff at a little Italian restaurant on New York Avenue, a block from the hamburger joint where he'd met his ex-cop informant.

Lou and Jeff were at a table in the back. The lighting was dim, the tablecloths checked red and white. The late-night, post-dinner crowd was light. There was no one within earshot of their table. I sat down, feeling as if I was dropping into a scene from *The Godfather*.

Lou had played the tape for me the day before. I wasn't thrilled—you could draw a straight line from my asking Lou if he was the target of a grand jury investigation to Lou's confrontation with the chief. But I was impressed that Lou had screamed at his boss. How many people have dreamed of doing that?

The waitress came to our table. Lou and Jeff each ordered a beer. I asked for a cranberry juice.

"I wish I knew what this was about," Lou said.

"This is a huge scandal," Jeff said. "If it gets out that the chief lied about the homicide commander, that he concocted a criminal investigation, he will be out—gone."

I sat there and said nothing. The waitress returned with our orders. Lou and Jeff nursed their beers.

Jeff threw out theories: Soulsby just lies. He can't help himself. That's what he did here. Or: Soulsby is jealous. He lied about Lou because he hates that homicide has gotten good press.

Jeff finished his beer and said he had to go home.

He said good night and left. I stared at his abandoned mug.

"Soulsby would run over his own mother to be chief," Lou said. "If Barry's doing dirt, Soulsby wouldn't hesitate to cover for him." Each of the theories had merit. At the moment, I was focused on my own role. I was in the middle of the story—a bad place for any journalist to be.

"I wished I'd handled it differently," I said. "Should have let you find out from someone else."

"You shouldn't sweat it," Lou said. Someone from the U.S. Attorney's Office had called him the day Soulsby was named chief, saying reporters were asking whether he was the target of a grand jury. "I would've found out anyway."

I wanted a beer. No, five beers. Maybe ten. I thought about where that would inevitably lead. How soon would I be back on S Street, copping rocks with a strawberry?

No, that wasn't an option.

I brooded about the situation. Where was this going? If things got hot, would my bosses stand by me? What would happen if Soulsby found out I was a crack fiend in recovery? Would he or his people attack me? What might Barry do with that nugget?

Lou was as stand-up a guy as anyone I'd ever met. I didn't know if I could count on my editors at the *Post*, but Lou was as steadfast as a thousand-year-old oak. I needed someone I could trust. Of course, by buying large volumes of crack, I'd helped fuel the violence that Lou had been combating. I wasn't sure how he'd react to that news flash. It was time to show some trust, I decided.

I took a deep breath. A handful of editors and co-workers knew about my addiction. I'd told my parents and siblings, though I hadn't gone into any detail. I'd told a couple of girlfriends. But no one else.

"Lou, there's something I should tell you. I wasn't in the best shape when I moved here to D.C. When I was in L.A., I started using crack. I tried to stop when I got the job at the *Post*, but that didn't last too long. I kept using, and it got pretty bad. I don't know how many thousands—tens of thousands—of dollars I spent scoring. I'd pick up girls, strawberries, to make the buys, to insulate myself from jump-outs. It got pretty bad. Right before Christmas four years ago, my boss took me to rehab. I stumbled once a couple months later, but I've been clean ever since. Just thought you should know."

Lou's expression didn't change. "You're okay now?" he asked. "Yeah."

Lou nodded. At that moment, I knew the trust went both ways. We resumed talking about Soulsby's lie.

A couple of weeks later, the whole episode seemed to be buried. Lou hired a lawyer, who met with an attorney for the police department. They worked out a deal. The D.C. Council was set to hold confirmation hearings for Soulsby in December. Lou agreed not to testify against Soulsby and to keep the audiotape of himself screaming at the chief under wraps.

In return, Soulsby took Lou off the night shift and assigned him to the training division. The chief also agreed, essentially, not to fuck with Lou anymore.

I was at my desk when Lou called with the news. "Good," I said. Part of me was disappointed that Soulsby wouldn't be exposed as a treacherous liar. But I was relieved to have the incident in my rearview mirror.

If the story ever became public, my role in tipping off Lou about Soulsby's lie would become known—and there was no predicting where that disclosure might lead.

CHAPTER 12

EXILED

Every morning, Lou reported to his new assignment at the training academy, an isolated outpost in Southwest Washington, hard by I-295. Every morning, he went through the same cloak-and-dagger routine: First he'd park his two-door Honda Accord in the facility's outdoor lot. Then he'd slowly turn and look in each direction, until he'd completed a careful 360-degree sweep.

When he was satisfied that no one was watching, he'd pull out a roll of Scotch tape, tear off a few pieces, and carefully attach them to the Accord's driver's- and passenger's-side doors and trunk. When he returned to his car at the end of his shift, he'd examine every piece of tape to make sure it was exactly as he'd left it.

A scene in the 1973 Robert Redford–Paul Newman movie *The Sting* had inspired Lou's Scotch-tape tactic. Redford's character, con man Johnny Hooker, enlists a veteran grifter, played by Newman, to exact revenge on the Mob boss who killed his partner. In one scene, Hooker wedges a piece of paper into the doorway to his apartment so he can tell if anyone slips inside while he's away.

At the outset of 1996, Lou didn't know what might be coming next. For that matter, he still didn't know why Chief Soulsby had suggested he was under criminal investigation, why he'd been transferred so suddenly out of homicide, or exactly how he might have crossed Mayor Barry. Whatever the case, it was clear that Soulsby wanted to wreck his reputation.

"It would have been easy for Soulsby to have someone plant drugs in my car," Lou would say later. "He was capable of anything. I had to try to protect myself."

Lou's windowless office was four by eight feet, just big enough for a small desk and a chair. He had no responsibilities, no teaching duties, no one to command. He was at the top of his game and he was in exile, tucked away in far Southwest near the U.S. Naval Research Laboratory and the Blue Plains waste-water treatment plant. The pungent smell from the plant assaulted him for the first few days, but eventually he became acclimated to it.

Lou made the best of his situation. In his tiny office, he studied for his law classes. To clear his head, he often ran the five miles from the academy to National Harbor and back, along the Potomac and into Prince George's County, Maryland.

The reason for his exile remained as murky as the waters of the river. It would be months before he had any inkling of why he might have been bounced from homicide.

One day that spring, Lou was walking on the street just outside Metropolitan Police Department headquarters, on his way to meet a friend for lunch. He ran into a homicide detective. The previous June, his prize informant, the ex-cop, had given Lou information about the abduction and murder of a gambler and racketeer named Carlton "Zack" Bryant.

Bryant was known to keep large sums of cash on hand and rumored to have made millions of dollars over the decades running off-the-books numbers games—his own lottery—in his Northeast Washington neighborhood. In late April 1995, he'd been kidnapped from his home and held for ransom. Without contacting the police, Bryant's relatives paid $50,000. That didn't save him, however: A few days after the abduction, Bryant's beaten body was found, dumped in a wooded area in Southeast.

No one had been arrested for the kidnapping/killing. But Lou's ex-cop source had given him a name: Roach Brown. Lou passed the tip to the detective on the case and arranged for the investigator to meet with his source. Now, a few months after Lou had suddenly been transferred out of homicide, the detective and Lou exchanged hellos and small talk.

"How's it going on the Zack Bryant case?" Lou asked.

"Oh, it turned out your guy was wrong," the detective responded. "It wasn't Roach Brown. It was Roach Henry."

Lou scratched the back of his neck. That couldn't be right, he thought. His informant had been sure. "No, it was Roach Brown," he said. The detective shrugged and soon went on his way.

This was the same Roach Brown who as a young man had been convicted of murdering a man whose home he and three others had broken into. The same Roach Brown whose work in a theater troupe in prison had caught the attention of President Gerald Ford, who commuted his life sentence. The same Roach Brown who, in 1987, was busted selling cocaine to an undercover agent and stole $45,000 from a charity for poor kids, then was let out sixteen years early by the D.C. parole board. The same Roach Brown who'd organized the ex-con vote for Marion Barry's triumphal 1994 mayoral campaign. The same Roach Brown who greeted everyone he met with a hearty "Merry Christmas!" all throughout the year—because, to Roach, "every day is Christmas."

There were dozens of guys in the city nicknamed Peanut or Spider. There weren't many guys known as Roach. And there was no one else with Roach Brown's remarkable history or larger-than-life public persona.

From the beginning of the Barry administration, Brown supposedly worked as the mayor's special assistant, as the director of the Office of Ex-Offender Affairs. But he wasn't on the mayoral payroll. In February 1996, D.C. Council members Kevin Chavous and

William Lightfoot had raised questions about what Brown actually did for the city and which department paid the ex-con. Lightfoot chaired the committee that had oversight of the District's Office of Emergency Preparedness, for which Brown was on the payroll as a "logistics assistant."

The previous November, a report by Russell A. Smith, the city's auditor, had noted that Brown had never spent a day at Emergency Preparedness. It recommended that he be fired from the position. The report further noted that when Brown applied for the job, he'd claimed to have earned a bachelor's from Morgan State University—even though he had no such degree.

Barry brushed aside the criticism. He simply shifted Brown to the Office of Employment Affairs. Brown would remain employed by the city until September 1997.

The scathing auditor's report was issued five months after Brown's city employment came to the attention of U.S. District Judge Oliver Gasch. It was Gasch who had sentenced Brown to life in prison in 1965. In June 1995, Gasch was unpleasantly surprised to learn not only that Brown was working for the city government instead of doing time, but also that Brown wasn't making good on the restitution he'd been ordered to pay to Hillcrest Children's Center, the charity he'd fleeced in 1987. Brown was on the hook for $45,000.

It was a lot of money for someone on a government salary.

In July 1995, about six weeks after Zack Bryant was kidnapped and killed, the mayor headlined a fund-raising event for Roach Brown at the historic Lincoln Theatre, on U Street Northwest. "He needs this forty-five thousand dollars," Barry said as he passed a hat around the theater, referring to Brown's restitution. The mayor would personally be kicking in $200.

That summer, shortly after Lou's informant said Brown had been behind Bryant's kidnapping and murder, Lou checked Brown's court file. Brown had paid a healthy chunk of the amount he owed in restitution, the file showed.

Brown had used some of the ransom money to pay down his restitution, the source had told Lou. At the time, Lou was unaware of the fund-raiser, but it wouldn't have allayed his suspicions of Brown. Even if Brown had used some of the fund-raiser money to pay down his debt, that wouldn't have meant that his source's information was wrong. After all, Lou's informant had always been on target. Besides, Brown had been convicted of murder, drug charges, and fraud and always seemed to be in trouble.

The chance meeting with the detective gnawed at Lou. After his lunch appointment, he returned to his office at the training academy. He checked a law enforcement database and found that Roach Henry had a good alibi for the Bryant kidnapping: He was incarcerated. Lou made a few phone calls and learned that Henry was also gravely ill, dying of cancer. Roach Henry died just eight days after Bryant was kidnapped.

Someone's sidetracking the investigation from the inside, Lou thought.

After his informant had come forward with information about Roach Brown, Lou had written up a memo for the Bryant case jacket. Now he couldn't remember whether he'd included the informant's name. If he had, the informant's life could be in danger. Lou kept copies of his write-ups in a computer file. He checked the file: The ex-cop wasn't mentioned by name.

The following day, Lou arranged for a friendly homicide detective to pull the case jacket and come to his office. His memo wasn't in the jacket. In fact, Brown's name had been scrubbed from the file. Someone had replaced the memo detailing Roach Brown's possible involvement in the murder with a flimsy write-up blaming it on the dying Roach Henry.

Lou was dumbfounded. It was the first and only time he'd ever seen such information removed from a homicide file. A homicide jacket was supposed to provide a history of the case; investigative leads were *never* dumped from such files. Suppose information turned up later that implicated a suspect who was named early in the investigation?

Lou handed the file back to the detective.

He ran through the sequence of events: Bryant is kidnapped and dies; his death is ruled a homicide. Lou's best informant passes him a tip that Roach Brown was behind the abduction. Out of nowhere, Lou starts hearing that Barry wants him relieved of his command. Soulsby not only transfers him but also tries to assassinate his character.

Suddenly it made sense that Barry would want him out of homicide. There was no evidence that the mayor had anything to do with the Bryant abduction or killing, but how would it look if a mayoral aide was arrested for murder? Lou was surprised that Brown hadn't already been indicted, based on the information provided by his informant.

That night, Lou called his source.

"The detective working the Zack Bryant murder says Roach Henry did it, not Roach Brown," Lou said.

"No way," the ex-cop replied adamantly. "It was Roach Brown. His office is down the hall from the mayor's office, and if you go in there you'll find drugs in one desk drawer and a gun in another."

Lou believed him. All the pieces fit: The mayor's newfound interest in him, his transfer out of homicide, Soulsby's attack on his integrity. The derailing of his police career seemed to be connected to his effort to investigate the Bryant murder.

But with Soulsby in charge of the police department, there was no one he could take his suspicions to. The U.S. attorney, Eric Holder, hadn't stood up for him regarding Soulsby's off-the-record lies about a grand jury investigation. Lou had hoped that Holder would make a public statement confirming that Lou wasn't and never had been the target of a grand jury probe, but the prosecutor had said nothing. Lou had no reason to believe Holder would buck the police chief on a murder investigation.

Lou kept taping his car, studying, and running.

*

For me, the Soulsby thing was dead. In the months since I'd relayed the chief's off-the-record statements to Lou, I'd continued on the crime beat. The paper sent me to New York to do a piece on plummeting violence in that city and the crime-fighting efforts of the NYPD.

My recovery from crack and alcohol was proceeding steadily. I'd become a faithful member of a support group that met weekdays at noon one block from the *Post*. Most of the core members were professionals who worked downtown. Their lives weren't perfect, but many of them had families, thriving careers, or their own businesses. A few of them, such as my friend Tom, had a level of peace and serenity I aspired to. There was no magic formula, but it was important to attend as many support-group meetings as possible, Tom advised.

There was no right or wrong way to do the program, either. When I started attending meetings regularly, right after my release from rehab, I'd worried about the program tenet that a belief in a "higher power" could restore alcoholics and addicts to sanity. I'd been raised Catholic but had fallen away from the church, and I didn't know what I believed about God.

My worries turned out to be unfounded. One of the regulars at the meetings I attended was known as "Godless John" because of his enthusiastic, almost gleeful atheism. Godless John had compiled more than a decade of sobriety. He faithfully went to meetings and was available whenever I wanted to talk. His example was crucial: Godless John showed me that adherence to a religious belief wasn't a prerequisite for staying clean.

Some people throw themselves into their recovery program, attending every support-group holiday gathering, developing a circle of exclusively sober friends, raising their hands and talking at every meeting. My approach was more reserved. I showed up and mostly listened. I remained close to people who weren't in the program, including one pal who liked to drink but wasn't an alcoholic.

In meetings, I listened closely to people who'd relapsed describe how miserable and dangerous it was to resume drinking or using drugs. I also listened to successful people with long-term sobriety who seemed to handle whatever life threw at them with grace and good humor. They had this in common: They stuck with the program. They went to meetings and helped fellow alcoholics and addicts whenever they were asked. They did the basics.

In my quiet way, I did the same. When Tom asked me to temporarily mentor a man who was a crack addict, I jumped in, meeting and talking with my fellow junkie. He eventually got sober. Whenever someone asked me to lead a meeting, I agreed.

After a year or so, I realized that on the few occasions I'd talked, it wasn't about struggling with alcohol or crack. It was about conflicts at work or with a disagreeable landlord. It was about dealing with life. I heard some old-timers say that the program could help a lot of non-alcoholics.

I had to agree.

Even though it seemed that I would escape the Soulsby–Lou skirmish with my career unscathed, I started having nightmares about the chief. In them, Soulsby was a dark, menacing presence who silently stalked me. More than once, my girlfriend awakened me to offer comfort after I'd tossed and turned during a particularly awful dream.

Not long after he ran into the detective outside of headquarters, Lou called me at my desk. I cradled the phone on my shoulder and furiously scribbled notes as he related what he'd learned about the Bryant murder investigation and Roach Brown.

I was about to say what a great story this was going to make when I remembered: I couldn't write it. Because I'd disclosed Soulsby's lie, I was part of the story. There was no way Metro editor Jo-Ann Armao would let me write something, no matter how explosive Lou's accusations might have been. And I couldn't simply hand the story to another reporter. For one thing, Lou didn't trust anyone else at the *Post*. For that matter, neither did I. I worried that a fellow reporter who didn't have all the background might be spun by the chief, especially if Soulsby implied or offered ongoing access. I wasn't even sure the paper's editors would want to pursue a story about the Bryant murder with another writer, given my involvement in the Soulsby–Lou conflict.

"What are you going to do?" I asked.

"What can I do?" Lou said. "Soulsby's the chief, Barry's the mayor, and I'm out of homicide."

Both of us were handcuffed. We finished the conversation and rang off. I put the phone down, thinking that Lou and I were living in a James Ellroy novel.

About a month later, on a Friday afternoon in mid-May 1996, I took the elevator down to the *Post*'s second-floor cafeteria for a snack. I picked up a blueberry muffin and took a seat in front of a TV mounted on the wall. It was set to a local channel, and the five o'clock news was coming on.

As I chewed on the muffin, an announcer trumpeted the lead story—something about a secret agreement between the chief of police and a former homicide captain. Video footage of Soulsby and Lou flashed on the screen. The reporter, Joan Gartlan, said she'd confirmed that the two had entered into the pact after the chief had made derogatory off-the-record remarks about Lou.

I froze mid-bite. *Oh, fuck, this thing's a zombie,* I thought. *It won't die. It won't go away.* I watched the rest of Gartlan's report in despair. She didn't say what the off-the-record remarks were, but it didn't matter. She'd nailed everything else. Gartlan was a good journalist. She'd stay on the story, I figured. My role in the episode was being resurrected, and there was nothing I could do about it. I suddenly lost my appetite and tossed the rest of the muffin into a trash bin.

Lou spent the weekend stewing over Gartlan's report. On Monday he was at the hospital with Loraine, who was about to give birth to their third child. The TV was on in Loraine's room. The local news started.

A doctor and a nurse watched the news with Lou. Gartlan appeared with a follow-up to her first story about the secret deal. Pictures of the chief and Lou appeared. The doctor and the nurse peppered Lou with questions. He told them the chief was assassinating his character. He was getting more upset by the minute.

Loraine wasn't too happy, either. When Lou had been head of homicide, he was never home; he was always out chasing after killers. Loraine had accepted that. She knew Lou would pour his heart into his command. Now, though, he was out of homicide and she was in labor. She needed his attention.

"Could you shut that thing off?" Loraine snapped.

Sheepishly, Lou reached up and flipped off the TV. The doctor and the nurse slinked away.

Moments later, Lou's pager went off. He took out his cell phone and made a call. Loraine shot him a look. Lou cut the call short.

The following day, Lou drove Loraine and newborn Jack home from the hospital. Lou and Loraine gave Jack the middle name Henry, in honor of Henry "Hank" Daly. Their other two kids— Megan, four, and Billy, two—squirmed in the back.

Loraine could barely walk. She held Jack as Lou helped her into the house. Megan and Billy scampered inside, bouncing off the walls, excited to have a baby brother.

The phone rang. Lou picked it up. He listened.

"Yeah, I'll be right there," he said.

Loraine glared at him, thinking, *Oh, no you don't!*

He did. Lou headed toward the front door, muttering something about a D.C. Council member wanting to hear the Soulsby tape, something about defending his name. He flew out the door.

Loraine managed to place Jack in his crib. Then she collapsed.

The pain was too great. She couldn't walk. Megan and Billy chased each other around the house. Loraine crawled to the nightstand and picked up the bedroom phone. She called Lou's sister, who said she'd come by to take Megan and Billy off her hands.

Loraine shook her head in disgust and disbelief. She thought, *When he gets home, Lou's going to have bigger problems than Soulsby.*

While Lou drove toward Washington and Loraine fumed, Soulsby lied. Twenty-five miles north of Lou's home in Charles County, Maryland, inside the District Building, William Lightfoot, the same D.C. Council member who'd gone after Roach Brown's job in February, summoned Soulsby to his office.

Four months later, the *Post* would publish a story in which Lightfoot related what Soulsby said to him about the controversy. The chief claimed that he'd told me and the other two reporters that the U.S. attorney was investigating a fatal shooting by a uniformed D.C. cop and that the results of the probe would reflect poorly on Lou. The homicide squad investigated all officer-involved shootings. Soulsby implied to Lightfoot that the homicide squad's investigation into the incident was, at the least, seriously lacking.

Soulsby's explanation was another lie. He'd never said anything like that to me and the other two reporters he'd talked to off the record. He'd said that Lou was the target of a criminal investigation. Soulsby had lied twice to me: once when I was with the two other reporters and again when he and I were alone in the elevator. In neither instance had he said anything about a questionable shooting.

In the article, Lightfoot said Soulsby admitted that entering into his secret deal with Lou, which prevented Lou from testifying at his D.C. Council confirmation hearing, was a "serious" lapse in judgment.

Lightfoot said he took Soulsby at his word. But he added that if he learned the chief had lied to me and the other two reporters, or to him, "I'd call for his resignation. That's where I draw the line."

⁑

A few days after Gartlan broke the Soulsby story, I was driving back to the office from a murder scene in Northeast Washington. Things seemed to have returned to normal. In response to Gartlan's reports, the *Post* assigned one of my co-workers to write a couple of brief stories about the controversy. The articles didn't mention my role in the mess. Soulsby refused to authorize the release of the audiotape of Lou berating him. He issued a brief public apology for the secret deal. The story seemed played out.

Then Marion Barry went after me.

As I headed toward the office, I turned on the radio and tuned to a local talk show. Barry's distinctive voice boomed from the speakers. The host asked the mayor about the Soulsby–Hennessy brouhaha.

My entire body clenched.

Barry defended Soulsby. Then he attacked me.

"Ruben Castaneda was off the record," the mayor said. "He was unethical by telling people about this." Barry repeated: *Ruben Castaneda, unethical. Ruben Castaneda, unethical. Ruben Castaneda, unethical.*

I pulled over to the curb as Barry verbally pummeled me. I dropped my head onto the steering wheel.

This was far from over.

The next day, Keith Harriston appeared at my desk. The boss wanted to see me about the Soulsby thing, he said.

I tried to steel myself as I walked into the Metro editor's office. It was on the South Wall, in the middle of the newsroom, with a glass door and glass walls. Everyone could see us.

In her forties, Jo-Ann was petite, with short dark hair and wire-rimmed glasses. She often wore a pinched expression that suggested she'd just taken a slug of sour milk. I could kid around with some editors. I couldn't imagine trying to joke with her.

"Close the door," she said. I shut the door and settled into a chair in front of her desk.

"You're fired," she announced, deadpan.

My heart stopped.

Jo-Ann smiled.

Ha, ha, ha. Didn't know she had a sense of humor.

The smile disappeared. My heart resumed beating.

Jo-Ann sat down. "Tell me about your role in this Soulsby–Hennessy situation," she said.

I recounted: Soulsby said what he said. I ran into him in the elevator and gave him a chance to take it back and he dug in deeper. In a total coincidence, I ran into Lou moments later. I hadn't intended to disclose the chief's comments, but I responded to Lou's question with a question, and he figured it out on the spot.

"It's a problem," Jo-Ann said. "Off the record means off the record. You're not supposed to disclose off-the-record information to anyone. If sources can't trust us, we won't have any sources."

"I know," I said. "I didn't intend to reveal anything."

"You violated *Post* policy," Jo-Ann said. "It's a problem."

The word *policy* was ominous. I sat up straighter in my chair.

"Look, I knew Soulsby was lying," I said. "In my mind, I wasn't violating any off-the-record agreement. Are we supposed to protect lies? Besides, suppose he was telling the truth—I'd have to check it out."

"Doesn't matter," she said. "You put the paper in a bad spot."

"What I did was a misdemeanor," I argued. "Soulsby's getting away with a felony. What about that?"

Jo-Ann was unmoved. "Makes no difference," she said.

We looked at each other.

"Anything else?" I asked.

"No, that's it. For now."

This isn't good, I thought as I got up and left her office. For the next couple of hours I tried to work, but I was too anxious to get much done. I decided to try to get ahead of whatever Jo-Ann might have in mind.

Some ambitious reporters and editors wore out the carpet walking to the offices of the *Post*'s top editors along the North Wall, getting face time with the people who could boost their careers. I hadn't been on that side of the building since my job interview, but I decided I needed to make a foray.

I walked to the office of Len Downie, the executive editor. I asked his secretary if I could see him. A couple of hours later, I settled into the chair in front of Downie's desk.

"What's on your mind?" Downie asked.

"I want to explain this Soulsby–Hennessy situation," I said. I recounted how I had run into Lou by coincidence. "I want you to know I never intended to violate an off-the-record agreement," I said. "I made a mistake, but I had no intention of violating any agreement with a source, even if Soulsby was lying, which I was pretty sure he was."

Downie listened, his face expressionless. "You know you made a mistake, but you had no intention of violating any agreement with a source, even if Soulsby was lying," Downie echoed. "And you believe he was lying."

"Yeah, that's basically it," I said.

"Okay," Downie replied.

I left his office having no idea where I stood.

Two months later, *60 Minutes* aired a piece on the situation.

In the segment, by Ed Bradley Jr., about a dozen of Lou's detectives stood up for their former boss. They lauded his command and attested to his integrity. Lou was interviewed. So was Soulsby.

Lou came off as calm, dedicated, and competent.

Soulsby seemed confused and shady. When Bradley asked if he'd release the reporters from the off-the-record agreement so they could reveal what he'd said about Lou, the chief hemmed and hawed and finally sputtered, "No."

I watched with a mixture of satisfaction and horror. It felt good to see Soulsby exposed nationwide as an untrustworthy buffoon. But the Soulsby thing wasn't just back from the dead. It was on the move. Fast. And I was standing helplessly in its path.

A few weeks later, Jo-Ann called me into her office. No warm-up jokes this time. She stood behind her desk, her arms crossed. I stood across from her.

"The Soulsby story isn't going away," she said. "We have to deal with it. We have to explain the *Post*'s role in these events." She said she was assigning another staff writer, someone who didn't know any of the history, to report and write the story. The reporter, Paul Duggan, would ask me for an interview.

"All right, fine," I said. "What should I say to Paul?"

Jo-Ann uncrossed her arms and put her palms out. "I can't tell you what to say," she replied.

I thought we were on the same team. I guess that's changed. "So there won't be any repercussions for me, will there?"

"I can't say," she shrugged.

I thought of my old editor, Phil Dixon, now at the *Philadelphia Inquirer*. During my first six months at the *Post*, I'd written a story about a convenience store in Northeast D.C. that posted photos of suspected shoplifters. Somehow, I'd screwed up the first name of one of the store managers I quoted. I didn't merely misspell it; I simply got it wrong. Phil was apologetic when he told me I had to write a correction.

"I couldn't save you on this one, man," he'd said.

A few months after I started the daytime police reporter job, Phil actually did take a hit for me. The *Washington Times* had a story about a controversial police shooting in Southeast—a story we didn't have. Downie called Phil into his office to ask why. Instead of blaming me, Phil explained that I was working on an enterprise piece about a series of burglaries in a well-off section of Northwest, and that he'd advised me to remain focused on that assignment.

It was clear to me that Jo-Ann was worried about the ongoing coverage of the Soulsby incident. I was certain Phil would have handled it differently. I don't think he necessarily would have taken the hit for me. How could he? I was the one who'd talked to

Soulsby and Lou. But if Phil thought I'd screwed up badly by revealing Soulsby's lies to Lou, he would have dealt with me right away, based on my actions alone. He wouldn't have waited for the fallout. He wouldn't have left me with a sense of uncertainty about my fate.

I knew that I wasn't one of Jo-Ann's favorite reporters. Maybe she didn't like me because she saw me as one of "Phil's people." It was true—I was loyal to Phil. And though no one involved in the decision ever asked my opinion, I also believed that he would have been a better Metro editor. Phil was the rare editor who was equally great with copy and with people. Still, I worked every bit as hard after he left as I had before.

"All right," I said to Jo-Ann. "Paul knows where to find me."

Two or three days later, Paul and I walked to a table in the *Post*'s cafeteria.

"So are you our version of internal affairs?" I said as we settled into our chairs.

Paul shook his head. "Yeah, it sort of feels that way," he replied. "This is a weird story. Sorry you got caught up in this. Let's just get through this."

Paul asked me about Soulsby's remarks and my subsequent encounter with Lou. I answered as best I could without revealing exactly what Soulsby said to me and the other two reporters. I was careful not to say anything that hadn't already been reported elsewhere. I figured Jo-Ann would pounce on anything that she believed was too revealing.

A week or so later, I woke up at dawn and picked up the paper from my doorstep. I sat on the edge of my living room futon and read the story. Including a reference to me in a quote by Jo-Ann, my name appeared twenty-two times. I winced every time I read it. In the story, Downie said that reporters shouldn't repeat off-the-record statements unless they have clear understandings with their sources. Jo-Ann said that I'd put the paper in an awkward spot.

It was in this article that Lightfoot related Soulsby's fabricated explanation involving a police shooting and said that he would call for the chief's resignation if he learned Soulsby had lied.

The moment I stepped into the newsroom that morning, Linda Wheeler, a fellow reporter, approached me.

"I read the story," she said apprehensively. "If I were you, I'd lay low."

"My knees hurt when I crouch," I joked.

Fuck it. I stood up straight, walked past my desk to the middle of the Metro section, lingered for a few minutes, then marched back to my desk.

They'd killed Lou's police career. This was nothing.

Marion Barry's fourth term in office wasn't nearly as successful as the campaign that got him there.

Sharon Pratt Kelly had inherited a financial mess from Barry when she became mayor, in January 1991. Barry inherited a financial disaster from Kelly when he returned to the mayor's office, in January 1995.

On February 1, after meeting with members of Congress, Barry announced that the city owed $355 million in debts it couldn't pay during that fiscal year. The deficit would grow to at least twice that amount in the following fiscal year, the mayor said. The two-year deficit represented nearly 22 percent of the city's $3.2 billion budget.

Massive spending cuts would be needed to keep the city from falling into bankruptcy, congressional Republicans said. Even with austerity measures, a federal takeover was possible, the legislators warned.

During his first three terms as mayor, Barry had won the loyalty of thousands of voters by growing the D.C. government payroll. In some neighborhoods, everyone seemed to either work for the city or be related to someone who did. This approach had helped create a flourishing black middle class, Barry's supporters said. His critics said it had created a bloated, unresponsive government.

As he announced the huge deficit, Barry acknowledged that he would have to make painful cuts to the city's workforce of 45,000. Congress, he said, wanted him to come up with a plan to attack the deficit. "They want recommendations from me," Barry said. "I get the impression they're not going to take any action unless I act, and I intend to act."

The mayor didn't act fast enough. On April 17, President Clinton signed a law creating the D.C. Financial Control Board. The board consisted of five presidential appointees who would run the city's finances as well as its nine largest agencies, including Public Works, Human Services, and the police department. That year, the Control Board would cut four thousand jobs from the city payroll. It would also take away much of the mayor's political power—though Barry would still have the authority to appoint the police chief, and that chief would still have the power to choose his commanders.

On April 27, 1996, a Saturday, two months after Barry had announced that a further ten thousand city positions would need to be cut and four months after he'd undergone prostate surgery, the mayor suddenly issued a written statement announcing that he would be taking a leave of absence. "I see tell-tale signs of spiritual relapse and physical exhaustion," Barry said in the statement. He would begin his sabbatical at the Skinner Farm Leadership Institute, a retreat in rural Maryland where Barry had spent some time following his release from prison in 1992. After a few days at Skinner Farm, Barry would go to the Thompson Retreat and Conference Center, near St. Louis.

Again Barry invoked language familiar to people who participate in support groups. He referred to the fourth step of the twelve-step Alcoholics Anonymous program, which suggests that "every person should take a 'fearless personal moral inventory' of oneself." That inventory, the statement noted, should include a level of "rigorous honesty." Barry and his supporters denied that he'd relapsed during his recovery from drug addiction. But many Washingtonians believed that the mayor was being less than honest about the reason for his sudden departure.

Barry returned to his duties in mid-May, proclaiming himself rejuvenated. But it wasn't long before he was embroiled in more controversy. In June, Secret Service agents raided the Logan Circle home of Roweshea Burruss, a self-proclaimed minister and ex-con who allegedly ran an illegal after-hours club that Barry reportedly frequented. Barry acknowledged that he'd been to Burruss's home, though he denied that it was for any nefarious purpose.

"I've probably been at his house a half-dozen times this year," he said. "That's about it. Sometimes I run by there to change clothes. I went by to have a quick sandwich."

Barry limped through the remainder of his term, powerless to launch bold initiatives or hand out city contracts because of the Control Board. By early 1998, political observers wondered whether Barry would even contend for a fifth term.

On May 21, Barry ended the suspense. He announced that he wouldn't be running for reelection. Without citing the Control Board directly, he decried the "restrictions" placed on the mayor. He vowed to keep fighting for the betterment of D.C. "Those who think I'm going to a rocking chair someplace, I've got news for you. You're not going to see me doing that," he declared.

Barry's decision left the race for mayor wide-open. In September, voters in the city's Democratic primary chose relative newcomer Anthony A. Williams over three veteran D.C. Council members. Williams had served as the city's chief financial officer for three years and was widely credited with balancing the District's books so effectively that it had a $185 million budget surplus by 1997.

Perhaps just as important, Williams was, in style and substance, the polar opposite of Barry. He wore bow ties and was widely perceived as lacking charisma. Williams didn't associate with ex-cons, carouse at nightclubs, or have a string of ex-wives. He wasn't publicly or privately struggling with cocaine addiction. He was viewed as steady and reliable.

That November, Williams defeated Republican D.C. Council member Carol Schwartz in the general election. It was as if the city's electorate was taking the first step toward recovery from Marion Barry. He was Mayor for Life no more—though perhaps not for long.

On March 6, 2002, his sixty-sixth birthday, Barry announced that he would be running for a citywide at-large seat on the D.C. Council. He was, he said, no longer using drugs. Some political observers wondered whether Barry planned on using the seat as a launching pad for another mayoral bid.

Supporters of Mayor Williams braced for a divisive campaign.

Two and a half weeks later, a federal law enforcement source called me at home: "The Park Police found Marion Barry with drugs." Officers had discovered Barry a couple of nights earlier in his Jaguar in Buzzard Point, an isolated section of Southwest. They'd found marijuana and cocaine in the car, my source said, though not enough to make an arrest.

I called the city desk downtown, passed the tip to an editor, and went about my day. The editor would assign someone else to chase down the lead.

It panned out: The following day, the *Post* reported exactly what my source had told me. The encounter between Barry and the police had begun when someone called to report a suspicious car in a no-parking zone. The officer who approached it saw that the occupant appeared to be "ingesting something." Sergeant Scott Fear, a Park Police spokesman, said that Barry appeared to have a powdery substance under his nose.

A police dog trained to detect drugs was called to the scene, and it "alerted" that drugs were in Barry's car, Fear said. A field test conducted on the interior of the Jag was positive for cocaine and marijuana residue.

Through his attorney, Barry denied being in possession of any illegal drugs. But the fallout from the incident was significant, for Barry as well as the city. His wife, Cora Masters Barry, left him shortly afterward, and on April 4 Barry announced that he was dropping out of the at-large race.

"My decision to seek office has to be weighed against the greater issue, which is what is the best overall interest of my family, this city, and its residents," he said in a statement.

In early 1997, Jo-Ann again summoned me to her office. She said she'd heard that everyone in the police department knew I'd disclosed Soulsby's off-the-record remarks. Word was out that I couldn't be trusted.

"Who did you hear that from?" I asked.

She named a local activist who worked with the police. I knew the guy. He was tight with Soulsby and had a hair-trigger temper.

I started to say something, but one look at Jo-Ann's face told me I'd be wasting my breath.

"So what now?"

"I'm taking you off the police beat and moving you to general assignment, in the city," she said.

"General assignment" meant just that—I'd have no beat; I would have to find stories that weren't part of someone else's beat. Editors could throw me into whatever stories they needed help with. Though general assignment in the city isn't necessarily a bad job, it felt like a demotion. It felt punitive.

I nodded, turned, and walked out of the office.

The new gig *was* punitive. My new editor was in a perpetually foul mood. She didn't seem to like me. She was critical about almost everything I did. When I told her I'd applied for a three-month stint with the *Post Magazine*, she sniffed, "I know, and you'll probably get it, though God knows why. You haven't done anything for Metro."

My stomach was knotted all summer. I hated coming to work. Dutifully, I cranked out stories about the weather, about traffic accidents, about a group of neighborhood kids who'd visited the National Mall for the first time on a school field trip. In August, Jo-Ann again called me to her office.

"We need someone in Prince George's County—on the court beat," she said. "I'm reassigning you there."

"But all my contacts are in the city," I said.

"It's better if you get out of the city, because of the Soulsby incident," Jo-Ann replied. "Change is good," she added.

I felt a swell of rage. I thought, *Are you fucking kidding me? Soulsby lies and Lou is bounced from homicide. And now I'm going to be exiled to some one-stoplight county?*

"I don't want to leave the city," I said.

Jo-Ann smiled. "I can assign you *anywhere.*"

It was a threat. The *Post* had news bureaus way out in Virginia, in Loudoun County and Prince William County. The tiny towns that dotted them weren't Mayberrys—they were places that *aspired* to be Mayberrys.

A few weeks earlier, I'd talked about my situation with Vernon Loeb, a highly regarded Metro reporter who years later, after Jo-Ann had moved on to a job as an editorial writer, would be appointed the section's editor. Vernon had said that he didn't think I'd done anything wrong in the Soulsby situation and that I should tell Jo-Ann to "pound sand." Part of me wanted to say just that, and more, but I decided this was a fight I couldn't win. If I didn't leave soon, I feared, I would do or say something that couldn't be fixed.

"I'll think about it," I said.

But I knew I had no choice. This reassignment didn't feel punitive.

It felt like a career killing.

CHAPTER 13

DEATH AND RESURRECTION

In between organizing files, fielding phone calls, and greeting clients, Gloria Lowery would often stand at her office window and watch drug deals. Gloria was the office manager of Manna Inc., the housing nonprofit Jim had founded. Initially, Manna operated out of a small office on 14th Street Northwest. But within a couple of years, shortly after New Community moved onto S Street, Manna moved to the two-story brick carriage house behind the church. In the late nineties, it would move to office space in Northeast. While Manna was located behind the church, Gloria had a prime view of the drug market in action.

Drivers would stop their vehicles in one of the alleys outside New Community Church. Slingers would approach the driver's side. Cash and drugs—heroin, meth, then mostly crack—would change hands.

Many of the buyers, Gloria noticed, were whites who drove cars with Virginia tags. Some of them apparently couldn't wait to get home before using. From her vantage point, Gloria could see them pull over in the back alley and tie up the crook of an arm with a rubber tube. She didn't see any of them actually plunge a needle in, but it was clear what they were doing.

"They didn't just speed off," like most people who'd just made an illegal drug buy, Gloria recalled. "That's where we'd find the discarded needles—back in the alley."

She sometimes saw arguments or fistfights. She heard gunshots more than once. Early on, whenever trouble was brewing, Gloria called a Third District captain, who would send a patrol car to roll through. The captain was Larry Soulsby.

"It was like a movie," Gloria said. "It was *Starsky & Hutch* all the time around there. I saw more than I needed to see."

Eventually, Gloria started volunteering with New Community's after-school program. She got to know Baldie's girls, Angie and Nicole, and she exchanged hellos and small talk with their father. Like everyone else who lived or worked on S Street, she soon learned that Baldie ran the drug traffic on the block.

Baldie never gave Gloria a hard time. "He was the notorious, lovable godfather," she said. "Back then, it was different. There was respect. He tried to show respect where it was given, and not let his activities cause us any harm. He saw the good the church was doing for his girls with the after-school program, and he was reciprocating. There was a code he lived by."

Gloria wasn't afraid of Baldie or any of his slingers. She never viewed them as "the other." For one thing, she'd grown up in a tough section of Northeast, in the shadow of I-295, where drug dealing and shootings were part of the landscape. Also, she had family members and one close friend who'd been incarcerated. The fact that they'd done bad things didn't make them bad people, she believed.

She was a member of the Spiritual Guidance Interdenominational Church of God, in Clinton, a community about five miles past the Maryland state line in Prince George's County. Her church had a prison ministry that visited the Lorton Correctional Complex. Gloria joined it in 1995.

The church volunteers and inmates would gather in the prison's small chapel. One Sunday, about a year after she started volunteering, Gloria saw a familiar face walk in for the service: Baldie. He'd put on some weight and seemed a little worn out. But he appeared to have achieved a measure of serenity.

Baldie was a "trusty"—an inmate who'd earned small privileges for being well behaved and having a good attitude. In addition to getting some minor perks, trusties are typically assigned responsibilities such as working in the laundry room or the kitchen mess. Baldie's responsibility was to keep order during the services, to make sure the inmates there for worship didn't get out of line.

There were eight rows of wooden pews, four on each side. About thirty inmates, including ten or so who sang in a choir, would fill the chapel for each service. Baldie would stand in the row between the pews.

No one ever acted out, Gloria said. Now and then, someone might behave as if he wasn't paying attention, whispering to another inmate or looking around distractedly. Baldie would give the guy a hard look—and his attention to the service would be restored.

"Baldie never missed a Sunday," Gloria said. "He wasn't the same Baldie. This was a man who was tired, who was grateful to have found peace in his later life. The drug-dealer part of him was gone. If you didn't know him before, you never would have guessed he'd been engaging in those kinds of activities."

After each service, Gloria and her fellow volunteers went to a small room off the chapel where they stored their belongings. There, she and Baldie would have a chance to speak briefly. They never talked about why Baldie attended the Sunday services, but she believes that he was there by choice—not that he'd been assigned to go by prison officials.

"He would greet me by saying, 'Bless you,' " she said. They discussed Bible passages, and Baldie would ask about Angie and Nicole and his granddaughter, the daughter of an older daughter. The granddaughter was probably the girl whose spontaneous statement had led the police to Baldie's stash, but the former dealer held no ill will against her.

"He encouraged me to encourage Angie and Nicole to do the right thing," Gloria said.

Gloria wasn't naive. She'd visited enough people who were incarcerated that she could spot faux jailhouse religious conversions. Baldie, she thought, was sincere. "I think toward the end he accepted Christ," she said.

Then, in late 1996, Baldie suddenly stopped coming to Sunday services. Gloria heard he was being treated for a serious illness at D.C. General Hospital.

On January 10, 1997, Baldie died.

Around the neighborhood, Jim heard that he'd been battling cancer.

The pastor had never visited the dealer while he was locked up.

"Baldie was a proud man. I don't think he wanted me to see him that way," Jim said. "He would have invited me if he'd wanted me to visit him in prison. But he didn't."

Baldie's memorial service was held in a tiny funeral home two blocks from the church. Someone in Baldie's family asked Jim to deliver one of the eulogies. On a brisk, bright day, Jim and Grace walked from New Community to the funeral home for the afternoon service.

The small chapel was dim, filled with a few of Baldie's relatives and some of his friends and associates, many of whom were drug dealers or street hustlers. A good number of the mourners had bloodshot eyes—and not, Grace suspected, because they'd been crying. They seemed drunk or high or both. She smelled marijuana. The darkness of the room unsettled her. "It was spooky," she recalled.

Jim listened as a handful of Baldie's friends delivered tributes to the former kingpin of S Street. They eulogized him as a kind and generous family man who would do anything for anybody who needed help. One of his daughters remembered Baldie as a "good father." No one talked about his drug dealing or the verbal abuse he'd heaped on his wife when he was drunk. She was absent from the funeral.

One of Baldie's relatives summoned Jim to the front of the chapel. Though they'd had different goals, Jim had always liked

Baldie. He considered him and his daughters part of his congregation. Though Baldie never took up Jim's invitation to come to church, Angie and Nicole had attended the after-school program and even occasional services and Sunday-school classes.

Jim still hated hypocrisy, however, whether it was coming from churchgoers in a small Arkansas town or associates of a D.C. drug dealer who'd run a city block for more than a generation.

"Baldie was a friend of mine. We liked and respected each other, and I treasured his friendship," Jim told the mourners. "Baldie did some good things. He loved his daughters and provided for them materially, though he set a terrible example for them. And as the benevolent godfather of S Street, he helped some people in the neighborhood."

Jim continued: "But Baldie was no saint. He sold a lot of drugs, which harmed a lot of people. He did terrible things to other people. His enterprise made life difficult for law-abiding people in the neighborhood. Like you, I mourn for Baldie. But let's remember him for who he truly was, not some mythical character he was not. Let's use his life and things he did wrong to be a lesson for us not to go in that direction."

A lot of Baldie's people, especially those who were still in the drug trade, seemed to squirm in their seats as Jim delivered his unvarnished description of the dealer's life.

They were visibly relieved when he wrapped it up.

After the eulogy, Jim and Grace walked back to the church, past only a couple of drug dealers. It was like that on most days now. Dealing on S Street was far from eradicated, but it had greatly diminished since Baldie's heyday in the eighties and early nineties.

In fact, dealing throughout the city had waned—especially crack dealing. In 1989, periodic urine tests taken by sample groups of District arrestees showed that 64 percent of them had used crack or cocaine within the previous forty-eight to seventy-two hours. By 1996 that number had dropped to 35 percent. Among younger arrestees, it fell from 39 percent to only 10 percent.

For a year or so after Baldie's arrest, in August 1993, dealing on the block had seemed to continue at about the same pace. As the years went by, however, it declined, slowly but steadily at first, then more rapidly. By the time Baldie died, traffic was down to a trickle. By the early 2000s, it was all but gone.

"It got better little by little," Jim said. "As time went on, there were fewer dealers on the street. There was no single event that brought about the change as far as the drug dealing."

The record-breaking violence of the crack era disappeared along with the drug. In 1994, the year Baldie was sentenced, D.C. recorded 399 homicides. In 2000, the city recorded 242. In 2012, there were only 88 killings. It was the first time since 1963 that the District had recorded fewer than a hundred homicides in a year. Most large cities throughout the country experienced similar trends.

There are many likely reasons for the decline. There was the work done by Lou and his detectives, and by FBI, DEA, and ATF agents, to lock up killers and dismantle violent drug gangs. According to at least one study, higher levels of incarceration coincided with a decrease in crime, particularly violent offenses.

There was also the U.S. Department of Housing and Urban Development's HOPE VI program to revitalize failing public housing projects by changing them into mixed-income, mixed-use developments. Beginning in 2003, District officials used more than $34 million in federal funds plus another $750 million in money from public and private investors to raze and redevelop the seven hundred dilapidated public housing units of the Arthur Capper/Carrollsburg Dwellings, between Capitol Hill and the Navy Yard in Southeast. The worn-out, crime-ridden buildings were replaced by an equal number of new public units, as well as by sixteen hundred new market-rate apartments, townhomes, and a building dedicated to senior citizens. Crime dropped dramatically during the redevelopment, according to an Urban Institute study.

On S Street, the renovation of the building that became New Community and the continued presence of the church set a tone.

Instead of providing a haven for drug users, slingers, and prosti-tutes, the building became a place of worship, a home to the after-school program, and more.

The church hosted Alcoholics Anonymous meetings. Jim helped ex-cons who were looking to turn around their lives, counseling them and helping them find jobs. Grace focused on providing educational opportunities for young people, launching an initiative to work with kids of all ages, particularly teenagers. After graduat-ing from college, Jim and Grace's daughter, Rachel, started an arts program for kids as well as adults.

Manna also had an effect on the immediate area, throughout Shaw, and eventually in other city neighborhoods, too. In the eighties, the nonprofit purchased and renovated forty properties within a two-square-block radius of S Street. A half-dozen of them were on S Street itself. Most of the dwellings were vacant, run-down single-family homes; some were apartment buildings that would become condos or co-ops. One building became a home for mentally ill people with AIDS. Over time, hardworking low-income people purchased the homes and moved in, transforming the neighborhood from an inner-city badland filled with drug dealers and strawberries to a stable community. Eventually, Manna renovated three hundred homes in Shaw.

Jim knows that simply having a job, particularly a low-paying one, doesn't necessarily allow someone to improve his or her finan-cial situation. Home ownership provides a permanent place to live and stability. It's the best foothold for climbing up the economic ladder, Jim believes, and Manna does everything the organization can to help working people gain it. Besides renovating homes, Manna provides financial-literacy programs, savings plans, and continued support once a sale is complete. The idea behind the organization is to provide an opportunity to climb out of poverty, not to offer charity.

"This is not do-gooderism," Jim explained. "Accountability is an important component of this."

In the mid-eighties, one Manna buyer purchased a renovated house on S Street. A few years later, it needed a new roof. The woman didn't have the money to pay for one, so she went to Jim for help. Manna replaced the roof, a job that cost thousands of dollars. The woman reneged on her promise to pay the organization back—so Manna sued her. Jim and the woman worked out a settlement: Manna helped her to refinance her home, which saved her thousands of dollars. She used some of those funds to pay for the roof.

"By becoming homeowners, they have a stake," Jim said. "They have equity they can use to pay off debts, start a business, go to school, or help their kids do the same. They feel they can move up the economic ladder."

By the summer of 2013, about one thousand Manna homeowners citywide had compiled $60 million in equity. The foreclosure rate for Manna home buyers was 2 percent. A survey taken a year earlier showed that although most Manna buyers could have sold their homes for a significant profit, about 85 percent were still in them.

It's possible that property values in Shaw would have risen without Manna. The May 1991 opening of the Shaw Metro station— planned for more than twenty years—on the northeast corner of 7th and S Streets, had a dramatic impact on the neighborhood. Through the end of 1991, there were on average 1,688 weekday passenger boardings at the station. In 1997, there were 3,027. By 2011, foot traffic at the Shaw station had more than doubled, to an average of 7,163 weekday boardings.

During the 2000s and 2010s, the area around S Street, and Shaw in general, experienced a development boom. John's Place, the nightclub that was popular with drug dealers and hit men, was torn down and replaced by a three-story brick apartment building. The Hostess bakery underwent an ambitious renovation. The interior was gutted. The rusting steps leading to the front doors were replaced by gleaming new ones. Huge new windows were installed overlooking the S Street entrance. Eventually, the lower floors would be home to restaurants and boutiques. The upper floors would become loft offices.

By the summer of 2013, S Street Northwest had been completely transformed from the lawless combat zone it was when Jim Dickerson first set foot on it. And Manna had paved the way, he believes: "We were doing renovations and development in the area when no one else was."

Nearly thirty years after New Community celebrated its first Easter in the neighborhood, the only original members remaining were Jim, Grace, and Nina Mason, who often plays the piano during services. Yet the church had stayed true to the "call and mission" statement that Jim had written at its founding: New Community would be a multidenominational church, with a racially, culturally, and economically mixed congregation. Lower-income and working-class people would be encouraged to take leadership positions within the church. There would be a special emphasis on helping children. Everyone's gifts would be nurtured.

"I had a vision about what the church could be, and in many ways that vision has been fulfilled. It's a place for everybody, a place where people can have spiritual growth and healing," Jim said. "We've done our own thing, which has emerged from our circumstances. We are local. We served the neighborhood." Though he devoted countless hours to helping run Manna, lobbying city officials for affordable housing funds, and helping congregation members and people who hung out on S Street, Jim didn't forget about his family back in Arkansas. Over the years, he reconciled with his mother, stepfather, and biological father before they died. For all their flaws, he never doubted that they loved him deeply. And he loved them deeply.

Jim never regretted launching his church in the middle of a combat zone.

"I knew God was there," Jim said of S Street in the eighties. "I was not bringing God to the street. God's presence was there, with those addicts, those drug dealers, those prostitutes, those murderers . . . I think what's held us here is God's calling.

"I could have been doing a lot of things. The call of this held me and my family here."

Bernice Joseph was one of those Manna homeowners who declined to sell her home for a big profit. In the summer of 2011, she received a handwritten note from someone representing a developer that wanted to buy her four-bedroom condo on Riggs Street Northwest. The offer was for nearly $1 million.

Bernice—B. J. to her friends—called a neighbor, a fellow condo owner, to talk about the proposal. The developer wanted to knock down her and her neighbors' homes in order to build luxury apartments. The project would require the agreement of fifty-four condo owners, most of whom, like B. J., had units near 14th Street Northwest. Some owned units a few blocks east, on 11th Street Northwest. All of the condos were in the Shaw neighborhood.

At the time, B. J., a single mother of four, had about $800 in her checking account and no savings. She was earning $28,000 a year as a teacher's aide at a D.C. charter school for developmentally disabled adults. Two of her own children had already left home, but money was still tight. On the phone, B. J. and her neighbor joked about what they would do with a million dollars.

Then B. J. tossed the letter into a wastebasket.

Within a few weeks, many of her fellow condo owners attended a meeting in a church basement to discuss the offer. Tempers flared. People who wanted to stay put yelled at people who wanted to take the developer's money. People who wanted to sell screamed at people who didn't. Others wanted to hold out for more money. During the meeting, B. J. weighed in: "I'm not selling," she said calmly.

The developer kept trying to woo B. J. and the other holdouts into the fall and early winter. In December, the developer hosted a holiday party for the condo owners at a restaurant on nearby U Street Northwest.

"I considered it a bribe," B. J. said. "I went and I ate their food, but I didn't change my mind."

B. J. was living paycheck to paycheck, but she saw no upside to selling—not for a million dollars, not for any amount. Ultimately, more than half of the owners decided not to sell. The developer's proposal went nowhere. Eighteen months after it died, in June 2013, B. J. still had no regrets about turning it down.

"This is not just a house," B. J. said. "This is my *home*. This is where my kids come home from school and bring their friends to visit. This is where we can have a barbecue in the backyard. It's a small backyard—but it's mine."

From the outside, B. J.'s condo appears unremarkable. Her unit is one of a series of fifteen identical-looking three-story row houses that line the western side of Riggs Street. One block north, fifteen more identical row houses line the western end of S Street. There's a common parking lot in between. Built as public housing in 1977, the brown brick buildings have the distinctly institutional look of a complex that would have "Dwellings" or "Gardens" in its name. Inside, there's a small living area that runs into a small dining area, as well as a modest kitchen. The second and third floors each have two bedrooms.

B. J. rides the bus for thirty minutes to get to her job, using the time to read history books and novels. She walks ten minutes to New Community, of which she's a core member. She also walks to a nearby high-end grocery store. Her two children still living with her—daughter Bethany, eighteen, and son Rovaughn, nine—like their schools and have close friends in the neighborhood.

"This is the first community I've built," B. J. said. "That means a lot to me. I love my house. I like everything about living here."

B. J. is certain she never would have had any of this if not for Jim and Manna. She and her then four-year-old son, Gary, came to D.C. in 1990 from their native Grenada. Her second child, daughter Leonis, stayed in Grenada with relatives. In Washington, B. J. and Gary moved in with B. J.'s mom, who lived in a house on S Street Northwest one block from New Community. One day, B. J. saw a flier advertising GED courses at the church. She'd never graduated from high school, so she signed up.

As she was leaving the church after class one day, a bunch of young kids from the after-school program were filing in. B. J. thought, *Wow, I need to sign up my boy*, and soon registered Gary. In 1992, B. J. moved to an apartment a few miles from S Street, but she and Gary liked the after-school program so much that she brought him to the church by bus.

In 1995, B. J. moved back to S Street to live with her mom. The same year, her third child, Bethany, was born. She asked Jim to christen the baby.

"Sure," Jim said. "But you have to come to church sometime. Not every Sunday, but sometime."

That fall, B. J. finally went to a service at New Community. She quickly assimilated into the congregation. Fellow church members took care of Gary and Bethany when she was working or running errands. Jim and Grace's daughter, Rachel, became Rovaughn's godmother when he was born, in 2003.

In 1998, Jim hired B. J. as a part-time church administrator. By then her family was living in a $600-a-month two-bedroom apartment at the Whitelaw Hotel, a building in Shaw that had been renovated by Manna. Jim started encouraging her to think about buying a Manna home.

"Becoming a homeowner was the last thing on my mind," B. J. said. "My friends were all renters, and most of them lived in run-down buildings."

Eventually Jim convinced her. In 1999, she joined the Homebuyers Club, a program Manna requires all of its prospective homeowners to complete before making a purchase. Every Saturday for two years, B. J. and her classmates learned about budgeting and saving money.

"They had us write down everything we bought throughout the week," B. J. said. "If I bought a muffin for $1.25, I wrote it down. I learned how to manage my money, and I learned how to save."

Never a big spender, B. J. became even thriftier. By the end of the program she had paid off $5,000 in credit card bills. The Homebuyers Club required her to save $25 a week, which she did faithfully. Manna kicked in $50 every week, as it did for all Homebuyers Club members.

In the spring of 2001, B. J. was walking on Riggs Street when she saw workers renovating one of the row houses. Manna staffers had offered to show B. J. properties she could buy, but she didn't feel the need.

"I decided that was going to be my house," she said.

B. J. started wandering over to watch the workers as they refurbished the condo. They would ask her what she was doing and she would reply, "I'm coming to look at my house."

That June, she bought the condo for $102,000. Between her part-time job with the church and her work as a child-care provider, she was earning about $18,000 a year while supporting three kids.

She didn't sleep well the first night in her new home. "The first night I slept here, it was so surreal," she recalled. "I stood on the steps and stared at my dining room table. I was afraid it was a beautiful dream and I was about to wake up."

In February 1997, a few weeks after Baldie's funeral, the D.C. Financial Control Board assumed more authority over the day-to-day operations of the police department. The board acted after a consulting firm recommended limiting Marion Barry's influence on the police force, particularly in personnel decisions.

The move was widely viewed as giving Chief Soulsby more power. When he was appointed, he'd faced budget cuts and a shrinking staff. "I don't think he's had a fair chance at managing the department the way he's wanted to," U.S. Attorney Eric Holder said. "The test of whether he's a fit person to run the department starts about now."

Ten months later, Soulsby admitted he wasn't a fit person to run the department.

Lou called me: "You heard about Soulsby?" he asked. He sounded excited.

"Yeah, I have." I was at my desk in the Prince George's County bureau, reading the budget of the following day's stories on my computer screen. It was November 25, 1997, two days before Thanksgiving. A story on Soulsby was at the top of the local budget.

Soulsby had suddenly resigned as police chief that afternoon, under multiple shadows of suspicion. He quit less than two hours before his best friend, Metropolitan Police Department lieutenant Jeffery Stowe, was indicted by a federal grand jury for shaking down married gay men and embezzling department funds. Stowe and Soulsby had been close for years. In fact, they were roommates, sharing a luxury apartment downtown.

"This is *great*," Lou said.

Stowe was the lieutenant in charge of investigating extortion plots. But instead of tracking down blackmailers, he'd been running his own shakedown scheme, an FBI affidavit alleged. He targeted patrons of the Follies Theatre, a gay bar in Southeast, not far from the Capitol. Stowe would prowl around outside the bar, looking for parked cars that contained baby seats, an investigator told me. According to the affidavit, he would then write down the license plate numbers and use a police computer to learn to whom the car was registered and where he lived. Two months earlier, court documents alleged, he'd tracked down a married man who'd gone into the Follies Theatre and demanded $10,000 from him. If the man didn't cough up the cash, Stowe threatened, he would send photos of the man inside the bar to his wife and boss.

Stowe and Soulsby's high-end digs also raised suspicion. Their apartment typically rented for between $1,700 and $2,000 a month. But the lieutenant and the chief were paying only $650 a month. Stowe had reportedly obtained the steep discount by lying to a building manager, claiming that the unit would be used for undercover police work. Soulsby said that he knew nothing about the discounted rent.

A little more than two years earlier, Soulsby couldn't stop grinning when Barry announced his appointment as chief. That afternoon, as he made public his resignation, Soulsby teared up.

"I cannot allow another controversy to impact on my officers and to detract from their accomplishments," he said. "My concern for the welfare of my officers and the people they serve transcends my own personal welfare."

Soulsby did not acknowledge any wrongdoing. He said he was stepping down for the good of the department, "not because I feel I have done anything wrong."

In an interview, Soulsby told a *Post* reporter that he was actually happy to be stepping down: "I need to take some time off and chill out. I'm just tired, very tired. I'm tired of fighting these silly battles."

The morning after the resignation, I called Lou early, as soon as I'd finished reading the articles on Soulsby and Stowe.

"This is awesome," I said. "And it's just the beginning."

Lou and I were convinced that it was just a matter of time before Soulsby was charged with a crime. Like any other defendant, Stowe would be looking to cut a deal with prosecutors to help himself. He *had* to have dirt on Soulsby. If Stowe dished on Soulsby and the feds could corroborate his accusations . . .

"I can't wait until that fat son of a bitch is marched into court in handcuffs," Lou said. "I'll be sitting in the front row."

"Save a space for me," I said. "I'll be sitting right next to you."

Soulsby's resignation was the main topic of conversation the next day when I went to Lou's house for Thanksgiving. He now invited me every year.

"What I don't understand is why he felt he had to lie about me, why he had to attack my integrity and reputation," Lou said. "He was the chief of police. He had the authority to transfer me. He could appoint anyone he wants. All he had to do was say he was going in a different direction—or nothing at all."

"Maybe he felt he had to discredit you because of the Roach Brown investigation," I said. "But I don't think it was premeditated. At the press conference, when I asked him what was going on with you, he got this look on his face—he seemed upset. I think he made it up on the spot. And when I gave him a chance to back away from it, in the elevator, he just dug in deeper."

"He's a sick guy," Lou said, shaking his head. "He's told so many lies, I don't think he knows what's true."

"But he's not *that* sick. He knows right from wrong. It's amazing someone like that could become police chief in a big city."

"He'd do anything to be chief, and Barry knew it. That's why he got the job. I can't wait to see him walk into the courtroom as a defendant," Lou said.

"They're going to need a really big orange jumpsuit," I said, imagining the nearly three-hundred-pound Soulsby finally doing his perp walk. "A whole cotton field's worth."

In federal court in January 1998, Stowe admitted to having lied to get reduced rent on the luxury apartment for himself and "another person" and pleaded guilty to wire fraud. Stowe also admitted that he'd embezzled $55,000 in MPD funds and pleaded guilty to two counts of extortion for shaking down two married men who'd visited the Follies Theatre.

"I know you all have a lot of questions—probably thousands of questions—and I wish I could answer them," Stowe told reporters. "Some of those questions concern other people that are in [MPD] and possibly others. Unfortunately, I cannot do that at this time. I wish I could."

For the next few months, Lou and I routinely swapped rumors we'd heard about Soulsby's imminent arrest or indictment. But nothing materialized.

Years passed. Federal prosecutors kept postponing Stowe's sentencing as the investigation continued.

In the end, the information Stowe spilled led the feds not to more police misconduct, but to union corruption. In October 2002, Jake West, the former president of the International Association of Bridge, Structural, Ornamental and Reinforcing Iron Workers, pleaded guilty to two counts of embezzling union pension funds. According to court papers, West spent more than $51,000 in union funds on golf, dinners, and items for his home in suburban Virginia. Six other union officials and employees would also plead guilty in the case.

West and Soulsby were golfing buddies who often dined together at the Prime Rib, a pricey downtown steakhouse. The feds wanted to know whether West had ever spent union money on Soulsby—and if so, whether he'd ever gotten anything in return. West's guilty plea inspired a new spate of rumors that the ex-chief would be the next to fall.

But Soulsby was never indicted. In October 2003, a federal judge finally sentenced Stowe to twenty-three months in prison, signaling the end of the investigation.

"What I did was reprehensible," the disgraced lieutenant said in court. "It's something I think about every night and sometimes through the day. It was a low point in my life. I had my financial back against the wall, and I made some very bad decisions."

He didn't say a word about his old roommate.

By then, Lou and I had pretty much stopped talking about whether Soulsby would ever be charged.

For a few weeks after Soulsby resigned, Lou had held out hope that interim police chief Sonya Proctor might offer him his old job in homicide or some other substantial assignment. They'd been at the police academy at the same time and had also worked together in 5D as young officers. Lou respected Proctor. She was smart and honest, the antithesis of Soulsby.

But Proctor never called. Though the Control Board was taking a greater role in running the police department, Barry was still mayor. Lou suspected that Barry could still pull a few MPD strings. In February 1998, three months after Soulsby's departure, Lou also left the police department.

His retirement dinner was held at the Bolling Air Force Base

Officers Club, in Southwest D.C. About two hundred people attended. Dozens of detectives who'd served under him in homicide were there. The retired chief of the U.S. Capitol Police, a former Prince George's County police chief, and a former lead agent for the Washington field office of the Secret Service all came. But only one current or former MPD white shirt showed up. After Lou's conflict with Soulsby over the chief's off-the-record attack was first reported, in the spring of 1996, many of his fellow officers had treated him as if he had a communicable disease.

"I wasn't surprised," Lou said years later. "I felt really good that my troops were there. The fact the event was well attended meant more to me."

Lou wasn't one to emote publicly, but he choked up briefly during his farewell speech as he addressed his former detectives directly. He spoke of how he'd aspired to lead the homicide command almost from the moment he joined MPD, twenty-four years earlier. He thanked the men and women who worked for him and told them they'd made a difference. "Commanding the homicide squad was the most rewarding experience of my time in MPD," he said.

By this time Lou had earned his law degree and passed the Maryland bar exam on his first try. By passing the Maryland bar, he was allowed to join the D.C. bar. He found office space in the District and began doing criminal defense work, along with personal-injury cases. By the early 2000s, Lou's private practice was prospering. During particularly good years, he was making more than triple his top police salary—close to $200,000.

In 2002, Lou ran for state's attorney in Charles County. The county was mostly rural, largely white, and somewhat conservative, if reliably Democratic in elections. But it was rapidly changing. Blacks were moving in at a brisk pace, and commercial and residential development was escalating. Lou waged an unconventional campaign, certainly for a Republican. He reached out to the county's burgeoning African American population, meeting with local NAACP leaders and speaking at black churches. His incumbent opponent, Leonard Collins Jr., a Democrat, was a hard-line, lock-'em-up prosecutor. Drawing on more than twenty years' experience as a cop in one of the country's most violent cities, Lou emphasized prevention over punishment.

Law enforcement alone isn't a fix for crime, Lou told voters. Only 50 percent or so of all crimes are reported, and only about 10 percent of those offenses are closed with arrests, he pointed out.

"I talked about how I could go out into the community and deal with a hundred percent of the population, talking about prevention," Lou said. "I could help people benefit from my experience in D.C. I could educate young people that the decisions they make when they're eighteen, nineteen years old will impact how they live the rest of their lives."

Lou also offset the incumbent's advantage in name recognition by appearing numerous times on TV news programs, where he was interviewed as a law enforcement expert about the D.C. Sniper case, raging that fall.

As the returns came in, the possibility of being the county's next state's attorney became a distinct reality. The result wasn't known until all of the 35,000 votes were tallied. Collins eked out a victory, but by only about two hundred votes.

But running for office raised Lou's profile, and not just with potential clients of his law practice. On the same day that Lou barely lost, another Republican, Robert L. Ehrlich, defeated Democrat Kathleen Kennedy Townsend, the lieutenant governor of Maryland and the eldest child of Robert F. Kennedy. Ehrlich became the state's first GOP governor since Spiro T. Agnew, in the late sixties. In January 2003, Thomas Hutchins, the delegate who represented Lou's district in Maryland's state legislature, resigned his seat to become Ehrlich's secretary of veterans' affairs.

Under the Maryland constitution, whenever a delegate steps down from his or her seat, whichever party the outgoing delegate belongs to gets to nominate a replacement to the governor. Hutchins was a Republican. The state's Republican central committee nominated Lou to replace him. Late that month, Lou was sworn in as a member of the Maryland legislature.

Lou was appointed to the Judiciary Committee, a plum assignment for a freshman lawmaker. Being a state delegate was a part-time job—the legislative session lasted only ninety days, near the beginning of each year. But between his legislative duties and his law practice, Lou was working almost as many hours as he had when he commanded homicide.

In late 2004, a member of Ehrlich's staff asked Lou whether he would like to be a judge. The governor had a vacancy to fill in Charles County. District court judges typically deal with misdemeanors such as traffic violations and low-level thefts—not exactly clashing with prosecutors with a client's liberty hanging in the balance. Taking the job would also mean a pay cut, a serious factor, given that Lou and Loraine were planning on paying for four college educations. At the time, the post of district court judge paid a little less than six figures.

But being a judge would have some advantages: The hours were regular, and the courthouse was a five-minute drive from Lou's house. He wouldn't have to trek all over the region to meet with clients or appear in different courthouses. No more endless hours spent investigating cases on behalf of clients. No more worrying that his kids were growing up without him.

Lou agreed to the appointment. On a frigid day in early February 2005, I drove to the Charles County Courthouse and joined about sixty of Lou's friends and relatives to watch him be sworn in, with Loraine and their kids at his side.

"Congratulations, Your Honor," I said as I shook Lou's hand after the ceremony.

One morning in 2008, a middle-aged black man walked into the well of the district courtroom in La Plata, Maryland, to stand before Judge William "Lou" Hennessy. Decades had passed since he and

Lou had last seen each other face-to-face. But Lou recognized the man the moment he saw his eyes.

The defendant, Gary Johnson, was charged with driving a truck with expired tags, driving without insurance, and driving without a seatbelt. He recycled old carpet pads and needed the truck to keep his business going, Johnson said, adding that he wanted to plead guilty.

Johnson was older and heavier, but Lou was certain.

"I think I remember you from back in 1977," he said.

Johnson wasn't so sure.

"You know a guy named Johnny McIlwaine?" Lou asked.

"Yeah, he just passed."

"You remember an incident at the Safeway store on 12th Street? I was one of the people involved in that case," Lou said. "I don't know if you want me to hear your case or not."

Lou wasn't more specific. He didn't want to embarrass Johnson in front of the other defendants. He didn't describe how he'd almost shot Johnson after he and a fellow bandit, both armed, stormed into a Safeway and ordered everyone down. Lou had been an arm's length from Johnson, his service revolver inside his coat pocket, leveled at Johnson's torso. He'd come very close to pulling the trigger.

Now, more than thirty years later, Lou offered to recuse himself from Johnson's traffic case. "I'm not saying I hold it against you," he said.

But Johnson apparently didn't recall the Safeway standoff. Or at least he didn't remember Lou. He was fine with Lou keeping the case.

Lou assessed him $75 in fines. "Fair enough?" he asked.

"Yeah," Johnson replied.

"Good luck to you," Lou said. "I'm glad to see you got yourself in good shape there."

Then he called his next case.

CHAPTER 14

SUBURBAN SUCCESS STORY

"Can I see?" I asked.

Julius LaRosa Booker bent down, grabbed the cuff of his pants, and lifted it up to display the damage inflicted by a Prince George's County police dog.

Booker was a large, powerful man with thick arms and legs. A chunk almost the size of a softball was missing from his right calf. I felt nauseated. And for a moment, I felt like I might cry.

I'd seen many terrible things during my reporting career. A man sprawled on the sidewalk in Northeast D.C., moaning, a bullet wound in his head. Thousands of bloated body parts gathered under a tent in Mexico City following the 1985 earthquake. And too many corpses to count—shooting and stabbing victims left lying in the street or slumped over the steering wheels of cars.

But nothing had struck me like the sight of Booker's leg, missing a huge chunk of flesh, courtesy of a police-dog attack eighteen months earlier. It was shocking. I fought back the encroaching tears—they wouldn't have been professional. I wondered what kind of pain Booker must have felt when the dog was ripping at his flesh. Then I nodded, indicating that I'd seen enough. Booker let go of his pants leg as I scribbled into my notepad.

Booker, thirty-four, walked with a pronounced limp. He'd

greeted me at the front door of his home in a blue-collar section of Prince George's and invited me inside. He'd shambled slowly to a couch as I settled into a nearby chair.

"How does it feel?" I asked after he'd rolled his pants leg back down.

If he stood for more than a few minutes, his right leg would swell painfully, Booker said matter-of-factly. He showed me a photograph of his four-year-old girl, Tanisha, who was afraid to sit on his lap.

"She asks me if it hurts," he said.

Booker wasn't a saint. But he wasn't a hard-core criminal, either. In October 1997, he'd been inside a stolen van with a prostitute in a tough part of Capitol Heights, Maryland, near the D.C. line. Someone called the cops. Patrol officers and a canine unit arrived. Booker blew out of the van and ran. The police dog ran faster.

I finished up the interview and walked out of his home. By the time I reached my car, I was no longer feeling weepy or queasy. I was feeling angry. Corporal Anthony Mileo, the canine officer who'd allowed his dog to rip away most of Booker's calf, hadn't been fired, hadn't been suspended. The department hadn't even given him a symbolic reprimand.

It was March 1999. Booker was one of a half-dozen police-dog-bite victims I would interview that month. I would read eighteen civil lawsuits alleging that Prince George's cops had brutalized someone with a police dog.

The fact that some cops use more force than is necessary on the street was hardly a revelation. One of my good Metropolitan Police Department sources had told me that if a suspect got too far out of line, he'd administer a "wood shampoo," raining baton blows on his head. It was an unwritten rule that both cops and criminals knew: "If you run, and you make us chase you, you're going to take a beating," my detective friend had said. I suspected he'd exaggerated some of his street escapades for effect, and I didn't think he'd ever maimed anybody.

This was something different, completely disproportionate and possibly illegal. Booker had been tortured and disfigured for life. I was outraged that police officers could use their authority to inflict such injuries with no accountability.

As I drove away from Booker's home, I felt a surge of adrenaline. It had been a while since I'd felt this excited about my job. For a year and a half, I'd been competently taking up space in my new assignment in Prince George's, covering the county courthouse and trying to figure out a way back to the city.

But now I had a *story*.

I hadn't been optimistic when I first drove out to the *Post*'s Prince George's bureau, located on the second floor of a cookie-cutter duplex in a nondescript office park. I'd covered the occasional trial or court hearing before. But I'd never been assigned to cover an entire courthouse, let alone two. In my new job, I was responsible not only for the county courthouse, in Upper Marlboro, but also for the Maryland federal courthouse in Greenbelt, about twenty miles away. That courthouse covered the southern district of Maryland.

On the D.C. crime beat, I'd been a natural at racing to shooting scenes and swooping into gang-controlled territory for stories. I'd become adept at interviewing gangsters and the survivors of homicide victims. And, of course, I had great contacts in the homicide squad.

All of that was now useless. And the idea of following cases through the court system had been vaguely unnerving. There would be indictments, pretrial hearings, trials, and appeals. Defense attorneys and prosecutors would file motions. How could I keep track of everything?

Prince George's hugs the Northeast and Southeast quadrants of D.C., with the Capital Beltway cutting through the county a few miles out from its boundary with the District. Most of the violent crime in Prince George's occurred in the poor and working-class communities situated inside the Beltway, close to the D.C. line.

Outside the Beltway, towns were generally wealthier, whiter, and more suburban or rural in nature, with lower crime rates. Inside the Beltway was predominantly black and Latino and more urbanized. Some local residents derogatorily referred to the area as D.C.'s "9th Ward." The District has eight wards, and the city's Ward 8, located in Southeast D.C., for years was plagued with high rates of crime and unemployment.

Still, it had taken only a couple of days for me to feel like I was a world away from the excitement of the city and my old beat. The courthouse and the county administration building were on opposite sides of Upper Marlboro's main street—which is, of course, Main Street. The street featured some modest law offices, a bail-bonds place, a small jewelry store, a bank, a pizza joint, a Chinese carryout, and a lone sit-down restaurant that went out of business and reopened under new ownership every few years.

I'd purchased court attire—a couple of inexpensive suits, a few nice ties, some dress shirts. I dutifully attended murder trials and sentencing hearings. In an effort to gain traction on my new beat, I chatted up prosecutors, defense attorneys, and the occasional friendly judge. I kept in mind something Lou had said when Soulsby exiled him to the training academy: "Any job is what you make of it."

Thirteen months into my new gig, in September 1998, a short, dark-haired woman named Sharon Weidenfeld had introduced herself in the hallway of the courthouse. She was an investigator who worked for private defense attorneys as well as the public defender's office. We'd both been in a courtroom where I was taking notes on a murder trial, and she'd quickly made me as a reporter.

Sharon told me she worked on a lot of civil cases involving brutality by the Prince George's County Police Department. In particular, she'd investigated some cases in which canine cops had supposedly urged their dogs to rip people up.

"You should think about doing a story about how the police use the dogs to hurt people," she said. "Some of the bites are really bad. I can help you. I've got lots of cases."

"Let me think about it," I said.

I stuck Sharon's card in my wallet but didn't give her idea much thought. She was an advocate for her clients, so of course she had strong views about police misconduct. It wouldn't have surprised me if police dogs got in an extra nip now and then, but I wasn't sure there was enough for a story.

The following month, something happened that convinced me there probably was: Within the span of three weeks, three unrelated civil lawsuits alleging excessive force by county police canine officers landed on my desk. All of the lawsuits claimed that officers had used their police dogs to inflict unwarranted injuries on the plaintiffs. And none of them involved the firm that usually hired Sharon to investigate police misconduct. They'd been mailed to the bureau independently.

I wrote a brief story on each of the lawsuits and started wondering: If three cases of alleged brutality by the canine unit could simply land in my lap, how many would I find if I went looking for them?

The Prince George's County Police Department was founded in the 1920s as a four-man force. Almost from the moment it was formed, the department earned a reputation for brutality. In 1967, a unit that called itself the Death Squad was led by a couple of white shirts and used informants to set up robberies of liquor stores and other businesses. Officers would then wait inside the stores to shoot the robbers. The existence of the unit was disclosed by one of its members in 1979. A county grand jury investigated, but none of the officers were charged or punished.

In 1969, hundreds marched on the Prince George's County Courthouse to call for the firing of an officer who'd shot and killed an unarmed man holding a baby in his arms. On the day before Christmas 1977, a county cop went after an unarmed man who'd allegedly shoplifted two $7 hams. The officer shot the man in the back of the head, killing him. Similar fatal shootings of unarmed men occurred throughout the eighties and into the nineties. In many cases, the victims were black and the officers were white.

Meanwhile, Prince George's underwent a dramatic demographic transformation. In 1960, its population was just under 400,000. By 1990 it had nearly doubled, even as whites steadily left. In 1960, only about 10 percent of county residents were black; by 1990 that number was 51 percent, with about 370,000 black residents, versus about 31,000 three decades before. Many of the blacks who moved in were college-educated and had high-paying jobs as lawyers and doctors, as well as in local, state, and federal government. Meanwhile, poverty and high levels of joblessness, addiction, and crime persisted in the communities on and near the D.C. border.

By the mid-nineties Prince George's was the wealthiest majority-black county in the country. In November 1994, Wayne K. Curry, a Democrat, defeated Republican Robert Ostrom for the open county executive seat. Curry, who'd also defeated a strong white candidate in the Democratic primary, became the first black county executive in the three-hundred-year history of Prince George's. He and other county officials ballyhooed Prince George's affluence as they lured businesses such as restaurants and big-box stores to previously underserved areas.

For all the changes, however, the culture of the police department remained the same. It was a haven for officers who didn't hesitate to use deadly force. In April 1995, the department's T-70 tactical squad was assigned to arrest Jeffrey C. Gilbert, who was suspected of killing county police corporal John C. Novabilski while he was sitting in his squad car, moonlighting as a security guard outside of a convenience store. Before the operation, a police commander showed squad members gruesome pictures of Novabilski's body, which had been shot repeatedly with a MAC-11 machine pistol. He also told them that Gilbert was a known hit man for drug gangs.

Six T-70 officers stormed Gilbert's girlfriend's apartment. They pummeled him, cuffed him, and took him to a hospital emergency room. He suffered a broken nose, a concussion, and a broken blood vessel in his brain. He remained hospitalized for four days and was in such bad shape that detectives were unable to question him. Sharon worked the case for Gilbert's defense attorney. A couple of days after the beating, she took photos of the blood-stained wall behind the bed from which the heavily armed officers had pulled the sleeping Gilbert.

"You would have thought somebody was murdered in that room," she recalled. "I think their mission was to bring him out alive—but barely."

Gilbert, it turned out, hadn't shot Novabilski. He wasn't a hit man for gangs. He wasn't a hit man for anyone. In its rush to capture a cop killer—and exact vengeance—the department had done everything wrong. Rather than conduct a methodical, thorough investigation to identify the culprit, police quickly decided on a suspect based on no solid evidence. Less than forty-eight hours after Novabilski's death, detectives wrote a charging document alleging that three eyewitnesses had identified Gilbert as his killer. The witnesses allegedly picked Gilbert's image from a photo array. Police took the charging document to a judge, who signed off on an arrest warrant.

It was, at best, slipshod detective work. Novabilski's killer had been wearing a ski mask, making an identification all but impossible. And two of the "witnesses" would later allege that police had shown them a photo of Gilbert and bullied them into identifying him from the picture as the killer.

When Gilbert was arrested, Lou called a Prince George's white shirt to suggest the department keep an open mind in its investigation. Four months earlier, two D.C. police officers had been ambushed much as Novabilski had. One was shot while sitting in a fast-food restaurant, the other while sitting in his squad car. Both officers had been wounded but survived. The attacker in one of the shootings wore a ski mask.

Lou's heads-up went unheeded.

Thanks, but we think we've got our guy, the Prince George's white shirt responded.

Lou and his detectives and the FBI continued to hunt the D.C. police stalker. In late May, they caught a break: Prince George's police interviewed a woman who alleged that she was being abused by her boyfriend. The woman was about to leave the police station when, almost as an aside, she added that her boyfriend had been the one who was going around shooting cops.

A witness to one of the D.C. shootings had told Lou's detectives that the attacker wore braces. Around that time, the woman recounted, her boyfriend had removed his braces—with pliers. His name was Ralph McLean.

MPD detectives and FBI agents set a trap: McLean's girlfriend would arrange to meet him at a gas station in Greenbelt, just down the street from the federal courthouse. An FBI agent who resembled McLean's girlfriend would pose as her.

McLean apparently sensed the setup. He arrived early, hid in a nearby wooded area, crawled on his belly toward the perimeter established by D.C. and Prince George's cops and FBI agents, and then sprang up and shot FBI agent William Christian Jr. in his unmarked Bureau sedan.

The shooting sparked a furious gun battle. McLean ran into the parking garage of a nearby shopping mall. Surrounded by law enforcement, he shot himself in the head. Next to his body was the same MAC-11 that had been used to kill Novabilski. McLean was also in possession of the slain officer's service weapon. McLean, not Gilbert, had killed Novabilski.

Prince George's detectives tried mightily to find a connection between McLean and Gilbert. They couldn't. The state's attorney dropped the charges against Gilbert. In time, Gilbert filed a federal civil rights lawsuit against the county police. The county would agree to pay him more than $1 million to settle the suit. The FBI and the U.S. attorney investigated the Gilbert beating, but none of the officers involved were indicted.

A few days after McLean killed Christian and himself, I wrote an article describing the rancor the episode had caused between the FBI and the local police.

At the time, I thought the brutish, ineffectual way the Prince George's cops had handled the killing of one of their own was an aberration, motivated by a desire to get payback for their fallen colleague.

In early 1999, Metro editor Jo-Ann Armao announced a new initiative. Metro staff writers were invited to propose story ideas that would entail more than the usual one or two days of reporting to complete. Ideas for investigative projects were welcome. Staffers who submitted proposals that were green-lighted would be given three weeks to report and write without having to worry about producing daily stories or responding to breaking news.

It was a terrific idea. If you were covering a busy beat, as I was at the courthouses, tackling an investigative project was nearly impossible. With three free weeks, I could look for more cases of alleged canine-unit brutality.

Sharon provided background on which current and former canine officers were known for being particularly zealous about releasing their dogs on people. She gave me about a half-dozen case files of police-dog attacks, including the one filed on behalf of Julius Booker. I wrote up a detailed proposal.

Jo-Ann approved it. I started working on the project in early March. For ten days or so, I did nothing but dig through dusty old files in the clerk's office in the Upper Marlboro courthouse. There was no way to look up civil suits filed specifically against canine cops, or even against the police department. First I had to go through a computer database to identify lawsuits filed against Prince George's County. Then I had to pull those files to see if the police department was a defendant. If it was, I'd read the beginning of the lawsuit to determine whether the allegations involved a police-dog attack. If so, I'd put that lawsuit aside and make copies. I went through a similar routine at the federal courthouse.

It was tedious, painstaking work. But it paid off: Counting the files Sharon provided, I amassed eighteen lawsuits, resolved or pending, against canine officers. A handful of incidents might have been explainable as anomalies. Eighteen suggested a unit on a years-long rampage.

In one case, a man suspected of stealing a car ran from the vehicle. A pursuing officer shot the unarmed suspect, Bryan Diggs, in the thigh. Diggs crawled into some nearby woods. He reached a barbed-wire fence and gave himself up, calling out that he'd been shot. The lawsuit contended that a canine cop, Corporal Stephanie Mohr, then ordered her dog to attack Diggs. It bit him in the left arm. Mohr also allegedly allowed her dog to bite sixteen-year-old Kheenan Sneed in the leg as he slept in a neighbor's hammock. She then arrived and hit the teenager on the head with a flashlight or a baton, according to the lawsuit. Officers told Sneed and his mom that they'd been pursuing a man suspected of breaking into a store. The teen had done nothing wrong.

In another case, a man named Robert Frank Taylor broke into a warehouse and was arrested by Officer Daniel Russell and his supervisor, Sergeant Joseph Wing. According to the court documents, Russell released his dog after Taylor was handcuffed. The animal, the lawsuit claimed, bit into Taylor's right leg as Wing yelled, "Tear it off!" Taylor filed the lawsuit while he was in prison. County attorneys, who usually defended lawsuits against police officers with great vigor, agreed to pay him $15,000 to settle the suit.

I reported on each lawsuit as thoroughly as I could, contacting the attorneys for the plaintiffs and, if possible, the dog-bite victims themselves. The police department ordered its officers not to talk to me and wouldn't make any white shirts available for interviews. Instead it responded to a list of written questions. County police dogs are trained to capture suspects by biting them in the right arm, the department explained.

For months, Sharon had been feeding information to the FBI, trying to persuade the Bureau to open an investigation into the canine squad. Internal police investigations were considered such a joke that the lawyers she worked with advised their clients not to bother filing reports of abuse directly with the cops. Reporting misconduct to the department only gave the accused officers a heads-up that a lawsuit was coming.

I spent my final week on the project writing a long story as well as a sidebar that profiled three current or former canine cops who'd collectively been named in eight lawsuits. The story explained how, unlike many other police departments, the Prince George's force maintained virtually no records of dog-bite incidents, aside from keeping track of the number of such encounters. It didn't keep detailed medical records of injuries or take photos of the wounds.

The piece would be published on April 5, a Sunday. Sharon called me the Thursday before: "The FBI's starting an investigation of the canine squad," she said.

I called the Bureau, which verified that it was launching a probe into whether the unit had a "pattern or practice" of violating civil rights. I folded this new development into the larger piece.

Wayne Curry, the county executive, had ignored my phone calls and e-mails requesting a comment. On Friday, I drove to his home, in an upscale section of Upper Marlboro. Curry was outside watering his huge lawn. He had a small dog, which barked and jumped excitedly when I arrived, leaving muddy paw prints on my light-colored pants. Curry laughed.

He seemed unconcerned about the allegations of canine-unit brutality. "That some people who are bitten by police dogs would file lawsuits is not surprising," he said.

The story appeared on the front page. I wondered whether the police department would try to push back and poke holes in my reporting.

It didn't.

*

A couple of weeks after the canine-unit story was published, the Prince George's police department sent three supervisors and a corporal to Los Angeles to study how the sheriff's department there had reduced biting incidents by training its dogs to corner suspects instead. The *Post* sent me, and I did a story on the new approach.

In May, Curry and police chief John Farrell held a news conference. By then, Curry wasn't so dismissive of allegations of brutality by the canine squad. The department's police dogs would be retrained to capture suspects by cornering them and barking, Curry and Farrell announced. They acknowledged that my articles had prompted them to reevaluate the way the unit operated. Canine officers who didn't get with the new program would be reassigned, Curry and Farrell said. Within months, virtually every officer in the canine squad had been replaced.

That summer and fall, I was inundated with tips. Sharon tipped me off about fresh police-dog bites. Lawyers called to tell me about other police-brutality lawsuits. Several defendants called to tell me how they'd been abused by the cops; some called collect from jail. Suddenly I was the go-to reporter for police misconduct in Prince George's County.

That September, *Post* executive editor Len Downie came to the Prince George's bureau to visit the troops and bat around story ideas. Before he headed to the door to drive back to the main newsroom downtown, Downie made a detour to my desk.

"You're doing a good job writing about police misconduct," he said.

"Thank you," I replied. "I've got lots more to write about."

A great sign, I thought. Downie was typically taciturn, and not promiscuous with praise.

The tips kept coming. I kept writing. On April 3, 2000, an attorney tipped me off to a staggering civil verdict: A federal jury in Baltimore had awarded Freddie McCollum Jr. $4.1 million in compensatory and punitive damages for a beating inflicted by three Prince George's County police officers in an encounter that began as a traffic stop for a missing license plate. The officers beat the fifty-year-old McCollum so badly that he lost his right eye and partial use of his left hand. The cops also released a police dog on him.

Just hours after the McCollum verdict came in, another civil trial, in an unrelated Prince George's police brutality case, ended in the federal courthouse in Greenbelt. That jury awarded $647,000 to Nelson Omar Robles, a Salvadoran immigrant who was arrested in Prince George's for a misdemeanor traffic warrant issued by neighboring Montgomery County. After MoCo cops said they were too busy to pick up Robles at the county line, Lieutenant James Rozar came up with a plan: "I've got a set of flex cuffs in the car," he told a dispatcher, "and I was just going to take him over to Montgomery County, handcuff him to a pole, pin his ID to the back of his shirt." Robles was left helpless for fifteen or twenty minutes before a Montgomery police officer arrived to uncuff him.

On the same day the McCollum and Robles verdicts came in, State's Attorney Jack B. Johnson announced that he was unable to obtain a grand jury indictment against seven Prince George's County cops implicated in the death of Elmer Clayton Newman Jr., who'd died in police custody with two broken neck bones the previous September. The state medical examiner had ruled his death a homicide, but the investigation had stalled because the officers refused to cooperate, Johnson said.

A couple of days later, Curry called a news conference to announce that he was forming a task force to review county police conduct. His tone regarding allegations of brutality was no longer glib. Speaking about the Robles verdict, Curry said, "I don't need a jury to tell me that chaining someone to a pole at night unprotected was an act of indecency beyond the conception of most civilized people. I am not the least bit surprised or upset with the jury's verdict. I am outraged by the conduct."

In the hypercompetitive *Post* newsroom, high-ranking editors often talked about how much they valued "accountability stories" that had "impact." The canine story and its follow-ups epitomized that kind of piece. Police misconduct had become the hottest issue in the county, thanks, at least in part, to my reporting. The feelings of exile I'd experienced when Jo-Ann assigned me to the county bureau were now a bad memory.

I felt great about my work. I felt great about working in Prince George's County. I believed that I was making a difference, and that my career was resurgent.

I was only partly right.

By the summer of 1999, I was part of the *Post*'s recruiting pitch at minority journalist conventions. That year, management put together a flier headlined "Suburban Success Stories" that featured photos of black, Asian, and Latino reporters who were supposedly thriving in suburban news bureaus. *Post* editors distributed the fliers at the National Association of Hispanic Journalists convention both that year and the next. Next to my photo was a brief biography and this sentence: "His recent front-page investigation of savage attacks by police dogs forced the Prince George's police department to immediately change its policies on training of the canines."

In June 2000, Jo-Ann and I shared a shuttle van that took us from the NAHJ convention in downtown Houston to the airport. Politicking didn't come easily to me, but I made an effort: "It was a good call, assigning me to Prince George's County," I told her. "These stories, they're really making a difference."

We made awkward small talk for the rest of the ride.

Three months later, in September, a federal grand jury indicted Stephanie Mohr, alleging that in September 1995 she had intentionally released her police dog on an unarmed, unresisting homeless man who was surrounded by officers. The incident occurred in Takoma Park, a city straddling the Prince George's–Montgomery County line. Mohr released the dog because it was new to the canine unit and needed to be broken in, federal prosecutors claimed. Her supervisor, Sergeant Anthony Delozier, had asked a Takoma Park Police Department sergeant who was on the scene for permission to let the dog "get a bite." The sergeant said yes, prosecutors alleged.

As I prepared to cover the trial the following spring, I kept knocking out stories about police misconduct. I was so focused that I missed a big development unfolding in my own office.

In early 2001, I learned that two Metro reporters and a staff writer on the investigative unit were working on two sets of stories about police misconduct in Prince George's. One would focus on forced false confessions in homicide cases, the other on excessive force.

At first I was puzzled that I'd been excluded from the project. Then I became angry. I felt as though I was being shoved out of my own hard-won turf. No one in management had even told me the project was in the works. It would be a high-profile series. The paper was clearly gunning for a Pulitzer Prize. Whoever got to work on the stories would likely get a career boost.

Maybe Jo-Ann or another editor thought it would be too much for me to cover my beat and work on a big project, too. Maybe I should have met with whoever had chosen the project team to make my case for inclusion.

Years later, I entered therapy to try to get through a painful breakup. I worked in some venting about the *Post* in general and Jo-Ann in particular. With the help of my therapist, I figured out that my identity was dependent on being a *Post* reporter. I took work slights too personally.

At the time, I didn't have such insight. I also didn't have it in me to meet with Jo-Ann or any other editor. I should have asked for a meeting and made a methodical case for inclusion. I had sources and knew background the other reporters didn't. I might have succeeded in persuading Jo-Ann and other editors that I should be part of the team.

But I was so caught up in my anger, I assumed that Jo-Ann and other editors would brush me off. So I seethed—mostly in silence.

That spring, Ashley Halsey III, the Maryland editor, sent me a message asking me to retrieve court records for a reporter working on the project. Typically, a news aide would be asked to conduct such a task. It felt like a deliberate dig. I shot a message back to Ashley, declining the assignment and offering to talk about my refusal. "Never mind," he replied.

In March, however, I did at least ask Jo-Ann for a raise, writing a detailed memo describing the impact of my reporting, which had led to officers being indicted or suspended, as well as policy changes.

A few weeks later, the jury in the first trial involving Mohr and Delozier deadlocked on the charges against Mohr and acquitted Delozier of a civil rights violation. The government retried the officers. In August, a second jury convicted Mohr of a civil rights violation and again acquitted Delozier of conspiracy.

There was a direct line from my first major story on police-dog attacks to Mohr's conviction. During the first trial, Terry Seamens, a Takoma Park city councilman, testified that he'd heard about the Mohr incident shortly after it occurred. He was troubled by the use of force, but he didn't know what to do. When he read my article, Seamens said, he learned of the FBI investigation into the canine unit and called the Bureau. The FBI wired up Seamens and had him talk to a Takoma Park cop who'd witnessed the biting incident.

The officer's recorded account gave life to the investigation. Eventually, Dennis Bonn, the Takoma Park sergeant who said he'd given Delozier permission to let Mohr's new dog "get a bite," pleaded guilty to being an accessory after the fact. Bonn testified for the government. In December 2002, federal judge Deborah K. Chasanow sentenced Mohr to ten years in prison, the maximum penalty.

The conviction and the tough sentence had a dramatic impact on the police department, Sharon said. "The police department was operating lawlessly. Officers felt they didn't have to answer to anyone. They felt they could do anything in their county. Until then, nobody had held them accountable—no county executive, no county council member, no chief of police. They ran wild. That was the first time they saw that if the federal government comes in and prosecutes a police officer, there's going to be serious prison time."

Before I started writing about police-dog attacks, the canine unit was registering more than a hundred biting incidents a year. By the time Mohr was sentenced, county canine bites were greatly reduced. In 2000, the first full year after the department retrained its police dogs, there were just nineteen biting incidents. The numbers remained low—nine in 2001 and eleven for each of the two ensuing years. County police dogs registered only three biting incidents in 2004, and the number of incidents remained in the single digits or teens throughout the next decade. Using less force did not seem to have any negative impact on the unit's effectiveness. Canine officers detained dozens of suspects every year—fifty-four in 2012, for example.

Sharon stopped hearing about unnecessary or excessive county police-dog attacks.

A month after Mohr was convicted, Jo-Ann turned down my request for a pay raise. Instead she gave me a $1,500 bonus. I was disappointed, but I kept working hard, knocking out stories about police misconduct. In December, I sent her a follow-up e-mail, reiterating my request for a raise. She didn't reply. Months passed.

In late September 2002, Jo-Ann asked me to lunch at the upscale restaurant in the Madison Hotel, directly across the street from the *Post*'s main office, downtown. Almost immediately, she handed me an envelope. Another $1,500 bonus. She was again turning down my request for a raise. Non-management employees, such as reporters, received modest raises, which are negotiated by the Newspaper Guild, which represents non-management employees at the *Post*. In addition to those pay bumps, editors doled out annual merit raises to reporters who'd done good work. Every year, Jo-Ann and the editors in charge of other sections, such as Style and Sports, decided who on their staffs would get merit raises. I would not have asked for a raise if I believed I had a very good or even great case. I requested a raise because I believed I had an overwhelming and undeniable case. The impact I was having in Prince George's was unmatched by any other Metro staff writer. It wasn't close. Also, when I had agreed to transfer from the D.C. staff to Prince George's, I had pointed out to Jo-Ann that the commute would cost me thousands of dollars a year in gasoline and car maintenance costs. "You do a good job out there, and I'll get you more money," she had promised.

Jo-Ann's refusal to give me a raise wasn't the only bad news. She said she wanted to reassign me to Montgomery County. I'd be on not only the courts beat but also the police beat. It would diversify my portfolio, she said.

I was stunned. Leaving Prince George's would mean losing all of my contacts and sources once more. I didn't know anyone in Montgomery County, a well-off, majority-white jurisdiction just north of D.C. Montgomery County seemed like a sleepy beat in comparison with Prince George's. The cops in Montgomery were accused of excessive force now and then, but they didn't seem to have a culture of brutality. Change was always hard for me, and I loved the work I was doing in Prince George's. There would be plenty more police misconduct for me to write about, I figured. I didn't want to start over in what seemed a far less interesting place from a journalistic standpoint.

I didn't say yes to the reassignment. I didn't say no. But Jo-Ann could clearly see that I wasn't thrilled at the prospect.

"Think about it," she said.

Two days after our lunch, a man was killed by a rifle shot while walking across the parking lot of a Montgomery County grocery store. The following morning, four more people in Montgomery were similarly killed, all in the midst of everyday activities—

mowing the lawn, pumping gas, sitting on a bench, vacuuming out a minivan. Police determined that each of the victims had been shot with the same gun. So began the three-week siege of the so-called D.C. Sniper.

While the rest of the newsroom mobilized, I stewed. I decided I needed to stand up for myself. I called Phil Dixon. He'd been away from the *Post* for seven years, but we'd remained friends.

I ran down my situation, then told Phil my plan: "I'm going to file a discrimination lawsuit. I know the paper could retaliate, could pick apart anything I do, could make my life miserable. I figure this could blow up my career. I don't care if I go up in flames, so long as Jo-Ann gets burned, too."

Phil suggested a more measured approach.

"That would be a really big step, filing a lawsuit. You *could* do that," he said. "Or you could try to work it out internally. Management always prefers that."

"Go over her head? Won't management just support her?"

"It's worth a try," Phil said. "If that doesn't work, you could still go the legal route."

I decided to take Phil's suggestion. I started with Milton Coleman, the former Metro editor who'd hired me. At the time, he was a deputy managing editor, the third in command of the newsroom, just below Len Downie and managing editor Steve Coll. I gave Milton copies of my memos requesting a raise. I included a copy of the flier touting me as a "Suburban Success Story." In a cover letter, I went for broke, asking not only for a bump in pay, but also that I be allowed to stay in Prince George's.

We met a couple of days later. "If you show these memos to Len Downie and Steve Coll, you will get a raise," Milton said.

My eyes lit up. "So I should go to them, right?"

"Go back to Jo-Ann," Milton said. "Give her another chance."

I wrote Jo-Ann an e-mail asking for a response to my latest request for a raise. Three days later, she hadn't responded. She was no doubt busy directing the coverage of the sniper shootings, but

I didn't care. I couldn't stop now. I sent her another e-mail advising her that I was taking my case directly to Downie and Coll. She replied immediately, saying that of course I had the right to go to upper management if I had an issue.

For three months, I heard nothing. Then, in January 2003, Jo-Ann called me to a meeting in her office.

She acknowledged the good work I was doing in Prince George's and said I didn't have to worry about being reassigned to Montgomery. She also said that I would be getting a raise. She'd been scripted, it seemed to me.

She continued, describing some of my shortcomings as a reporter and writer: I didn't have enough respect for daily deadlines. I didn't always stay in touch with my editor. I focused too much on what happened in the courtroom. I crammed too many details into the ledes of my stories.

I was in a state of shock—in a good way. The North Wall had sided with me. I felt like I'd pulled a David and slain Goliath. That was great—in the short term. In the long run, the victory had a price, I figured. I thought there was no chance Jo-Ann would promote me within the Metro staff. And if I applied for a plum assignment elsewhere within the paper—say, with the National staff—the editor of that section would ask Jo-Ann about me. In a newsroom packed with talented and ambitious journalists, anything less than a full-throated recommendation would torpedo my chances.

As I walked out of Jo-Ann's office, I was sure of two things: That unless I screwed up spectacularly, Jo-Ann would leave me alone and let me keep working in Prince George's. And that any chance I'd ever had for a promotion or a choice new assignment was now gone.

CHAPTER 15

"A PERFECT EASTER STORY"

The group of uniformed Prince George's County cops who sat together in one row of the courtroom death-glared me as I walked past. Another twenty or so cops were scattered throughout the room. I felt their eyes on me as I headed toward the hallway.

As I passed the clustered uniforms, some of them hissed. I thought about saying something but decided not to react. I simply walked out. There was a break in the trial, and I had to check in with my editor. I allowed myself a brief smile when I reached the hall.

It was April 2006. The mood in the Upper Marlboro courtroom was grim, angry, and tense. By then I was accustomed to such antagonism from Prince George's cops, many of whom held me responsible for the criminal conviction of former canine cop Stephanie Mohr and the revamping of the police-dog unit. I'd also written plenty of other stories that had led to officers being suspended or investigated, as well as to criminal charges being dropped against suspects because of questionable police tactics.

Five years earlier, I'd covered the trial of Brian Catlett, a county cop who was charged with involuntary manslaughter for fatally shooting Gary A. Hopkins Jr., a college student who'd allegedly been trying to grab another cop's gun. Catlett was acquitted.

Moments after the trial ended, the state's attorney at the time, Jack B. Johnson, took me aside in the hallway.

"I've overheard a couple of officers say how great it would be to 'get' something on you," he warned me.

Some cops, without identifying themselves by name, wrote me angry e-mails. "I have to wonder what it would be like to make a living in the vile way that you do," one wrote in January 2003. "You sit back and report half truths and innuendoes about a job which you know nothing about. Ever faced a gun? Have you ever been in a fight for your life over a weapon?"

The Prince George's officers who were hostile to me apparently took my reporting personally—many of them seemed to assume I hated cops. I didn't. Some of the finest people I knew—Lou included—were with the Metropolitan Police Department. I did loathe bullies, though, and the abuse of power.

I respectfully responded to every message, offering to write a correction if any of my reporting was in error.

None of the senders ever asked for one.

The day I was hissed at, I was covering the murder trial of Robert M. Billett, forty-four. He was charged with killing a county cop the previous June, during a confrontation that had begun as a traffic stop. An officer in a squad car had tried to pull over a Chevy Tahoe. The driver hit the gas, ran two red lights, and pulled into the parking lot of an apartment complex in Laurel, a community in the northern part of the county.

Billett and two other men in the car jumped out and ran. Corporal Steven Gaughan, forty-one, was working nearby as part of a plainclothes detail looking for stolen property. At the apartment complex, Gaughan got out of his vehicle and joined other officers in chasing the men. Billett pulled out a gun and fired.

One round hit Gaughan in the shoulder. Another slipped by his protective vest and hit him in the abdomen, police said. He was taken to a hospital, where he died a few hours later. Police shot Billett, who was seriously wounded. He survived.

Near the end of the trial, the defense called a witness, Terri King, a woman who lived in the apartment complex where the gun battle erupted. She testified that Gaughan had fired first and that Billett had shot back in self-defense. Under a withering cross-examination by Deputy State's Attorney John Maloney, King acknowledged that she'd worked as a prostitute in several cities and been convicted of theft in Prince George's in 2003. The admissions were damaging to King's credibility.

I wrote up the story, reporting King's account of the shootout and her acknowledgment of her checkered past. It was a basic news story, thoroughly fair.

But someone with a badge and a gun apparently thought differently. The day the article was published, I received an anonymous e-mail reminding me of my detention by the LAPD, some twenty years earlier, when I'd gotten roaring drunk and tried to pick up a woman who turned out to be a plainclothes cop. I felt a sense of shock as I read the brief message about one of the worst nights of my life.

The taunting message was almost certainly written by a Prince George's County cop. Only an active member of law enforcement could have looked up such a record on the police computer database. It was a federal offense to use the database for non-law-enforcement purposes.

I took the incident seriously enough that I told a *Post* editor about it. I didn't know how far the e-mailer was willing to go. He or she had risked catching a federal charge just to mock me in an e-mail. What if that person learned about my crack addiction? By that point, I'd told some relatives and close friends, including a couple of co-workers and a girlfriend or two, that I'd struggled with addiction. A handful of editors who knew the newspaper had arranged for me to go to rehab, such as Milton Coleman and Len Downie, knew I'd battled substance abuse, though neither editor had ever asked for details, and I hadn't volunteered them. Could the e-mailer obtain my hospital records? That would be illegal, too—not that it seemed to matter.

I was a different person from the man who'd drunkenly tried to pick up the wrong woman. I attended support-group meetings and tried to help fellow alcoholics and addicts. I worked hard and did my job well. When I traveled to California to visit my family, I doted on my young nieces and nephew, and I gave their parents no reason to distrust me.

But someone hated me enough to break the law to goad me. Police officers had been overheard talking about getting something on me.

"They're afraid of you," Lou said when I told him about the glares and hisses. He mentioned one of his friends on the Prince George's force. "He said you wrecked the police department."

I thought I'd misheard. "You mean he thinks the *Post* has wrecked the police department?"

"No, he thinks you personally have wrecked the department."

Just how far could an angry and enterprising cop go?

A few months later, in early 2007, I wandered into the office of Tracey Reeves, a *Post* editor. We started out discussing news stories, but we eventually began talking about our lives. I sensed that I could trust her, and I told her the broad outlines of my struggle with and recovery from crack addiction and alcoholism.

Tracey's eyes lit up: "You have to write that story!"

She suggested I pitch it to the *Post*'s Sunday magazine. I wasn't so sure.

But Tracey's reaction made me think about a popular saying in my support group: "Your secrets will kill you." In the context of the program, that meant that we needed to disclose our misbehavior to a trusted fellow recovering alcoholic. It was part of the process of cleaning the slate and moving forward.

But I began to think the saying could have broader applications. What if my addiction wasn't a secret? A pissed-off Prince George's cop couldn't use my addiction against me if I revealed it myself, I decided. Late that summer, I met with Sydney Trent, a *Post Magazine* editor, and pitched the idea of writing about what it was like to cover the crime beat during the crack era while I was an active crack addict.

"Go for it," Sydney said.

That fall, I wrote the article on weekends and before and after my work shift. In December, as the publication date neared, I called relatives in California to let them know what was coming. I told Lou and other close friends. I notified judges, prosecutors, and defense attorneys I routinely worked with. I told the other reporters in the Prince George's bureau. I called friends throughout the country. One, a fellow journalist, wondered whether the disclosure would harm my career.

"What career?" I replied.

I still loved my job, but I knew I was just about maxed out at the *Post*, a fact that was oddly empowering. And the newspaper industry as a whole was imploding. Newspapers throughout the country were folding, and many of those that were left standing were laying off tens of thousands of journalists a year. Career-wise, I realized, I had nothing to lose.

I met with the president of the county police union and called a Prince George's white shirt I was friendly with. I told them I was writing about being a crack addict while covering the police beat in D.C.

"I know a lot of officers don't like me, and I expect some of them will attack me," I said. "That's fine—I'm putting myself out there, so I'll be fair game. But they need to keep it legal."

I told the union chief and the white shirt about the e-mail that referred to my L.A. detention. "If any cop goes there, well, I know the number to the U.S. Attorney's Office," I said. "How long would it take the FBI to figure out which police computer was used to look up my name?"

*

The article was published on December 30, 2007. The issue's cover featured a cartoon of Paris Hilton wearing a tiara and a sash emblazoned with "2007." The cartoon character was carrying a Chihuahua. The cover went with a year-in-review piece by humorist Dave Barry. My story was anything but humorous: I described my encounter with Big Man, how I picked up female addicts to make crack buys in exchange for sex, my forays on S Street, and my stint in rehab.

I woke up before dawn, retrieved the newspaper from outside my building, read the article, and braced for the blowback.

There was none. In the ensuing days, more than six dozen readers sent e-mails saying they had a loved one who was struggling with addiction. The article gave them hope, they wrote. Some friends whom I hadn't tipped off called to congratulate me—for getting clean and for the piece. Later that week, Greg Shipley, a Maryland State Police spokesman, looked at me after he completed a press statement about a prison inmate who'd been taken to a hospital for treatment of chest pains and had escaped.

With a handful of fellow journalists looking on, Shipley asked if I was the reporter who wrote the magazine article.

I felt my neck muscles tense.

"Yes," I said.

"Man," Shipley said. "You are *tough*."

The day after the story was published, I wandered into the main *Post* newsroom downtown to pick up a couple of additional copies of the magazine. Publisher Don Graham spotted me a few feet from the elevator and walked over.

"Glad you made it," he said as he patted my shoulder.

There were no taunting e-mails or phone calls from Prince George's County police officers.

Just like old times, I pulled up in front of the hulking bakery on S Street. The slingers quickly surrounded my car. I made the buy and drove through the alley behind the church that looked like a castle. Minutes later, I was back at my old apartment on 10th Street Northwest. Quickly, greedily, I loaded half the chunk of crack into the end of my pipe and lit up. The rock crackled and hissed. Trembling, I closed my eyes and brought the pipe to my lips . . .

I woke up in a panic. The nightmare was so realistic, so detailed, it took me a few terrifying seconds to realize it was just a bad dream. It was August 2008, eight months after I'd come out in the magazine as a crack addict.

The publication of the story didn't change my day-to-day routine. My friends remained my friends. My sources continued to provide tips. The judges, lawyers, clerks, and security officers at the state and federal courthouses didn't treat me any differently.

In January 2008, a few days after the article was published, I received a breezy congratulatory e-mail from Mark, a former *Herald Examiner* colleague. We'd been out of touch for eighteen years, ever since I'd left Los Angeles. I quickly wrote back, saying I needed to talk to him to make amends and asking for his phone number. He was part of the wreckage of my past, and I needed to clean it up.

When Mark and I had worked together at the *Herald Examiner*, in the late eighties, we were seemingly barreling toward doom on parallel tracks. Everyone knew that I drank hard, but Mark was considered the real wild man of the paper. It was common knowledge that he indulged in marijuana, cocaine, and maybe other drugs. He often dragged himself into the newsroom around noon, his eyes bloodshot.

Mark was a few years older than me. I was introverted and had a small number of friends, mostly *Herald Examiner* colleagues. Mark was gregarious and charming and had a large circle of friends inside and outside the newsroom. Six feet tall and lean, with angular features, thick black hair sprinkled with gray, and eyes that often seemed to be twinkling in bemusement, he was as handsome as some of the TV and movie stars he covered as a feature writer in the Style section. He seemed never to lack for female companionship.

A few months before I left L.A. for Washington, someone organized an office Fourth of July picnic. A sign-up sheet was posted on the bulletin board in the middle of the newsroom. Staffers wrote down their names and what they would bring to the party: potato salad, hot dogs, hamburgers, soda. When no one was looking, I forged Mark's name and printed a single word: "narcotics."

It was completely juvenile and thoughtless, but I meant no malice. Mark had always been friendly to me. One night when I was at Corky's, drowning my sorrows over my latest ruined romance, he had hung out with me, listened, and gently counseled me about the temporary nature of setbacks and victories alike. I felt better.

From my desk I watched as a handful of people read the list and snickered or chuckled when they got to Mark's name. But when Mark wandered over and saw it, his face went dark.

He sputtered, "If I ever find out who wrote this . . ."

Then he tore the list off the wall, flung it into the nearest trash can, and stormed away. I figured it was better to let my authorship of the gag remain a mystery.

When I called Mark a couple of days after our e-mail exchange, he quickly made me laugh: "So, where's Carrie now?"

We talked easily about our respective misadventures. Mark told me he'd been clean for a few years, said he got tired of the chaotic drug life and simply quit. He was working at a newspaper in Florida, living in an apartment near a bay where he had a boat. Mark and I had both tumbled into the hellhole of crack addiction, and, improbably, we'd both climbed back out, more or less intact.

Mark said he was curious—why did I have to make amends with him? What had I done to harm him? I told him about my dumb prank and recalled how upset it had made him at the time.

For a couple of beats, Mark said nothing. I braced for his angry rebuke. Then he laughed.

"I don't remember," he said. "You're forgiven."

Mark had relatives in the D.C. area. We made plans to have lunch or dinner the next time he was in town.

It seemed we were on our way to forging a new friendship based on our shared escape from addiction.

Less than two weeks later, Mark was dead.

I learned about his death when I signed on to a website that covered the journalism industry. The site had a brief item describing how Mark hadn't shown up for work one day, prompting worried co-workers to go to his apartment, where they found his body. There was no evidence of trauma or foul play, the story said. An autopsy would determine the cause of death. But I already knew.

A few weeks later, a mutual friend confirmed it: Mark had died of a drug overdose.

Mark's death reminded me that, no matter how well I thought I was doing, I was always one drink or hit away from a nasty end. Some people can get clean for a few months, or even years, relapse, then start over. I knew I wasn't like that. I had no margin for error. The monster that was awakened when I relapsed after I got out of rehab in 1992 would be exponentially more powerful now. It was inside me, waiting patiently for the smallest of opportunities.

The crack dreams crept back into my sleep that spring. My nighttime teeth grinding and wrist snapping intensified. I chomped through another mouth guard. I had my dentist make me one double the usual thickness. For my wrist, I upgraded from a soft brace to one outfitted with a steel spine.

I knew, though, that I was just treating the symptoms.

And I worried that the nightmares weren't just an expression of my subconscious fears, but a harbinger. Mark had had everything going for him. He was smart, charismatic, talented, and handsome. In the weeks after his death, his family posted a page online where people could share their recollections about Mark. Relatives and friends posted messages making it clear that Mark was beloved. In the years since I quit using, I'd reestablished ties with my family, made some lasting friendships, and written stories that changed a police department with a legacy of brutality.

Did any of it matter? I kept up with my program of recovery, but if someone like Mark could fall, what chance did I have in the long run? I had no problem being around people who drank. How would I respond if I was offered a hit of crack? Suppose the offer came from an alluring young woman?

On a warm, sunny September day in 2008, much like the one on which I first drove to S Street with Champagne, I went back to the neighborhood where I'd made hundreds of crack buys.

I hadn't been on the block since I'd gotten clean, sixteen years earlier. I wondered whether the street was still dominated by slingers. It was a whim. I wanted to know if I could be near them without making a buy. I felt the need to test myself.

It was Sunday. Traffic was light. I turned right onto S Street, parked, and took in the block.

The abandoned bakery remained derelict, the windows boarded up, the big doors padlocked. But there were no slingers in sight on either side of the block. The street was quiet.

John's Place was gone. Instead of the low-slung concrete nightclub, a gorgeous three-story brick apartment building anchored the corner. A sign on the ground floor, which had large glass curtain walls, touted a day care and learning center.

New Community Church looked the same. How had it survived? Maybe there was a story there.

I slipped a notebook and pen into the back pocket of my jeans, hopped out of the car, and wandered over. It was midafternoon. A sign in the front yard said Sunday services were held from 11:00 A.M. to 12:30 P.M. The worshippers were long gone. But maybe I'd luck out and find the pastor or a church worker.

A stout, middle-aged black man answered my knock on a side door. He wore glasses and had graying, close-cropped hair. The man was holding a broom.

"Hi, my name's Ruben Castaneda," I said. "I work for the *Washington Post*. I'm a reporter on the local staff. I remember what this block was like in the late eighties and early nineties, and I've always wondered how a church could survive in the middle of a crack zone. I was hoping I could talk to someone about how the church got by during that time."

The man motioned me inside and introduced himself: Billy Hart. He talked as he resumed sweeping.

"We were fine because of Baldie. He looked out for the church," the man said.

"Okay. Who's Baldie?"

"He was a drug dealer. He lived next door. He pretty much ran the block." Goose bumps from the top of my head to the soles of my feet. A great story if it checked out. I casually pulled out my notebook and pen.

"What did Baldie do?"

Billy told me about the time he summoned Baldie to deal with the three intruders who were stealing items meant for the kids in the after-school program. I slipped in a few questions and wrote it all down, trying not to look too anxious.

"How else did Baldie help the church?" I asked.

"You should talk to Pastor Jim," Billy said. He pulled out a cell phone and punched in a number.

"Jim, some guy's here. Says he's from the newspaper. He wants to talk to someone about how Baldie protected the church," Billy said. "Uh-huh."

Billy handed me the phone. I introduced myself.

"Jim Dickerson. I'm the pastor," the man on the other end of the line said. The name was vaguely familiar. Had I read about him? Something about affordable housing?

"I've been around long enough to remember what the street was like fifteen, twenty years ago," I said. "I remember when S Street was a 24-7 crack zone. Mr. Hart said the church was protected by a drug dealer named Baldie. I'd like to talk to you about it."

"We've had reporters come around now and then," Jim said. "Not all of them have been trustworthy. I suppose we could talk." He sounded guarded.

Jim gave me his cell phone number. Adrenaline whooshed through me as I walked back to my car. I could barely believe the story that I'd stumbled on. I hadn't given much thought to where my money went after I made all those crack buys. Now I had a name—and, better still, the broad outlines of a terrific narrative. I wanted to know more.

I decided to call Jim as soon as I could to set up an interview.

Guilt and fear held me back. September, October, and November passed without my following up with Jim.

I thought about it. I kept his number on my nightstand. I even picked up the phone and began dialing a few times. But I never finished.

It was a great story, no doubt. But on the day I met Billy and talked to Jim, I hadn't thought the whole thing through. In our brief discussion, Jim had given no indication he'd read my Sunday magazine article. Most of the response to the story had been positive. But the people who'd given me a thumbs-up weren't directly impacted by my addiction. I'd contributed to the pathology that had affected the people of the church, as well as the people who lived around it.

I would have felt dishonest interviewing Jim without disclosing my role in making S Street a combat zone. And I wasn't sure he'd want to talk about his connection to the neighborhood crack dealer anyway. I understood immediately why a pastor would reach an accommodation with such a character. The late eighties and early nineties were a lawless time in dozens of D.C. neighborhoods. I could see how, in the midst of chaos, a pastor might make nice with the local drug peddler. But people who hadn't been near the drug markets may not understand. They might see any accord with a dealer as collaboration with the enemy.

Christmas and New Year's Day slipped away, and I still hadn't gotten in touch with Jim. But I couldn't get the story out of my mind. Finally, in early January, I called him.

"Did you happen to read an article I wrote for the *Post Magazine*, published about a year ago? It described why I was so familiar with the way S Street used to be."

Jim said he hadn't.

"I think it would be helpful if you read it first. It would give you an idea of where I'm coming from, why I'm so interested in S Street."

"Fine," Jim said. "You can bring the article to the church. If no one's there, just drop it in the mail slot at the front door."

The next day, I made a copy of the story and took it to the church. No one answered at either the front or the side door, so I slid it through the mail slot.

I hoped for the best.

I waited a few days, then called Jim again.

"I read the article," he said. He didn't sound guarded anymore. He sounded enthusiastic. "When do you want to meet?"

"I was worried you wouldn't want to talk to me after reading the article," I said. "I was part of the problem back then."

"The fact you went through that gives you more credibility with us," Jim said. "Everybody's in recovery from something."

For the next three months, we met weekly at the church, usually for an hour at a time. Jim was completely open and forthcoming about his friendship with Baldie. He described his efforts to reach out to the kingpin and his slingers and recounted his own life story and how he had come to establish the church on S Street.

Jim was generous with his time. There were no conditions on any of our interviews.

About two months into our talks, Jim invited me to attend a service at New Community. "You're welcome to come anytime," he said.

"Thanks. I'll think about it," I replied. Jim didn't put on a hard sell, and he didn't attach his cooperation to my church participation. That was appealing. So was Jim's notion of Christianity, which seemed very different from the fire-and-brimstone brand of Catholicism I was brought up in as a boy. The Catholic Church of my youth taught that following God, as specifically defined by the church, was the only way to avoid eternal damnation.

Jim, on the other hand, spoke often about the impact the "healing power of God's love" had had on his life. And he was clearly dedicated to helping poor people in the neighborhood and throughout the city.

But I wasn't looking for religion. I was looking for a story.

Six days before Easter, I was in the parking lot of the Prince George's County Courthouse when my cell phone rang. I checked the number—it was Jim.

"Hello, Jim."

"Hello, Ruben. I was wondering, would you be willing to come to church next Sunday to tell your story to the congregation?"

"I've never spoken at a church," I said, surprised. "What would I talk about?"

"Just tell your story."

"Next Sunday is Easter."

"Yes. It's the perfect Easter story. It's about redemption and rebirth."

I hesitated. I hadn't done much public speaking—just a few journalism classes here, a couple of awards banquets there. And some members of Jim's congregation lived on or near S Street. I'd helped make their neighborhood a combat zone. Would they be as understanding and forgiving as Jim?

But my recovery program called for making amends to all those I'd harmed, unless doing so would cause more damage. The response wouldn't always be positive, but that wasn't the point. Making a sincere effort to own up to my past transgressions was what mattered.

"I'll do it. How long do I have to speak?"

"Ten minutes. I'll let you know when your time is up."

"Ten minutes—that's a long time."

"You'll be fine."

"Okay," I said. "What should I wear?"

Jim laughed.

"Be yourself," he said. "Just keep it real."

I smiled at the sandwich board set on the sidewalk outside the entrance to the church: NEW COMMUNITY CHURCH. WORSHIP 11 A.M. BELOVED SINNERS WELCOME. THERE IS ALWAYS ROOM FOR ONE MORE.

Brightly colored balloons bumped up against the high ceiling of the sanctuary. Fifty or so worshippers, a full house, sat in chairs and pews. I hadn't known what to expect, but I was surprised.

Washington, like many cities, is starkly segregated on Sunday mornings. There are black churches, white churches, Latino and Asian churches. I'd never seen or even heard of a truly integrated church. But the worshippers on hand were almost evenly split between black and white. There were young people, middle-aged women in their best dresses, and a handful of older congregants, including a woman in a wheelchair.

After an abbreviated sermon, Jim introduced me as a guest speaker and motioned me to the middle of the room, directly in front of the crucifix constructed from bricks donated by Baldie.

Jim took a seat. I faced the congregation, my pulse racing. My story wasn't what I would have thought of as sermon material. I'd written down some talking points, which I pulled out of my pants pocket.

I introduced myself and gestured to my right, toward the large bay windows that provided a view of S Street and the bakery. In my mind's eye, I saw the slingers surrounding Champagne moments after she'd hopped out of my Escort, saw her calmly making the buy before slipping back into the car.

Turning back to my audience, I slowly scanned the faces of the worshippers, left to right. For the first time, I noticed several young children in the congregation, a few young enough to sit in the laps of their mothers and fathers, some a bit older, up to about age ten. I'd have to go with a G-rated version—I wouldn't mention Champagne or Carrie or how we'd used each other.

I described how S Street used to be a nonstop crack zone, paused, and looked at my shoes.

It was one thing to write about what I'd gone through and what I'd done. Writing was at the same time emotionally intimate and removed. Writing the magazine article, revealing myself as a junkie who had fed D.C. pathology during the crack era, had been exhausting. True, reaction to the story had been generally positive. But I hadn't been in the room with the people who'd read my article.

Now I was standing right in front of some of those whom I had harmed by making hundreds of buys in the combat zone in which they lived. I wouldn't have blamed any of the people who lived on or near S Street during that time if they were angry with me. And I would have to suffer their wrath, face-to-face.

I glanced at Jim. He nodded in encouragement. I remembered what he had said: "Just tell your story."

So I did. I talked about how I'd started using crack in L.A. and begun making buys on S Street when I moved to D.C.

As I spoke, I scanned the congregation again, left to right, then back. The worshippers were listening; they were with me. The sanctuary was dead quiet.

Something inside me changed. It felt like a small bit of healing.

I recounted my awful spiral, my encounter with Big Man, how my boss drove me to rehab just before Christmas 1991.

Some of the middle-aged and older women in the crowd were glassy-eyed, near tears. I wondered: Had they lost someone, a family member or a close friend, to addiction?

Jim pointed to his watch. I was almost out of time.

I looked straight at two of the older black women sitting in the back of the sanctuary. There were virtually no white residents in the neighborhood during the crack era, and the younger people would be too young to remember the combat-zone years. But it was quite possible that these women had lived through them.

"For those of you who lived in the neighborhood during that time, I want to say I am sorry. By buying drugs, I contributed to the pathology and crime you had to endure. I know I bear some responsibility for the chaos, and I am truly sorry."

Jim stood up, came to my side, and put his arm around my shoulders. I let out a deep breath. I was emotionally spent.

"Thank you, Ruben, for that powerful story," Jim said. "It's appropriate for this joyful season of redemption and reconciliation."

Jim led the congregation in a closing prayer.

When the prayer was over, more than a dozen worshippers, black and white, surrounded me. They were smiling. A middle-aged woman gently clasped my shoulder. In that moment, whatever remnants of anxiety I'd been carrying vanished.

Another woman, one of the ones I had been looking at when I apologized for contributing to the chaos on S Street, hugged me.

"Thank you for sharing your story," she said. "I remember how it was—it was bad, just like you said. We're glad that you're here."

No admonishments. No accusations. Just acceptance and encouragement.

Jim took me aside and put his hands on my shoulders.

"Thank you again for speaking. Remember, you are welcome here anytime."

"Thanks, Jim. Thank you for inviting me. This wasn't what I expected."

I stepped through the large double doors and paused on a set of steps above S Street. It was a crisp, clear day, and the sunshine felt good on my face.

ACKNOWLEDGMENTS

This book was made possible by the sterling and resolute efforts of my agent, Bonnie Nadell. She worked with me on multiple versions of the book proposal until we got it right, and throughout the process provided indispensable guidance, encouragement, and, when I needed it, tough love.

I am grateful to Nancy Miller, editorial director at Bloomsbury, who took a chance on a first-time author with an unconventional and complex memoir.

A book like this is a collaborative effort, and I am indebted to the finest editors a writer could ever hope to work with. When I thought the narrative was as good as it could be, Bloomsbury's Lea Beresford's inspired and skillful edits made it better. Copy editor Will Palmer provided a sterling final polish.

Leonard Roberge's brilliant edits helped me structure a complicated story in a way that was thematically and narratively cohesive. His instincts regarding which sections of the story required deeper reporting and better writing were unerring.

I am indebted to Lou Hennessy and Jim Dickerson, both of whom generously allowed me to interview them for countless hours, and who provided the kind of candor and insight that writers dream of. Thanks are due to Lou's wife, Loraine, and Jim's wife, Grace, both of whom provided terrific anecdotes and crucial perspective in multiple interviews. Rachel Dickerson shared her memories and several photos which can be seen at www.sstreet rising.com. Church members Billy Hart and Bernice Joseph graciously described what Jim, New Community Church, and Manna Inc. have meant to them.

Many current and former law enforcement officers shared their stories with me. They include FBI agents John David Kuchta and Mark Giuliano and some of Lou's former MPD colleagues, including Bill Ritchie, Vernon Gudger, Donald Bell, Neil Trugman, Jeff Greene, and Anthony Brigidini. I owe profuse thanks to Sharon Weidenfeld for pointing me in the direction of police brutality in Prince George's County.

Milton Coleman saved my life by taking me to rehab. My early recovery was fortified by the unwavering friendship of Phil Dixon and Courtland Milloy. Special thanks to Phil for his wise career advice.

I am grateful to my brother, Javier, and sister-in-law, Stephanie, for their forgiveness, and my sister, Laura, for her support and unconditional acceptance.

This book may never have been written if not for Tracey Reeves, who insisted that I had a story worth telling.

When I faced doubt or exhaustion, encouragement from a handful of close friends kept me going. They include Gordon Dillow, Betsy Bates Freed, Maria Verdugo, Kathy Culliton-Gonzalez, Anne Folan, JoAnn Goslin, Lisa Frazier Page, Joe Ottrando, Barbara Yuill, and, of course, Lou, Jim, and Phil. I thank my cousin Horacio "Buddy" Rodriguez for his quiet and steadfast confidence in me.

I am indebted to the staff at Suburban Hospital, who gave me a fighting chance, and Tom, Godless John, Ned, Frank, and many other fellow alcoholics and addicts who showed me how to keep the monster within in check.

Finally, thank you, Roxanne, wherever you are, for nudging me away from the monster when it threatened to destroy me.

A NOTE ON THE AUTHOR

Ruben Castaneda worked for twenty-two years as a staff writer at the *Washington Post*. His *Washington Post* Sunday magazine piece on struggling with addiction while covering the police beat won first place in feature writing from the Washington-Baltimore Newspaper Guild's Front Page Awards. He is the recipient of numerous other journalism awards. He lives in Washington, D.C.